EUROPA-FACHBUCHREIHE
für wirtschaftliche Bildung

Office now!

Englisch für Kaufmann/ Kauffrau für Büromanagement

2. Auflage

VERLAG EUROPA-LEHRMITTEL
Nourney, Vollmer GmbH & Co. KG
Düsselberger Straße 23
42781 Haan-Gruiten

Europa-Nr.: 24640

Verfasser und Leiter des Autorenkreises

Dr. Dieter Wessels 58452 Witten

Mitarbeiter früherer Auflagen

Sebastian Barisch 74080 Heilbronn-Böckingen
Christian Müller 75015 Bretten

Sprachliche Beratung

Chris Abbey

Verlagslektorat

Anke Hahn

Produktion der MP3-Audiodateien: Buchfunk – Hörbuchverlag GbR, 04105 Leipzig
Sprecher: Chris Abbey, Johannes Ackner, Tom Bailey, Sophia Baron, Deborah Bode, David Fischbach, Felicity Grist, Robert Günschmann, Angela Hodgson, Hilary Sams, Nicola Seaton-Clark, Dan Wesker

2. Auflage 2023

Druck 5 4 3

Alle Drucke derselben Auflage sind parallel einsetzbar, da sie bis auf die Korrektur von Druckfehlern identisch sind.

ISBN 978-3-7585-2272-7

Bei Fragen zur Produktsicherheit wenden Sie sich bitte an produktsicherheit@europa-lehrmittel.de.

Umschlag, Satz: Grafische Produktionen Jürgen Neumann, 97222 Rimpar
Umschlagkonzept: tiff.any GmbH, 10999 Berlin
Umschlagfoto: ©sborisov-fotolia.de
Druck: Elanders Waiblingen GmbH, 71332 Waiblingen

Vorwort

Office now! ist ein neu konzipiertes Lehrwerk für das Unterrichtsfach „Englisch" an beruflichen Schulen. Es orientiert sich an den Rahmenlehrplänen für die Ausbildung zum Kaufmann/zur Kauffrau für Büromanagement und bildet somit die dort beschriebenen Lernfelder ab. Insofern will **Office now!** die schulische Fachausbildung durch eine entsprechende sprachliche Fortbildung gezielt begleiten bzw. ergänzen. Darüber hinaus kann **Office now!** auch in der außerschulischen, d. h. vor allem in der betrieblichen und außerbetrieblichen Aus- und Weiterbildung genutzt werden.

Das Lehrwerk knüpft an Englischkenntnisse an, die bis zum Abschluss der Sekundarstufe I erworben wurden (Niveaustufe A2 des Europäischen Referenzrahmens). Ausgehend von Kompetenzen in wesentlichen Bereichen der englischen Grammatik und von einem Grundwortschatz von ca. 1000 Wörtern will **Office now!** die Lernenden befähigen, die Anforderungen der KMK-Zertifikatsprüfung (Niveaustufe II) – das entspricht der Niveaustufe B1 des Europäischen Referenzrahmens – erfolgreich zu bewältigen.

Die Texte und Übungen sind überwiegend **handlungsorientiert** angelegt. Sie greifen also gezielt Themen und Situationen aus den Lernfeldern auf, in denen fremdsprachliches Handeln erforderlich oder vorstellbar ist. Diese Handlungsorientierung spiegelt sich in der Fokussierung auf die sprachliche Fortentwicklung in den Kompetenzfeldern Hörverstehen, Leseverstehen, schriftliche und mündliche Kommunikation sowie Sprachmittlung wieder. Somit sind **Dialoge, Telefonate, Schriftverkehr auf elektronischem Wege, Diskussionen, Rollenspiele, aber auch Mediationsanlässe** häufig verwendete Formate in Texten und Übungen.

In 14 Units entwickeln die Lernenden ihre handlungsorientierte Sprachkompetenz themenspezifisch weiter. Hierzu werden neben dem variantenreichen Übungskanon zahlreiche Übungen für Partner- und Gruppenarbeit wie auch Gelegenheiten zur Präsentation und Diskussion in der Klasse angeboten. Auf die Erfahrungen der Lernenden im betrieblichen Alltag greift **Office now!** gezielt zurück. Mit dem systematischen Angebot von **binnendifferenzierenden Aufgaben** können auch leistungsstärkere Lernende angesprochen werden. Darüber hinaus gibt das Lehrwerk Gelegenheit, wichtige Gebiete der englischen Grammatik aufzufrischen.

Zusätzlich zu dem Lehrwerk besteht die Möglichkeit, die mit Digital+ DIGITAL+ gekennzeichneten Hörverstehenstexte sowie einzelne Aufgaben (durch gekennzeichnet) in unserer EUROPATHEK zu nutzen. Nähere Informationen befinden sich auf der vorderen Umschlaginnenseite.

Wenn Ihnen dieses Lehrwerk gefällt, sagen Sie es weiter. Aber helfen Sie uns auch, die vorhandenen Texte und Übungen zu optimieren. Sagen Sie uns, was es im nächsten Druck, in der nächsten Auflage zu verbessern gilt. Schreiben Sie uns unter lektorat@europa-lehrmittel.de.

Das Autorenteam freut sich auf Ihr Feedback. Vor allem aber wünschen wir Ihnen erfolgreiches Arbeiten mit **Office now!**

März 2023 Autoren und Verlag

Unit 1 My first day at work

1.1 How to introduce yourself

[1] Ausbildung
[2] Kaufmann/frau für Büromanagement
[3] Unternehmen
[4] sich vorstellen
[5] Kollege/in
[6] Arbeitsplatz

Track 1

You are going to start your training[1] as an office management assistant[2] on August 1st. Your company[3] is called Bulten Electronics LTD. While you are thinking about your first day at work, you remember that you will have to introduce yourself[4] to your new colleagues[5] and you are considering carefully how to do so correctly. After that they will probably take you to your workplace[6] and explain your tasks to you.

[1] Teamleiter/in

Hello. My name is Ann Wilking. I'm the teamleader[1] of this team.

©contrastwerkstatt-fotolia.com

[1] Praktikum
[2] sich bewerben

Good morning. I'm Jane Rodriguez, and everyone calls me Jane. I'm doing an internship[1] at the moment, which takes six months. Maybe I'll apply[2] next year.

And I'm George Bayrak. I'll finish my training as an office management assistant next summer.

©contrastwerkstatt-fotolia.com

[1] eine Ausbildung machen
[2] (beruflich) werden
[3] jüngere/r Mitarbeiter/in im Büro

Hi, I'm Simon Lange. I'm training[1] to become[2] an office junior[3]. It's my first year.

©contrastwerkstatt-fotolia.com

Note

workplace is the place/desk where you work
place of work means job/post/position

Read the introductions below and decide who it might be. Give reasons for your choice. Then listen to the recording.

Track 2

Hi there. My name is ______. I'm 19. After finishing secondary school[1] I started my training in this company. I was born in Hanover. I like playing computer games and I like snorkelling[2]. I'll take my final exams[3] next year and I really hope I'll pass[4].

Hello everyone. I'm ______. I'm 19 years old. After my A-levels[5] this year I started my training in this company. I like playing soccer and meeting friends. My hometown is Bremen. At the moment I'm looking for a new flat, which is difficult to find in Hanover.

Hi guys. I'm ______. I'm 20 years old. I was born in Barcelona, Spain. I've been living in Germany for five months now. After my language course in Berlin I decided[6] to stay in Germany for a while. I like to go window-shopping and I also like travelling.

Hello. My name is ______. I'm 39 years old and I live in Hanover. After studying economics[7] in Hanover I started working for this company. I like reading books and love to go swimming.

1 Realschule, Hauptschule
2 Schnorcheln
3 Abschlussprüfung
4 (Prüfung) bestehen
5 (*etwa*) Abitur
6 sich entscheiden
7 Wirtschaftswissenschaften

Info

Introducing yourself

When you introduce yourself, you state your full name. You could also mention[1] when and where you were born, where you live, where you went to school, what your interests and achievements[2] are and what you are doing right now. Depending on[3] who you are talking to and the situation, the amount[4] and the kind of[5] information and, of course, the language you use may vary[6]. Introducing yourself seems easy, because you know all the facts. But you must decide how much you say and what kind of facts you give. You will have to consider[7] the situation, and what your audience[8] is like, what may be important for the audience to know and also, of course, what the people listening to you may be interested in. It just takes[9] a little bit of practice. So try it right now.

Useful phrases

My name is …/I am (called) …
I live in …
I went to/I attended school[10] in … and just graduated[11]/passed my finals[12] in June this year.
In school I liked … most. – I didn't like … at all.
In August/September I started my training in … company/at … (name of the company)
I have been doing part-time work in a supermarket/delivering newspapers …
My favourite sport is …
I like playing/watching … . But I don't like …
In my spare time …/Outside school I …

1 erwähnen
2 Erfolge,Leistungen
3 abhängend/abhängig von
4 Betrag, Menge
5 die Art von
6 variieren, sich (ver)ändern
7 in Betracht ziehen
8 Zuhörer
9 man braucht nur
10 Schule besuchen
11 Schule abschließen
12 Abschlussprüfung

Note

Simon, Ann, Jane and George use short forms such as *I'll*, *I'm*, *we've* etc. These forms are mainly used in spoken English and in private written communication (text messages, e-mails, letters).

Write out the long forms.

1 *We'll go* to the cinema tonight. __________
2 They *aren't* watching. __________
3 *I'm* coming to your party. __________
4 He *hasn't* read the text yet. __________
5 They *can't* see us from where they are. __________
6 I *mustn't* smoke at work. __________
7 They *won't* go to the fun fair. __________
8 She *shouldn't* have brought up this problem. __________
9 You *didn't* answer the phone last night. – Why *weren't* you at home? __________
10 You *needn't* worry. – *We've* got everything under control. __________

Revision

Use the **simple present** to express the idea that an action is repeated or usual. The action can be a habit, a hobby, a daily event, a scheduled[1] event or something that happens often. It can also be something a person often forgets or usually does not do.

The simple present is the 1st form of the verb: *I work in London. – I go to work every morning.* But the 3rd person singular (he/she/it) adds an *-s* or *-es: She work**s** in London. – She go**es** to work every morning.*

Note: Verbs ending in *-y* have *-ies* in the 3rd person singular: *He worr**ies** a lot.*

If there is a vowel *(a, e, o, u)* before the *-y*, you just add "*-s*" *(she pla**ys**, she enjo**ys**).*

[1] geplant

Write these verbs in the 3rd person singular.

I forget	- she	_____	you go	- he	_____	they carry	- she	_____
we believe	- he	_____	they have	- it	_____	I tidy up	- she	_____
you enjoy	- she	_____	we write	- he	_____	you empty	- she	_____
they do	- he	_____	you hope	- she	_____	they fly	- it	_____

Now practise introducing your partner to the class and say a few words about her/him. To find out about your partner ask her/him questions beginning with *who, when, where, what* etc.

Track 3

[1] Abteilung

©Production Perig-fotolia.com

Simon's first day at work

Simon begins his first day at work. He is very nervous. His boss, Ann, takes him to her department[1] and introduces him to her team.

Ann: Good morning, everybody. – Excuse me! May I have your attention please? – Thank you. I'd like to introduce our new colleague. Please meet Simon – Simon Ballard.

Simon: Hello, everybody.

Ann: Simon is our new trainee[2] and has started work today. He's just finished school and wants to start out[3] as an office management assistant. His training in our company will last two years. And as I've already told you, he'll spend the first three months of his training in our department. Now, I hope you'll do all you can to make Simon feel welcome. – Well, Simon, first I want you to meet[4] everyone in our department. Now, this is Jane. Her desk is over there by the window.

Simon: Hello, Jane, pleased to meet you.

Jane: Hello, Simon, welcome to our team.

Ann: And this is George. He sits opposite[5] Jane. George will look after[6] you for the first couple of weeks[7].

George: Hi, Simon, hope you'll like it here.

Simon: Hello, George.

Ann: And this is Jonathan …

[2] Auszubildende/r
[3] beginnen
[4] kennen lernen
[5] gegenüber
[6] sich um jdn. kümmern
[7] ein paar Wochen

©Syda Productions-fotolia.com

Please answer these questions.

1 In your own words describe what happened.
2 How does Ann call the members of her team?
3 How does Simon greet the team?
4 For how long will Simon be in Ann's department?
5 What are the names of Simon's new colleagues?
6 Where do they sit?

Ann is really pleased about the way Simon has introduced himself to his new colleagues. This is why she tells Simon to write a short memo on how to introduce oneself for future applicants[1].

[1] Bewerber/in

Info

Writing skills: How to write a memo

Business memos have a special format which is informal[1]. They are used for internal[2] information only. If you have something private to say, do not write a memo.

The tone of memos usually is informal and friendly. Keep them short (not more than 100 words). The memo is written to inform the reader about important facts and give answers to these questions: *who?/when?/where?/what?/which action?*

Memos generally have the same structure. And you will find these elements:

- **Addressee[3]:** Flush left[4], in capital letters[5], near the top of the page
- **Sender:** Flush left, in caps, immediately[6] below the addressee's name
- **Date:** Flush left, in caps, immediately below the sender's name
- **Subject:** Flush left, in caps, immediately below the date

[1] formlos
[2] innerbtrieblich
[3] Empfänger/in
[4] linksbündig
[5] Großbuchstabe
[6] unmittelbar, direkt

Write a memo: "How to introduce yourself."

1.2 How to equip one's workplace

Track 4

Jonathan takes Simon to his desk. On their way Jonathan explains that Simon will be spending many hours at his desk every week and that he will be using the equipment[1] and tools[2] that his employer[3] gives him. Then they arrive at Simon's desk. At first Simon is quite amazed. – There is just an empty desk!

Jonathan starts laughing. "That's what happened to all of us. But Ann wants all employees[4] to arrange[5] their workplaces according to their needs so that they feel comfortable[6]," he says. Simon is very excited now and keen[7] to start. "Would you please help me to get the information I need?" he asks Jonathan.

"Yes, of course. It's a pleasure. Let's get started," Jonathan answers.

1 Ausstattung, Ausrüstung, Geräte
2 Werkzeuge, (Hilfs-)Mittel
3 Arbeitgeber
4 wollen/mögen, dass jd. etw. tut
5 einrichten, anordnen
6 sich wohl/zuhause fühlen
7 begierig, sehr interessiert

Get to know your office equipment.

1 Look at the items of office equipment below and link the words to the pictures. Then decide which you really need.

2 Which would be useful?

3 Can you think of any other items of office equipment that you might want to have around?

Use your dictionary if you don't know.

©marog-pixcells-fotolia.com

©Tsiumpa-fotolia.com

©Style-Photography-fotolia.com

©MEV Verlag GmbH.ccm

©teerawit-fotolia.com

©SakisPagonas-fotol a.com

©MEV Verlag GmbH

paper clip

printer

file folder

punch

smartphone

ring binder

memory stick

computer keyboard

mouse

computer

screen

writing pad

staples

printer paper

?

©Damian-fotolia.com

©Andreas Mueller-fololia.com

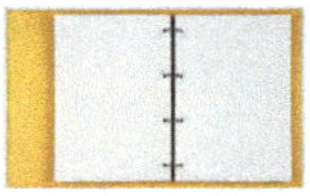

bjphotographs-shutterstock.com

©geniuskp-fotolia.com

©pbombaert-fotolia.com

©Costin79-fotolia.com

©MEV Verlag GmbH

©PrettyVectors-fotolia.com

Your office seems to be fully equipped now. There are a lot of items which you need to do your job. Decide which of the definitions below fit the terms. There are more words than definitions.

1 window envelope
2 board marker
3 sticky tape*
4 highlighter
5 pen tray
6 index cards
7 printer cartridge
8 post-it note
9 staples
10 hanging file
11 printer paper
12 memory stick

a – open box where you can keep your biros[1], pencils, rubber etc.
b – container[2] with ink[3] used to produce texts on paper
c – cover for business letters where you can see the address of the letter inside
d – hard paper where you can write down information
e – holder of documents that hangs down
f – little device[4] used to save information and transfer it to another computer
g – special pen that helps you to mark words or passages of a text
h – little metal devices used to stick paper together
I – writing tool often used in seminars, meetings[5] or school

1 Kugelschreiber, Kuli
2 Behälter
3 Tinte
4 Gerät
5 Sitzung, Konferenz

Note

*In the US they call it *Scotch (tape)*; in GB it is called *Sellotape*. Both these names are trade names. *Tesa* is a German trade name.

1.3 How to become an office junior

Track 5

It's a good career[1] to get into as your hours will usually be 9 am to 5 pm Monday to Friday. At particularly[2] busy times there might be some overtime[3]. It's an office-based[4] job. Don't expect to spend a lot of time at your desk, as there is a lot to be seen all around the office.

As you'll be greeting visitors, you should always look clean and tidy to make a good first impression[5] for your company.

Your most likely career path[6] is to take on more responsibility[7] and work your way up to become an office manager[8] if you work hard and obtain further qualifications[9]. But since it is junior role[10], you won't always have the most exciting of tasks to do – so be ready for lots of routine work.

Most employers will expect you to have reached at least[11] GCSE standard[12], including English and Maths.

Depending on the tasks in the job description[13] and the level of support that you will get, some employers expect you to have either two good A-levels[14] or a few years of experience[15] in office administration[16].

Most of the training[17] will be on the job[18]. You'll be taught how to use the equipment and about office procedures[19] by more experienced[20] colleagues. If you work in a bigger company, you may get the chance to work towards[21] some vocational qualifications[22] in Business Administration[23].

Adapted from http://totaljobs.com/carees-advice/job-profile/admin-jobs/ accessed 19 Sept. 2015

1 Karriere, Berufslaufbahn
2 insbesondere, besonders
3 Überstunden
4 Büro-
5 Eindruck
6 Berufslaufbahn, beruflicher Werdegang
7 Verantwortung
8 Büroleiter/in
9 sich weiterqualifizieren
10 Stelle von untergeordneter Bedeutung
11 zumindest, mindestens
12 Abschluss Sekundarstufe I
13 Stellenbeschreibung
14 Fachprüfung im engl. Abitur
15 Erfahrung
16 Büroverwaltung
17 Ausbildung
18 im Betrieb
19 Büroroutine
20 erfahren
21 hinarbeiten auf
22 berufliche Qualifikation
23 Betriebswirtschaft

Please answer the following questions.

1 What does the text say about the job of an office junior?
2 Why should an office junior look smart?
3 Describe the career of an office junior.
4 What kind of education should young people have who want to become office juniors?
5 How are office juniors trained?

©tigatelu-fotolia.com

1.4 Talking about school

Britain	U.S.A.
After primary school[1] (age 5-11) students move on to secondary education[2] (age 11-16) which they complete with GCSE exams (GCSE O-levels = general certificate of secondary education – ordinary level[3]). The number and the subjects[4] can be chosen by the student, but must include[5] English and Mathematics. Students can then start an apprenticeship[6], go to college to get a vocational qualification (NVQ = national vocational qualification[7]) or continue their secondary education. The NVQ can be obtained in many different areas: plants and land, extracting[8] and providing natural resources, engineering[9], manufacturing[10], transporting, providing[11] business services, communicating[12]. If students stay on at school for another two years they can take A-level (advanced level) exams in two or three core subjects which will then qualify them to continue[13] their education at university. The school-leaving age[14] is 18. The Scottish school system of education is a little different.	There are several systems of school education in the U.S.A. The data below show the most common one. American children generally start school at the age of 5. Age 4-5 — Pre-school education[15] Kindergarten (these programmes must be paid for by parents) Age 5-10 — Primary education[16] Elementary school[17] Age 11-13 — Middle school – Junior high school[18] Age 14-18 — Secondary education[19] High school – Senior high school[20] Age 18+ — Tertiary education[21] – College or university In the U.S.A. compulsory schooling[22] ends at the age of 16. Students can then take up a job or go on to high school. When students have graduated from high school[23] they can choose whether they want to start to work or go to college. Graduation from high school or senior high school is required for students wanting to go to college or university.

[1] Grundschule
[2] Schulbildung in der Sekundarstufe I
[3] allgemeines Niveau
[4] (Schul-/Studien-)Fach
[5] einschließen, umfassen
[6] Ausbildung (meist gewerblich)
[7] staatlicher Berufsbildungsabschluss
[8] *(Rohstoffe)* Abbau
[9] Ingenieurwesen
[10] Herstellung, Produktion
[11] bereitstellen
[12] Kommunikation(-swesen)
[13] fortsetzen
[14] Ende des schulpflichtigen Alters
[15] Vorschulerziehung
[16] Grundschulausbildung
[17] Grundschule
[18] Mittelschule
[19] Sekundarschulausbildung
[20] Oberschule, Gymnasium
[21] Hochschulausbildung
[22] Schulpflicht
[23] Schulabschluss machen

A friend of yours wants to know about the education system in Britain. Tell her/him the basic facts in German.

Some of your classmates can do the same for the U.S.A.

Info

What is mediation?

Mediation means that the content of a text is told in another language. It is not a translation! You choose your own words and sentence structures. But you must make sure that you "transport" the main ideas and/or facts.

Decide which is the right German translation for the English terms and phrases.

English	German
at the age of	(bei einer Prüfung) durchfallen
average grade	(Zeit) im Ausland verbringen
comprehensive school	die Schule/den Unterricht besuchen
form teacher	Durchschnittsnote
grade	ein Jahr wiederholen
pupil	ein Praktikum machen
school report	eine Prüfung machen/bestehen
school year	eine Prüfung wiederholen
student	Gesamtschule
summer holidays/vacation *[AE]*	im Alter von
to attend school/classes	in den Kindergarten/ in die Schule gehen
to decide to go to … (school)	junge/r Schüler/in
to do a work experience	Klassenlehrer/in
to fail an exam	Klassenfahrt
to leave school	Note
to pass an exam	Schüler/in
to repeat a year	Schulferien
to resit an exam	Schuljahr
to spend (time) abroad	sich entscheiden, auf die … (Schule) zu gehen
to start kindergarten/school	Sommerferien
	(Schul-)Zeugnis
	(von der Schule) abgehen

Note

There is no one-to-one translation for the following:

*Gymnasium** ≈ *grammar school*

Realschule/Hauptschule ≈ *secondary school*

Berufsschule ≈ *vocational school*

Abitur ≈ *A-levels [BE]; (senior) high school [AE]*

Abitur machen ≈ *to do one's A-levels [BE]; to graduate from high school [AE]*

Mittlere Reife; Realschulabschluss, Hauptschulabschluss ≈ *high school diploma [AE], GCSE O-level exams [BE], secondary school leaving certificate*

Realschulabgänger(in) ≈ *secondary school leaver [BE]/high school [AE] graduate*

* The English term *gymnasium* (or short: *gym*) stands for a hall where you do physical exercises.

Do you know the terms for the subjects you had in secondary school? Make a list.

Did you have any of these subjects? In which year?

English	German
PE (Physical Education)	Sport
Fine Arts	Kunst
Design & Technology	Gestaltung & Technologie
Computer Studies	Informatik
Environmental Management	Umweltmanagement
Home Economics	Hauswirtschaft(-slehre)
Combined Sciences	Naturwissenschaften
Business Studies	Betriebswirtschaftslehre
Food & Nutrition	Nahrung & Ernährung
Commercial Studies	Handelskunde

Note

In English, school subjects are often capitalised[1], especially in official documents.

[1] großschreiben

Explain your school career to an English-speaking visitor to your company/institution. Also give reasons for your decision to join a particular school and do the subjects that you finished your final year with.

Unit 2 Working in an office

©Vibe Images-fotolia.com

©stokkete-fotolia.com

©WavebreakMediaMicro-fotolia.com

Office work through the ages

Let's get going!

1 What is your experience after the first few weeks in your company/institution?

2 What are the things you like most about your new life?

3 And what is there that you don't like at all?

2.1 Office work What's it like?

Track 6

Like any other job, office work has its pros and cons[1]. Much depends on how you feel about your work – which is difficult to say, because you, as an office junior, are just beginning to see what it's like. You've met new people – your team. You're getting to know new people almost every day, colleagues and possibly customers[2] as well. Some of them are interesting to talk to, others less so.

You're given things to do. Some of them you find challenging[3]; others are definitely boring – but they've got to be done. You'll have many things explained to you[4], some are really complicated; others you find easy to understand. Maybe you find it difficult to accept that there are always people telling you what to do and how to do things, when to do them and then look over your shoulder[5] to see how you're getting on[6] and whether you're doing it right. Sometimes there are meetings, and you may have to talk to business partners and customers.

Your daily routine has changed. You're no longer free to organise your afternoon as you like. Maybe you can't dress as you used to, because your company has a dress code[7]. In the end, it all comes down to[8] what you make of it.

1 Vorteile und Nachteile
2 Kunde/in
3 schwierig, anspruchsvoll
4 man erklärt Ihnen
5 jdm. über die Schulter sehen, jdn. kontrollieren
6 vorankommen, klar kommen
7 Kleiderordnung
8 darauf hinauslaufen

Based on what is said in the text, how has your life changed? Give examples.

List the pros and cons of office work that you find in the text.

Find one or two examples to explain the expression "*what you make of it*" in the last line of the text.

Now study these comments about office work.

I love this office. It's so easy to meet people and have a chat.

I hate making small-talk[3] with everyone I meet.

What I really like about office work is the coffee breaks. You can get up and walk around.

My boss is really nice to me.

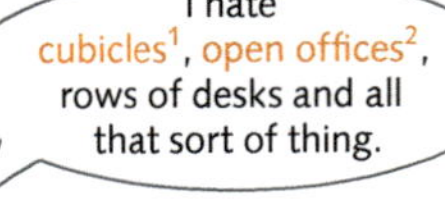

It's interesting. I learn new things every day.

Regular working hours? That's not for me, really.

You've got clearly defined times when you start and finish. And that helps me to organise my day.

Although it's a complete waste of time[4], chatting[5] gives you a chance to get to know your colleagues better.

I miss meeting my school-mates every day.

Some of the older people in my office are really interesting to talk to.

[1] Bürozelle, Kabine
[2] Großraumbüro
[3] Smalltalk machen, sich unterhalten
[4] Zeitverschwendung
[5] plaudern

What do you think? Can you make such statements about life in your office? Say why or why not.

2.2 The ideal office junior

When you were interviewed[1] for the training to become an office junior, your prospective[2] employers were not only interested in your school career. They also wanted to find out about your activities[3] and achievements outside[4] school. They wanted to know what kind of person you are and whether you would fit into the existing team. Here is a list of qualities and skills they may have been looking for.

- friendly and helpful
- super organised[5]
- flexible
- able to put first things first
- detail-oriented[6] and accurate[7]
- trustworthy[8] and reliable[9]
- self-motivated[10]
- articulate[11] and good communicator[12]
- good verbal and written[13] skills in German
- experienced in using a computer (especially Word and Excel)
- able to work in a team
- punctual
- tidy[14] with a neat appearance[15]

©sylv1rob1-fotolia.com

[1] Vorstellungsgespräch führen
[2] zukünftig
[3] Tätigkeit
[4] außerhalb von
[5] blendend organisiert, mit super Organisationstalent
[6] detailbewusst, detailgenau
[7] genau, präzise, sorgfältig
[8] vertrauenswürdig, verlässlich
[9] zuverlässig
[10] (selbst)motiviert
[11] wort-, sprachgewandt
[12] mit verbindlichen Umgangsformen
[13] mündlich und schriftlich
[14] sauber, ordentlich
[15] gepflegte Erscheinung, gepflegtes Äußeres

Becoming an office junior

1 Looking at your experience of talks with prospective employers, which of the descriptions on p. 18 (all of them found in British job adverts[1]) would you consider important for a trainee in office management? State your reasons.

2 Find other aspects which you would add to this list.

3 Rearrange[2] the list above together with your own ideas by order of importance. In class, give reasons for your choice.

[1] Stellenanzeige
[2] neu anordnen

4 Find out why your partner decided to begin her/his training as an office junior. Present your results in class. Discuss the reasons given by your classmates.
Use phrases such as the following:
- I always liked … That's why I decided to (do) …
- It seemed a good idea to me to (do) …
- I chose this training/traineeship because …
- I like/enjoy …ing. Therefore …
- I very much wanted to (do) …
- When I heard about … it was clear to me at once that …
- My friends told me that … Therefore …
- During my work experience I got to know … That's why I …

5 Describe what your first few weeks were like and what you had to do. Discuss your experience with your classmates.

Revision

The time

There are several ways of telling the time. Please note the following:

It's seven o'clock. I'll meet you at seven (or: *at seven o'clock*).
It's a quarter past seven. Or: *It's seven fifteen.*
It's ten (minutes) past seven.
It's half past seven. Or: *It's seven thirty.*
It's twenty (minutes) to eight.
It's a quarter to eight. Or: *It's fifteen minutes to eight.*

Use *o'clock* only for full hours. The short forms *am* (= *ante meridiem* meaning *before midday*) and *pm* (= *post meridiem* meaning *after midday*) are used only to make clear which half of the day is meant.

In connection with timetables (train, bus, etc.) people also use the 24-hour clock and they say: *eight fifteen (= 8.15), fifteen thirty-seven (15.37).*

Examples: *The train leaves at seven twenty-nine.* Or: *The bus arrives at nineteen twenty-two.*

Note the prepositions: *at noon* (meaning 12 o'clock sharp), *at midday, at night, at midnight* (meaning 12 o'clock at night)

But: *in the morning, in the afternoon, in the evening.* Similar to German usage you may add: *early* or *late (in the early morning, early in the morning, in the late afternoon, late in the afternoon)*

Learn these expressions of time: *today, tomorrow, yesterday, the day before yesterday, the day after tomorrow, two/three … days ago, in two/three … days' time, in a week's/month's time, in a fortnight, last/next week/ month/year, in 2017*

Practise using the time and translate these sentences.

1 Der Film beginnt um 8 Uhr.
2 Das Konzert dauert bis viertel nach zehn.
3 Mein Zug fährt um 12.42 Uhr ab.
4 Es ist jetzt genau 12.00 Uhr.
5 Die erste Stunde beginnt heute um 9.45 Uhr.
6 Mein Flug kommt um 19.25 Uhr in Düsseldorf an.
7 Wir treffen uns um 15.00 Uhr.
8 Um 18.30 Uhr gibt es Abendessen.
9 Ich treffe dich heute Abend um halb acht am Bahnhof.
10 In zwei Wochen beginne ich meine Ausbildung als Bürokaufmann/-frau.

Use these verbs:
begin/start
last/go on (until)
arrive
leave/depart
meet so.

2.3 The time spent at work

Compare your normal days at work and find out how your working hours[1] are organised (regular hours, extra hours[2], holidays etc.). Start with the time you arrive at the office and finish with the end of your working day[3]. Also say what breaks you have and how long they are. Before you start, make sure you understand the words and phrases in the list below.

[1] Arbeitszeit
[2] Überstunden
[3] Arbeitstag

Vocabulary

Find the German for the following. When you have finished, check your solutions in an online dictionary.

standard working week	(to take) a day off
regular working hours	(to take) time off
(to work) flexitime	employee benefits
flexitime account	lunchbreak, coffee break
core hours/time	holiday entitlement
to start/leave early	annual holiday/leave/vacation *[AE]*

2.4 The job

Searching the internet (search words: *administrative assistant*[1], *team assistant*[2], *office assistant*[3], *office junior*), you will find long lists of tasks. Some of them are listed in the table on p. 21 (Columns 1 & 2).

[1] Verwaltungsassistent/in
[2] Teamassistent/in
[3] Büroassistent/in

Note

Mind the spelling: Assistent *[German]*, **but** assistant *[English]*.

Decide which of these tasks you do regularly, often, sometimes or not at all. Tick (√) the boxes as required.

Note

When filling in forms in Britain and the U.S.A. it is customary to mark boxes with a tick (√) rather than a (X) as we do in German-speaking countries.

1	2	3	4	5	6
Function	**Tasks**	**Regu-larly**	**Often**	**Some-times**	**Never**
General office work	• picking up[1] mail from the post office/ mail room[2] every morning • coordinating outgoing mail[3] • doing administrative[4] and general clerical work[5], such as photocopying, faxing, filing[6], sorting[7] etc.				
Writing	• answering general enquiries[8] • writing and layouting[9] reports[10] • corresponding in German and English • creating spreadsheets[11] and charts • preparing project documents[12] in MS PowerPoint and MS Word				
Phoning	• answering telephone calls • taking and passing on messages[13]				
Office organisation	• watching over office equipment • checking out[14] the supplies[15] needed and placing orders[16]				
Helping others	• working under the direction of[17] managers and senior staff[18] • assisting[19] senior staff with their duties[20] • tracking[21] information for others • helping with monitoring[22] deadlines[23]				
Organising	• researching[24] the best travel connections[25] • booking flights, trains, hotels etc. • arranging[26] and coordinating[27] business trips[28]				
Docu-mentation	• helping with the preparation of documents/presentations • collecting data[29] • helping with regular reports • preparing simple analyses[30] of information or data for executives[31] • handling[32] statistics and project data[33] • helping with project documents				
Meetings	• helping with the organisation and follow-up[34] of meetings or conferences • copying materials for meetings • preparing meeting rooms[35] • ordering meals and refreshments for clients • assisting with events[36] and receptions[37]				
Customer contacts	• supporting[38] customer-related[39] activities (appointments[40], internet research[41]) • greeting and directing[42] visitors				

1 mitnehmen, abholen
2 Postzimmer
3 Postausgang
4 Verwaltungsarbeit
5 Schreib-, Büroarbeit
6 Ablage machen
7 sortieren
8 Anfrage
9 gestalten
10 Bericht
11 Tabellen/Diagramme anlegen
12 Projektunterlagen
13 Nachrichten annehmen und weiterleiten
14 überwachen, prüfen
15 Vorräte
16 Auftrag erteilen
17 unter der Anleitung von
18 ältere Angestellte
19 helfen, unterstützen
20 Pflicht, Aufgabe
21 verfolgen, suchen
22 überwachen
23 Frist
24 heraussuchen, finden
25 Verkehrsverbindungen
26 planen, organisieren
27 aufeinander abstimmen, koordinieren
28 Geschäftsreise
29 Daten zusammenstellen
30 Analyse
31 leitende/r Angestellte/r, Führungskraft
32 bearbeiten
33 Projektdaten
34 Nachbereitung
35 Sitzungs-, Konferenzraum
36 Veranstaltung
37 Empfang
38 unterstützen
39 kundenbezogen
40 Termin
41 Nachforschung, Recherche
42 führen, (Weg etc.) weisen

Note

The distinction between *customer* and *client* is not always very clear. Generally speaking *customer* is used for people/companies who/which buy things (e.g. in shops), whereas *client* is used for people/companies requiring services (bank/marketing/insurance[1]).

[1] Versicherung

Talk about your work as an office management trainee.

1 Add any tasks which you do and which are not listed on p. 21.

2 List the tasks you do or don't like. Say why or why not.

3 In groups of three or four, look at Column 2 and try to find nouns for the first word after the bullet point (words ending in *–ing*). Use your dictionary if necessary. In some cases this may not work. But where it does, you may need to make changes in the language. Which?

4 Now write an e-mail or a WhatsApp message to your friend telling her/him what you do in the office. Use adverbs of time such as *early in the morning, at noon, in the early afternoon*. And use adverbs of frequency (*often, seldom, rarely, regularly, occasionally, every day, once a week, hardly ever, all the time*, etc.) The phrases below may be useful.

It is my task/job to …

I get a chance to …

In my training as an office junior I …

I'm learning to …

I'm (also) responsible for …

They ask me to help to …

My colleagues/boss ask(s) me to …

But I never ...

One of my main tasks is to …

I (certainly) like/enjoy (doing) …

It takes … hours/minutes to do sth.

(However,) I'm not very keen on (doing) ...

5 Say how often you or your senior colleagues use English in your/their job and for which activities. Find out what the situation is like in the companies/institutions where your classmates work.

6 Photocopying and filing are something that few people are very keen on. This task is usually given to office juniors or young people doing a work placement[1]. Can you think of the reasons? Who else should do it?

1 Praktikum

Revision

Singular and plural

In English the plural of nouns is formed by adding *"s" (town – towns)*. For nouns ending in *"ss", "ch", "sh"* or *"x"* the plural form is *"es" (dress – dresses; match – matches; dish – dishes, fax – faxes)*.

The plural form of nouns ending in *"y"* after a consonant is *"ies" (city – cities)*. If the noun has a vowel *(a, e, o, u)* before the *"y"*, there is no change *(toy – toys, play – plays)*.

For some nouns ending in *"o"* the plural form is *"es" (tomato, potato, echo)*. For many others the plural form is regular (*photo, radio, kilo* or *studio*).

For nouns ending in *"f"* or *"fe"* the plural form changes to *"ves" (calf – calves, life – lives, half – halves, knife – knives)*. The plural is regular for the following: *chief(s), proof(s), roof(s), belief(s)*.

The numbers *hundred, thousand, million, billion* do **not** have a plural when combined with another number: *two thousand, twelve million*. **But note:** *hundreds of people, millions of euros*.

Note these irregular plural forms: *foot – feet, child – children, man – men, woman – women, tooth – teeth*.

Also note: Contrary to German practice, currencies are expressed in the plural form when there is more than **1** of something (e.g. *two dollars; €1.01 = one point one euros; €3.45 = three euros and forty-five cents*). And do not forget that the words for **currencies** are written in **small letters**.

Practise using the plural.

1 Choose the correct plural form *-s, -es, -ves, -ies*. In some cases you may need to change the spelling.

printer	___	secretary	___	knife	___	keyboard	___
office	___	party	___	boss	___	colleague	___
bus	___	house	___	centre	___	category	___
dictionary	___	storey	___	inch	___	yard	___
mile	___	memo	___	bottle	___	toy	___

2 From singular to plural. Find the right plural form.

1 Our company has office___ in several African country___.

2 Our supply___ are a bit low. So we need some potato___ and tomato___

3 In my office there are five wom___n and only two m___n.

4 He won five million___ pounds in the lottery.

5 The dentist had a good look at my t___th.

6 Four and a half thousand___ fans are waiting to get into the football stadium.

7 Million___ of dollars were spent to rebuild this bridge.

8 These measure___ should help to protect the life___ of our child___.

9 Your photo___ of our office part___ are excellent.

10 All of these box___ are three f___t long and two f___t wide.

2.5 The workplace

©Picture-Factory-fotolia.com

©virtua73-fotolia.com

©Rawpixel.com-fotolia.com

©photowahn-fotolia.com

©Monkey Business-fotolia.com

©trekandphoto-fotolia.com

Look at the photos above.

1 Which of the offices shown in the photos comes closest to what your office looks like? Briefly describe the similarities[1] and the differences.

Here are some points to consider:

- The work environment[2] (size of the office, layout[3], furniture, technical equipment; type and size of the business, the type of work, the rank of the employees);
- Health and safety issues[4] (daylight and electric light, fire escapes[5], sizes of corridors and staircases, emergency exits[6]);
- Employee needs[7] (some like to work on their own; some prefer to work in a team environment; some can work very well in a big office; some want to be able to talk to their colleagues easily etc.).

[1] Ähnlichkeit
[2] Arbeitsumfeld
[3] Anordnung, Gestaltung
[4] Arbeitsschutzfragen
[5] Feuerleiter
[6] Fluchtweg, Notausgang
[7] Bedürfnisse der Mitarbeiter/innen

2 Form groups of three or four students and describe your office to your classmates. Here are some ideas you could think/talk about.

- Number of people working there
- Arrangement of the desks also in relation to windows, doors
- Positions of wall units[1], filing cabinets[2], other furniture
- Location[3] of photocopier/printer and fax machines
- Heating and ventilation[4], opening windows
- Place for your personal things (coat, bag)
- Distance to kitchen, toilet, lift, staircase
- Place to have a break or to smoke
- Seating arrangements[5], preferred positions for managers
- Arrangements for receiving visitors or having team meetings

[1] Wandschrank, -regal
[2] Aktenschrank
[3] Standort
[4] Belüftung
[5] Sitzordnung

3 As a group, decide on a single plan which you will then present to the class. To support your group presentation draw up a plan of your office or the floor on which you work on a large sheet of paper and put it up in the corridor or on the wall of your classroom. Have a close look at the different plans. Compare your results in class. Which of the layouts described by your classmates would you prefer for yourself? State your reasons.

4 Considering the room plans in your company, would you change the current arrangements? If so, in what way?

2.6 Office layouts: Pros and cons

DIGITAL+ Track 7

Life in the office has changed considerably in the past fifty years, as have the forms and content[1] of office work. Thus, office work without electronic equipment would be difficult to imagine nowadays. In some businesses there are not enough desks for all the employees. More and more jobs can now be done by employees working from home (home office[2]). Most teachers do that for part of their work (marking[3], preparing lessons etc.). But also think of employees who travel around in certain regions of the country to see customers regularly and tell them about products and services (sales staff[4]). They have their fully equipped[5] home office and come into the company office only once in a while[6]. So they need little more than somewhere to connect their laptop and put their coat.

A very modern form of workplace is called "coffice[7]" – the office in a coffee shop which provides a Wi-Fi[8] connection in a relaxing environment[9], where, of course, you can also obtain food and drink. It is a home office away from home, so to speak. There is a certain noise level[10] as in an office; and there are people around you all the time, but you do not have to talk to them. You may have seen this form of office work in your hometown – a form of working which is popular especially with young people.

©Wessels

1 Inhalt
2 Büro zu Hause, häuslicher Arbeitsplatz
3 Durchsicht/Bewertung von Arbeiten
4 Verkaufspersonal
5 ausrüsten, ausstatten
6 ab und zu
7 Kombination aus coffee (shop) und office: Arbeitsplatz im Café
8 WLAN
9 entspannende Umgebung
10 Lärmpegel, Geräuschkulisse

The **cabinet office**[1] **system** usually consists of[2] an office for the department head and a secretariat[3], a meeting room or two and a number of small cabinets/rooms with one or two workplaces each. The rooms are often found on either side of a corridor.

1 Büroflucht, -etage
2 bestehen aus
3 Sekretariat

Advantages	Disadvantages
• There are few problems among employees. • Employees can work independently. • They can concentrate on their work. • Receiving visitors does not create too much disturbance[1].	• Difficult for teamwork • Contacts with other colleagues are reduced. • There is no free flow of information. • Monitoring[2] and helping employees is not so easy.

1 Störung
2 überwachen

1 Zellenbüro
2 (ab)getrennt
3 schalldämmende Trennwand
4 Privatsphäre

In a **cubicle office**[1] **system,** the individual workplaces are often separated[2] by sound-absorbing partition walls[3] to create an atmosphere of privacy[4]. The walls may be up to six feet high. The space needed per workplace is fairly small. This system is often used in call centres.

1 Arbeitsfläche, -bereich
2 überhören, mitbekommen
3 erschöpft

Advantages	Disadvantages
• The cost for office space is kept low. • Employees have their individual work areas[1]. • Communication is possible over the walls. • There is some degree of privacy.	• The sound level can be fairly high. • Discussions and phone calls can be overheard[2]. • Working in a team is not easy. • Discussions need to take place elsewhere. • Employees often feel exhausted[3].

1 Großraumbüro
2 *hier:* einnehmen
3 anordnen
4 auf verschiedene Art und Weise

The **open-space** or **open-plan office**[1] often covers[2] the whole floor of a building. Workplaces can be grouped[3] in a variety of ways[4]. They are often separated by sound-absorbing walls.

1 Möglichkeiten, Einrichtungen
2 Erholung, Entspannung
3 Pausenraum
4 Ruhezone

Advantages	Disadvantages
• The cost of office space is kept very low. • Contacting colleagues is easy. • Information can flow freely. • Teamwork is fairly easy. • There are good facilities[1] for work and recreation[2], e.g. breakrooms[3], rest areas[4], etc.	• There is no privacy for the employee. • There is a risk of conflicts, because it is impossible to avoid contact. • The noise level can be very high and lead to exhaustion. • Discussions need to take place elsewhere.

Talk about the "ideal" office.

1 In the text, find words and phrases that come closest to the following:

1 … work by themselves ____
2 … supervise employees ____
3 … office of a secretary/PA ____
4 … talking to one another ____
5 … stressed ____
6 … in many different ways ____
7 … divided by ____
8 … talking to people ____

2 Use the information in the boxes to complete these sentences.

1 Some people prefer the cabinet type office, because …
2 The cabinet office system is not so good, because bosses …
3 The cubicle office system is good for people who …
4 If you want to have a discussion with people working in cubicles, …
5 Open-plan offices can be found in many businesses, because …
6 But some people say they would prefer another type of workplace, because …
7 The home office can be a good solution for people who …
8 For people who can work on their own and like contacts to the outside world, the paperless coffice is a good alternative, because …

Look at these illustrations and describe the different types of offices.

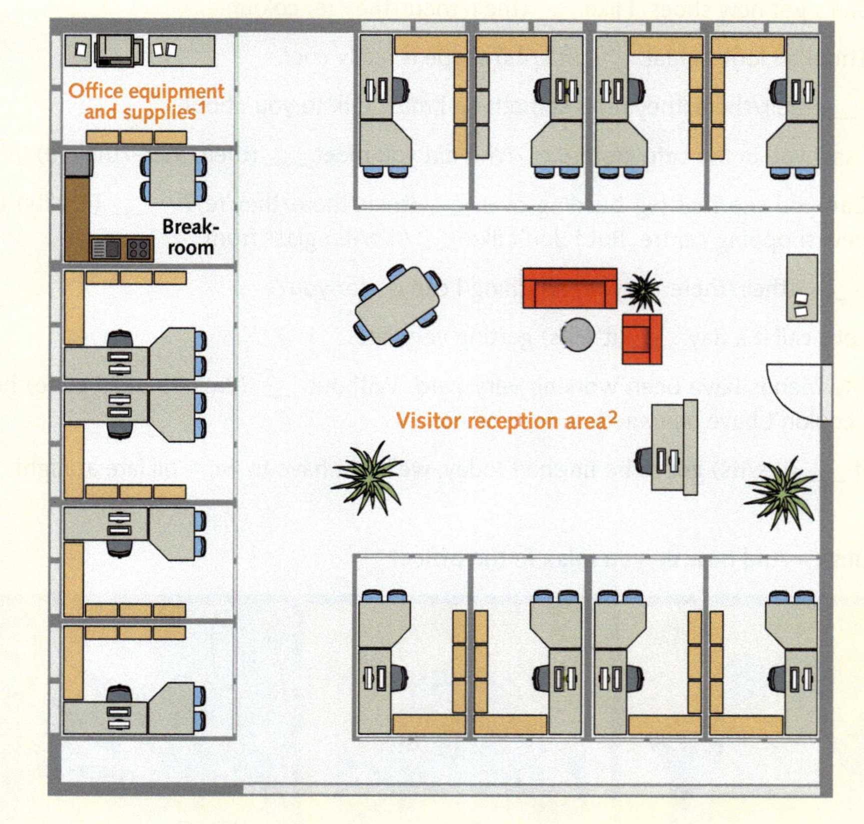

[1] Bürogeräte, Büromaterial

[2] Besucherempfangsbereich

Which type of office shown above would you prefer? State your reasons. Discuss your views in class.

Write an e-mail.

Imagine that as part of your training you have just moved to another department. Write an e-mail/a text message to your friend in Britain/the U.S.A. and tell her/him about your experience after your first day in a new office environment.

Note

Don't mix up ***it's*** and ***its***. ***It's*** is short for ***it is*** or ***it has***; ***its*** replaces a thing (example: *I've got a new mobile.* ***Its*** *colour is white.* – ***Its*** stands for mobile.).

It's also easy to mix up ***their***, ***there*** and ***they're***. ***Their*** means that something belongs to someone or something (example: *I went to* ***their*** *house today.* – the house of my friend's parents). ***There*** is the opposite of *here* and means some distance away (example: *What did you do* ***there***? – in your friend's house). It is also used in expressions such as *there is* or *there are*. ***They're*** is short for ***they are*** (example: ***They're*** nice people.).

Choose the correct short forms for these sentences.

1 ___ (it's/its) good to see you. - ___ (it's/its) been nice talking to you.

2 She's got new shoes. I like ___ (their/there/they're) colour.

3 This iPad looks great. ___ (it's/its) shape is really cool.

4 ___ (their/there/they're) is something I must talk to you about.

5 I saw you in the café yesterday. Who did you meet ___ (their/there/they're)?

6 Can you see that big building over ___ (their/there/they're)? - ___ (it's/its) our new shopping centre. But I don't like ___ (it's/its) glass front.

7 Is ___ (their/there/they're) anything I can do for you?

8 Let's call it a day. ___ (it's/its) getting very late.

9 My friends have been working very hard. Without ___ (their/there/they're) help I couldn't have managed.

10 If ___ (it's/its) got to be finished today, we'll just have to work till late at night.

"It's been hard work for the penguins. – And how do you relax in the office?"

Unit 3 Finding my way in the company

3.1 Learning about companies

These logos stand for businesses whose products are sold worldwide. You will certainly have come across[1] many of their products. Maybe you even use some of them sometimes or regularly.

[1] zufällig treffen auf

What do you know about these businesses? What are their main fields of activity[1]? Where are they based[2]? Use your mobile and find out.

In small groups, collect some information and present your findings[3] in class.

Are there any similarities[4] in what you and your classmates found? – If so – which?

[1] Tätigkeitsfeld
[2] Sitz haben
[3] Ergebnisse, Resultate
[4] Ähnlichkeit

3.2 Presenting a company

Track 8

Presenting a company is very similar to presenting yourself. Every company has a beginning, a history, that is to say, it has developed over a period of time[1] from small beginnings into a larger business. Its range[2] of products or services[3] may have changed. And this may also be true of the location it operates[4] from. Furthermore[5], that company is organised in a certain way. Most likely, it employs many people and makes a contribution to the local community[6]. The occasions where you may have to present your company, and maybe your function within the organisation, vary (meetings with colleagues from outside[7], visits by customers and trade partners[8], visits of the general public[9]). For each group, the approach[10] and the volume and type of information required[11] will be different.

[1] über eine Zeitspanne hinweg
[2] Sortiment, Auswahl
[3] Dienstleistung
[4] *hier*: tätig sein
[5] außerdem, darüber hinaus
[6] Standortgemeinde
[7] von außerhalb
[8] Geschäftspartner
[9] allgemeine Öffentlichkeit
[10] Herangehensweise
[11] *hier*: erforderlich

Track 9

Now read/listen to a brief company presentation given to a group of visitors.

Ladies and Gentlemen,

©vetkit-fotolia.com

Good morning to you all! I hope you had a good journey and didn't have any problems finding us. Thank you for having made the effort[1]. On behalf of the whole management team[2] of Brown & Sons Limited, I'd like to welcome you here in our head office[3].

My name is Daniel McInnes. And I'm responsible for marketing and customer relations[4]. I'd like to introduce Leslie Howard. Leslie is our senior customer relations officer[5]. Good of you to be with us, Leslie.

And before I go on, just help yourselves to coffee or tea or cold drinks, if you prefer.

Well now. I'll just give you a short overview[6] of who we are, what we do and where we are planning to go. If you have any questions, I'd be pleased to answer them as we go along[7]. So, don't hesitate[8].

Our company was founded by Jonathan Brown in the 60s, in 1965 to be precise[9], and at first provided logistics services[10] for the local farming community[11] here in Lincolnshire. A few years later, with a sound customer base[12] firmly established[13], Jonathan decided to branch out into[14] trading in farming supplies[15] generally, that is to say buying and selling fertilisers[16], seeds[17] of all kinds, pesticides[18] and general farming equipment[19], etc. He set up a network[20] of sales outlets[21] not only here in Lincolnshire, but step by step also in the neighbouring counties[22].

As the business grew, he involved his two sons, Richard and Dennis, who are now jointly responsible[23] for the management, while his daughter, Miriam, looks after the administration[24] in our head office here. Jonathan retired[25] a good 30 years ago. And the time has come now for the third generation to take over.

Brown & Sons Ltd today employs more than 150 people in various locations. Here in Lincoln we have our headquarters[26] and the central goods depot[27]. Our sales[28] passed the 150 million mark last year. Now, our plans are to consolidate[29] the business first before continuing to expand[30] further northwards into Yorkshire and beyond.

We are very proud of the fact that many of our customers have remained loyal to us for so many years. We aim to[31] build on this trust[32] by providing a first-class service to cover the specific needs[33] of our customers in the agricultural community[34].

Well, that's it for the time being[35]. Thank you for your attention. – Are there any questions? – If not, you can put them either to me or to Leslie as we go along. – And now I'll explain what the plan is for this visit …

1 Anstrengung unternehmen
2 *hier*: Unternehmensleitung, Führungsmannschaft
3 Hauptverwaltung
4 Kundenbeziehungen
5 Leiter/in der Abteilung Kundenbeziehungen
6 Überblick
7 *hier*: bei Bedarf
8 zögern
9 um genau zu sein
10 Logistikdienstleistungen, Transportdienste
11 *hier*: landwirtschaftliche Betriebe hier vor Ort
12 Kundenstamm
13 gut aufgebaut, stabil, solide, ordentlich
14 *hier*: Neuland betreten
15 landwirtschaftliche Güter
16 Düngemittel
17 Saatgut
18 Pflanzenschutzmittel
19 Agrarmaschinen
20 Netz(-werk)
21 Verkaufsstelle
22 angrenzende Grafschaft
23 gemeinsam verantwortlich
24 Verwaltung
25 in Rente gehen
26 Hauptverwaltung
27 zentrales Warenlager
28 Absatz
29 das Erreichte festigen
30 sich ausbreiten, expandieren
31 wollen, beabsichtigen
32 auf dieser Vertrauensbasis aufbauen
33 besondere Bedürfnisse
34 Landwirtschaft
35 zunächst einmal, fürs Erste

Comment on points in the text.

1 What are the key points in the history of Brown & Sons Ltd?
2 Which sectors does the company operate in?
3 To what extent are the members of the family involved in the business?
4 What are the points Daniel covers in his introduction?
5 Comment on the language. Try and find expressions that make the text easy to listen to.

©contrastwerkstatt-fotolia.com

Work with language.

Use terms from the box below to replace the terms in italics in sentences 1–10. There are more terms than you need.

• activity • branches • consolidate • customised[1] • established • expansion • • headquarters • our key account manager[2] • location • managing directors • • provision • a short survey[3] •

[1] auf die Kundenbedürfnisse zuschneiden
[2] Hauptkundenbetreuer/in
[3] Überblick

1 I am pleased to welcome you here in our *head office*.
2 To begin with, here is *some information* about our business.
3 My colleague here is *responsible for our big customers*.
4 Our company was *set up* twelve years ago.
5 We offer *customer-specific* IT solutions for doctors and lawyers.
6 Our latest *business venture* is to provide similar services for marketing companies.
7 In the last five years we set up *sales outlets* in the regional market towns.
8 Our company now has two *general managers*.
9 *Growth* is not our most important goal. We want our customers to be happy with our service.
10 After a period of fast increasing sales, we aim to *stabilise* our customer base.

©alotofpeople-fotolia.com

Info

A few key points to structure a company presentation:

- Welcome the visitors to your company.
- Introduce yourself (State your name and function.).
- Introduce a colleague who may be helping you or let her/him introduce themselves.
- Present your company:
  - State the name and the type of organisation.
  - Mention a few facts (annual sales[1] – at home and abroad[2]; number of employees; locations; affiliated companies[3], if any).
  - Talk about the beginnings.
  - Talk about the company's current[4] activities (products, markets/customers).
  - Talk about what is special about the company.
  - Talk about plans for the future.
- Outline the plan for the meeting/visit.

[1] Jahresumsatz
[2] im Inland & Ausland
[3] angeschlossene Gesellschaft
[4] jetzig

Prepare a presentation.

Collect information about your company/business/office. You may wish to use some of the phrases below for your presentation.

Introduction:	*My name is …* *I'm responsible for …* *I deal with …*
Company setup:	*Our company is based in …; and we have branches[1] in …* *Our head office is/headquarters are in …* *Our main production plant[2] is in …* *We also have offices/sales outlets in …* *We have … subsidiaries[3] which deal with/trade in[4] …*
History:	*We were founded/established in …* *Even today … is a family-owned business[5].* *In … we set up a subsidiary in …* *We merged[6] with … (company) in …*
Activities:	*Our company produces/makes/manufactures …* *We supply[7]/trade in/buy and sell …* *We provide (…) services for …* *We develop …*
Performance:	*We are among the top five …* *We are one of the leading … in … (region).* *For the past … years we have seen a steady[8] growth …* *From small beginnings we have grown very fast to become …* *Our turnover[9] has/sales have now reached …* *We now have branches/subsidiaries in …*

[1] Zweigstelle, Filiale
[2] Werk, Produktionsstätte
[3] Tochtergesellschaft
[4] handeln mit
[5] Familienunternehmen
[6] sich zusammenschließen
[7] liefern
[8] stetig, kontinuierlich
[9] Umsatz

3.3 Company organisation

In any business, the responsibilities for the various activities are shared out among the staff. And obviously, the bigger the business, the more complex the organisational[1] structure is likely to be. The business is often organised by function, by regions, by product groups, in work teams or very often by a combination of all of these. Most companies have adopted a hierarchical[2] structure which, usually depending on the size of the company, can be fairly flat or very complex.

[1] Organisations-
[2] hierarchisch

Learn about job titles[1].

[1] Stellenbezeichnung

1 Decide which of the English and the German terms belong together.

Accountant Bookkeeper Driver Foreman Managing Director Product Development Officer Production Manager Recruitment Officer Sales Manager Sales Representative Wages Clerk Warehouse Manager	Außendienstmitarbeiter/in Buchhalter/in Fahrer/in Geschäftsführer/in Lagerleiter/in Lohnbuchhalter/in Meister/in/Vorarbeiter/in Produktentwickler/in Produktionsleiter/in Rechnungsführer/in Sachbearbeiter/in für Personaleinstellungen Verkaufsleiter(in)

2 Copy the structure below and fill in the empty boxes. Use the job titles from the box in the bottom left corner of p. 32. Think about the position in the structure of the organisation.

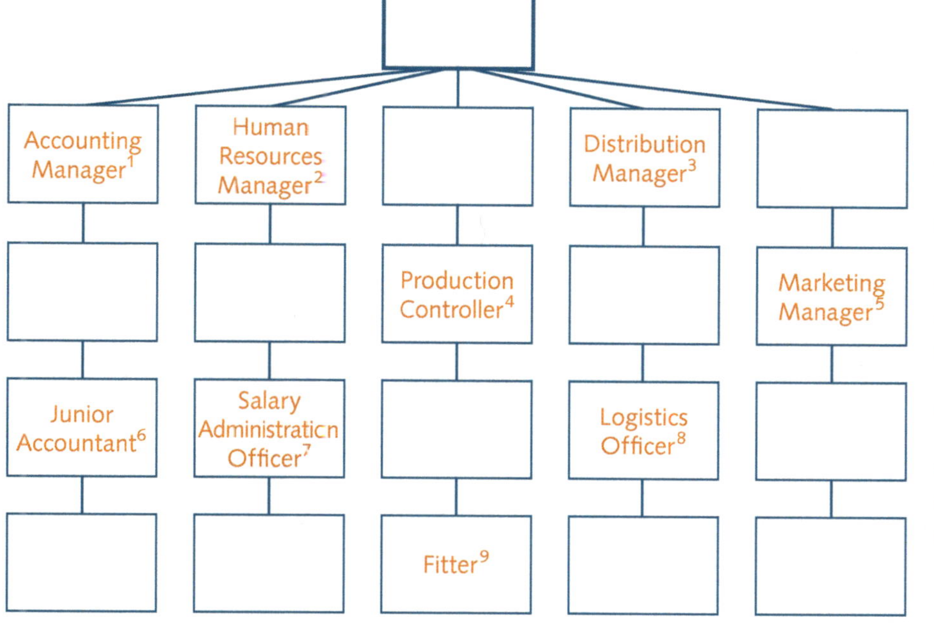

[1] Leiter/in des Rechnungswesens
[2] Leiter/in des Personalwesens
[3] Vertriebsleiter/in
[4] Produktionskontrolleur/in
[5] Leiter/in der Marketing-Abteilung
[6] Nachwuchskraft in der Buchhaltung
[7] Gehaltsbuchhalter/in
[8] Leiter/in der Logistik
[9] Schlosser/Monteur

The organisational structure in your company/business

1 Decide which of the German and English job titles belong together.

English	German
dispatch manager	*Büroleiter/in*
facility manager	*Chef-Einkäufer/in*
head buyer	*Lagerarbeiter/in*
office manager	*Mitarbeiter/in am Empfang*
production supervisor	*Objektleiter/in, Gebäudemanager/in*
project manager	*Produktionsleiter/in*
purchasing officer	*Projektleiter/in*
quality controller	*Qualitätskontrolleur/in*
receptionist	*Sachbearbeiter/in Einkauf*
secretary	*Sekretär/in*
sales agent	*Software-Entwickler/in*
software engineer	*Verkäufer/in*
warehouse worker	*Versandleiter/in*

2 Now draw a chart and explain it to your classmates.

State which departments you will go through in the course of[1] your training and/or those you have been through already.

[1] im Verlaufe von

In class, draw up a list of all the departments mentioned.

Revision

Adjectives, comparatives and superlatives

In English there are two ways of forming comparatives.

Short adjectives (one syllable) and two-syllable adjectives ending in *-y* take the ending *-er*, *-est* (which is similar to German). The ending *-y* changes to *-i*.

Examples:	*small*	*smaller*	*smallest*
	heavy	*heavier*	*heaviest*

More and *most* are used for the comparative forms of some adjectives with two and all adjectives with three syllables or more.

Examples:	*urgent*	*more urgent*	*most urgent*
	favourable	*more favourable*	*most favourable*

For some two-syllable adjectives, both modes of forming comparatives exist side by side.

Example:	*polite*	*politer/more polite*	*politest/most polite*

This is also the case with these adjectives: *unhappy, clever, common, simple, stupid, narrow, gentle.*

All adjectives take *less* and *least* to indicate a "reduction": *less happy, the least favourable result.*

Note these irregular comparisons:

little	*less*	*least*
old	*older*	*oldest* (*elder/eldest* for family members)
good	*better*	*best*
bad	*worse*	*worst*
much/many	*more*	*most*
far	*further*	*furthest* (*farther/farthest* only for distance)

Also note: *fewer/fewest* are used for countables, i.e. people and things *(fewer visitors, fewer tourists)*. For uncountables use *less/least (less water, less money (!), the least trouble)*.

Put these sentences into idiomatic English.

1. Mein älterer Bruder studiert in Leipzig.
2. Ich werde meine Ausbildung in weniger als einem Jahr beenden.
3. Das ist das schlechteste Ergebnis in den letzten fünf Jahren.
4. Heute hatten wir weniger Besucher als am vergangenen Samstag.
5. Unsere Kunden sind jetzt zufriedener als vor einem Jahr.
6. Mit einer geringeren Zahl von Produkten ist das Verkaufsgespräch (*sales talk*) viel einfacher.
7. Der schwerste Koffer wiegt 23 Kilo (*kilogram*). Die drei anderen sind weniger schwer.
8. Wir hatten einen günstigeren Preis erwartet.
9. Wir müssen versuchen, am Telefon höflicher zu sein.
10. Vielleicht sollten wir doch etwas weniger Geld für Werbung ausgeben.

3.4 Telephoning

3.4.1 Some basics

Everybody can use the telephone. So you might think: Why bother? But there is more to it than meets the eye.

Find telephone vocabulary in this wordsearch.

There are 14 terms. But first check the terms in the margin in your (online) dictionary.

	a	b	c	d	e	f	g	h	i	j	k	l	m
1	r	i	n	g	i	n	g	t	o	n	e	s	s
2	g	a	x	e	x	t	e	n	s	i	o	n	m
3	a	n	d	j	l	n	o	w	x	e	p	m	a
4	r	s	w	i	t	c	h	b	o	a	r	d	r
5	e	a	n	b	r	u	h	q	r	u	p	j	t
6	a	p	h	g	m	e	s	s	a	g	e	e	p
7	c	h	m	s	a	d	c	r	u	c	c	n	h
8	o	o	w	d	z	e	v	t	a	f	g	g	o
9	d	n	s	p	l	d	m	l	o	x	w	a	n
10	e	e	m	o	b	i	l	e	h	r	h	g	e
11	t	z	t	r	k	a	j	k	b	s	y	e	m
12	p	l	a	n	d	l	i	n	e	r	e	d	a

- Anrufbeantworter
- Vorwahlnummer
- wählen
- Telefonverzeichnis
- besetzt
- Durchwahl(nummer), Nebenstelle
- Kopfhörer mit Mikrofon
- Festnetz
- Nachricht
- Klingelton
- Telefonzentrale

Use the words from the wordsearch to fill in the gaps.

1 The _______ for London is 020. Of course, this applies only if you use the _______ .
2 I'm finished with the old _______. The _______ is so much more fun.
3 When you've finished keying in the subscriber's number, you should hear the _______.
4 If there's nobody at home, you can leave a _______ on the _______.
5 Just call the person at the _______, and they will put you through.
6 I couldn't get through, because your phone was _______ all morning.
7 People doing a lot of their work over the phone find it easier to use a _______.
8 For my _______ just drop the 0 und dial 251 instead.
9 Our telephone company doesn't issue _______ anymore, because most people get the number they need via the internet.
10 Sorry, I couldn't answer your _______ . I was in a meeting.
11 In Britain, the number to _______ for emergencies is 999.

[1] eingeben
[2] Nummer des Teilnehmers
[3] Notfall

Info

Some dos and don'ts for telephoning

- Speak slowly and clearly.
- Say who you are and mention the name of your company/business/institution.
- State the time of day and ask what you can do for the caller[1].
- Don't forget to be friendly and polite. Say *please* and *thank you*.
- Listen carefully.
- Don't interrupt your partner.
- Ask the caller to repeat when you have not understood.
- Don't try to solve all the problems yourself. Put the call through to the person responsible.
- Try and be helpful.
- Have a notepad[2] and pen ready to take notes.
- Repeat numbers and names so that people can be called back.
- Keep any background noise to a minimum.
- Don't keep a caller waiting for too long. It's better to call them back.

1 Anrufer/in
2 Notizblock

Learn about telephoning.

1 Mediate. Your boss has asked you to produce a German-language version of the dos and don'ts. Do not translate word for word, but try and find a kind of language that flows and sounds natural.

2 From your experience, is there anything you would like to add to this list? What is the policy regarding telephone manners at your place of work? Share your experience.

3.4.2 Telephone alphabet

Obviously, it is useful to know the German telephone alphabet for national calls. Make sure you learn it. If your company does business with other countries, it is equally[1] important that you know the international telephone alphabet as well. You may be talking to people from other countries who have a very strong local accent or who do not speak English well. Even callers from Britain and the US or Canada are sometimes difficult to understand. So, when saying names or telephone numbers, you want to be sure that you understand your partners and also that they understand you. And of course, good telephone skills leave a good impression.

1 ebenso, ebenfalls

Track 10

International spelling alphabet

A Alpha	G Golf	M Mike	S Sierra	Y Yankee
B Bravo	H Hotel	N November	T Tango	Z Zulu
C Charlie	I India	O Oscar	U Uniform	
D Delta	J Juliet	P Papa	V Victor	
E Echo	K Kilo	Q Quebec	W Whiskey	
F Foxtrot	L Lima	R Romeo	X X-ray	

Note

The spelling of the letter "z" is pronounced *[zed]* in British English and *[zi]* in American English. Note also the differences in the pronunciation of the letters "e" *[i]* and "i" *[ai]* and also "g" *[dschi]* and "j" *[dschei]*.

Now listen to the international telephone alphabet.

3.4.3 Good to know

When saying names, addresses and e-mail addresses on the phone, you need to know the words for special signs.

Learn to use signs.

1 Write down a list of the words for the signs that you use in normal texts. Here they are:

.	,	;	:	?	!	"…"	…'

Note

The hyphen (-) links two words. [The symbol is short]. The dash (–) [the symbol is long] indicates the beginning of a new idea in a sentence. In e-mail addresses the – is called "hyphen" or "minus sign".

©Tanusha-fotolia.com

2 For these signs you often add the word "sign", e.g. $ = the dollar sign. Now make your own list for the following:

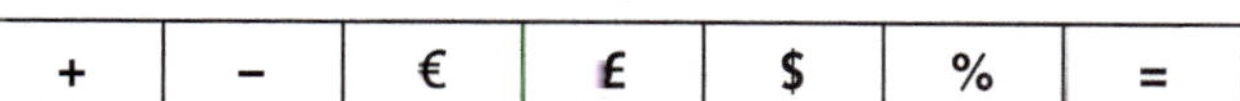

+	–	€	£	$	%	=

3 Choose the right signs from the table for the terms listed below. Make sure you know the German words.

I	_	*	\	#	(…)	@	~	[…]	/

asterisk[1] | at (sign) | backslash
forward slash | hash(tag) | left/right round bracket
left/right square bracket | vertical bar/slash[2] | tilde
underscore[3]

[1] Sternchen
[2] senkrechter Strich
[3] unterstreichen

With your partner, practise using the international alphabet.

1 What is the (registration) number of their father's/mother's car?
2 What is their e-mail address in their company or the contact where one can get information?
3 What is the name of their company's website?

Practise saying these internet sites.

1 http://www.allareacodes.com/
2 https://countrycode.org usa
3 www.telephonebook.bt.com
4 www.linguee.com
5 www.dict.cc
6 https://dict.leo.org

Note

The last three are good sources for vocabulary search.

3.4.4 Telephone numbers

©Vgstudio-fotolia.com

Info

In Britain and the U.S.A. telephone numbers are usually stated singly. The number 0 is stated as *oh* and sometimes also as *zero* or *nought*.

Examples: *75674 = seven – five – six – seven – four*
The area code for Berlin is oh – three – oh

Numbers such as *44* are stated as *double four*; *11* is stated as *double one* and *00* is usually stated as *double oh*.

Example for a British phone number: *0044-1372-8004332 = double oh – double four – one – three – seven – two – eight – double oh – four – double three – two*

Note

It is still customary in Britain to answer the phone by just saying *Hello* or by stating the place where you live and your number. So you need to listen very carefully when you answer the phone.

Practise using telephone numbers.

1 With your partner, practise using the international telephone alphabet and say telephone numbers. Use your own name and number and those of your company. Spell your full address (*Postleitzahl* = postal code *[BE]* or ZIP code *[AE]*).

Track 11

2 Listen to the recording and write down the numbers and also the names of the towns.

3 Say these telephone numbers. Use them in full phrases, e.g. *Our/Their/My number is …; We/They/I can be reached under …; For more information phone …*

020 (for London) 480 77 11
0161 (for Manchester) 899 12 68
0121 (for Birmingham) 879 55 12
0151 (for Liverpool) 635 40 21
0212 (for New York) 130 00 75
0213 (for Los Angeles) 398 55 77
0248 (for Detroit) 254 88 00
0786 (for Miami) 434 85 44

It is useful to know some country codes.

Country	Country Code	Country	Country Code
Belgium	0032	Italy	0039
France	0033	The Netherlands	0031
Germany	0049	Australia	0061
Switzerland	0041	Canada	001
USA	001	United Kingdom	0044
Spain	0034	Poland	0048

1 Now practise using these country codes. Use phrases such as the following: *The country code for … is ….* Or you may say: *… is the country code for ….*

2 Find out the country codes of other countries that your company may be dealing with or where some of your classmates come from.

Try to understand a telephone conversation.

Track 12

1 Listen to the recording and fill in the gaps. Because of a bad line, some of the information in this phone call has got lost.

A: Could you please give me your number so that I can call you back?

B: That would be a good idea. My number is: ______ for Germany, the area code for Cologne is 0221, but you drop the 0. And my number is 58 23 176.

A: Thank you. I repeat: ______ for Germany, 221 for ______ . And your number is ______ 3 166.

B: Sorry, that's not quite correct. The last but one digit[1] is 7.

A: OK, so your number is 58 23 ______ ?

B: That's it. Quite correct!

A: And what did you say your name was?

B: My name is Felizia Brinkmann. Shall I spell that for you?

A: Yes, please do. That would be kind. It sounded rather difficult.

B: So my first name[2] is Felizia spelt F E L I Z I A. And the surname[3] is Brinkmann, spelt B R I N K M A N N.

A: OK, I think I've got that. Good. And may I also trouble you for your e-mail address please?

B: No problem. My address is: felizia.brinkmann as before. And then @t-online.de.

A: I repeat: Felizia ______ Brinkmann ______ t ______ online – one word?

B: Yes, that's right. Online – one word.

A: OK. And then dot ______.

B: That's it. Exactly.

[1] Ziffer, Stelle
[2] Vorname
[3] Nachname

©Minerva Studio-fotolia.com

2 Now practise reading the text. Then listen to the dialogue once again.

3 Use this dialogue and write your own list of useful phrases and their German equivalents.

Note

Mind the difference in the spelling of the words *Adresse* (German) and *address* (English). This also applies to the verbs etc.: *adressieren = to address; Adressat = addressee.*

3.4.5 Telephone phrases

Write down the German for these terms and phrases and make sure you learn them.

1 automatische Ansage
2 außerhalb der Bürostunden/Bürozeiten
3 dienstliche Nummer
4 private Rufnummer
5 Notrufnummer, Beratungsstelle
6 Empfang
7 speichern
8 löschen, tilgen
9 Tonsignal

Telephone	Digital
to call/phone so., to give so. a ring, to make a call	I don't have a signal[6].
The line is bad.	text message
recorded message[1]	to text so.
out-of-office hours[2]	to save[7] a text
office number[3]	to delete a message
home number[4]	Please leave a message after the tone.
hotline, helpline[5]	cellphone *[AE]*

Below find useful phrases in parallel boxes that relate directly to what the caller and the person answering are saying.

1 sich entschuldigen
2 jdn. durchstellen zu/verbinden mit
3 Nachricht weiterleiten
4 nicht genau verstehen
5 in der Leitung/dran bleiben
6 Nachricht hinterlassen
7 Nachricht aufnehmen

Person calling	Person answering
• Hello, this is Peter Jones. • Jones/Peter here. • My name is Jennifer O'Connor. • I'm Deborah Leighton. Good morning.	• This is GTD Limited. Reception. My name is Tina Greer. • Reception. Sharon speaking. How can I help you? • Good afternoon. This is Emily at the Howden Trade Centre. What can I do for you? • Who is calling, please?
• So sorry, but I think I dialled the wrong number. • So sorry. – I do apologise[1].	• Never mind. That can happen. • I'm sorry, but you must have got the wrong number.
• I'll spell that/it for you. ... My surname is ... (And now my first name ...)	• I didn't quite get[4] your name. The line is (very) bad. Could you please repeat that?
• I'm calling about ... • My reason for calling you is ... • Could I speak to David Huxley, please? • Could you please put me through to[2] your Marketing Department? I would like to speak to Mr/Ms ... • I would like to speak to Laura Bingley in your Logistics Department, please. • Could you pass on a message[3], please?	• OK, just hold the line[5], please. I'll put you through (now)./I'll try to connect you. • She's just put the phone down. • I'm afraid he's/she's not in at the moment. • He's very busy just now./She's in a meeting all morning. • Would you like to leave a message[6] perhaps?/Can I pass on/take a message[7]?

Person calling	Person answering
• Could I leave a message, please? • Yes, thank you, that's very kind of you. • When do you think I could reach her/him? • When do you expect her/him (to be) back in the office? • When do you expect the meeting to be finished? • When do you think he/she will be free? • Right, then I think I'll call again later/tomorrow/next week.	• Her/His phone is engaged just now. Would you like to wait a moment? • Would you like to ring/call back later? • If you leave me your number[1], he'll/she'll call you back later. • He's/She's away on business. Perhaps there's someone else who could help you if it's urgent[2]. Let me try. • Or would you like to speak to someone else? • Her/His extension is 435.
	• Hello … , there's … wanting to talk to you. Can you take the call? – Or are you busy right now? • I was just about to pick up the phone, when …
• Thanks a lot. • Thank you for your help. Goodbye. • Thank you very much and goodbye.	• You're welcome./Thank you. • Thanks for calling. • Thanks a lot. Goodbye. • OK then. Bye-bye.

[1] jdm. die Nummer geben
[2] dringend

Learn about telephone language.

In groups of three or four students, work out idiomatic German sentences for the phrases listed here. Leave out the first and last boxes. Find ways of sharing your work in class.

Listen to this telephone call. Make notes of the details.

Lena Westermann is taking the call. But the caller, Patricia Soames, wants to talk to Mr Sven Braukmüller.

You will find the text on pp. 201–202.

Track 13

Listen to the telephone conversation again and then answer these questions, please.

1 What are the names of the two ladies?
2 Who do they work for?
3 What is the problem?
4 What message does Pat leave?
5 What does Lena promise to do?
6 What is the number of Pat's company?
7 What does Pat say about Lena's English?

Write a memo of the telephone conversation in German for Herr Braukmüller.

Role play

Situation: A caller, Jessie Montague, wants to talk to the person responsible for visits to Sampson Engineering Ltd. The call is answered by the switchboard operator/receptionist. Use the phrases in the box on pp. 40–41. Practise being polite at the beginning and at the end of the conversation.

Role card

A You are Jessie and you are trying to arrange the visit of a group of sixteen-year-old students to Sampson Engineering Ltd. You ask to be put through to the person in charge. Explain why you are planning the visit (getting students to learn about the world of work in manufacturing). Be prepared to give your name and telephone number.

You will find the text for Role B on p. 202.

Learn to leave messages.

There is no answer to your phone call. Instead, you hear this recorded message:

"I'm sorry. But the person you're calling is not available at the moment. However, you can leave a message. Please speak after the tone."

And this is what you can say:

- State your name and the name of the company you work for.
- State why you are calling (change of an appointment; your boss needs more information/details about …; your boss wants to discuss details of the planned visit; etc.).
- Say that you/your boss would like to be called back and give your telephone number and the extension.
- At the end say "Thank you and goodbye".

Practise saying an ansaphone message. Use the pattern explained above. Reasons for your call:

1 Sie brauchen weitere Informationen für das Alpha-Projekt.

2 Das Treffen kann leider erst nächste Woche stattfinden.

3 Sie haben noch Fragen zum Termin für das Treffen.

4 Sie benötigen noch einige Tabellen für die Präsentation.

5 Sie wollen noch Einzelheiten über die Firma wissen.

Of course, you can also use a reason of your own choice.

Unit 4 Getting organised

4.1 From school to work

©shutterstock-fotolia.com

©shutterstock-fotolia.com

Moving from the sheltered[1] life at school – to many that does not seem to reflect[2] reality; they hated school. Entering the world of business[3] and administration clearly is like a watershed[4]. You step into what many people call the "real world". So let's take stock[5].

1 geschützt
2 wiederspiegeln
3 Wirtschaftswelt
4 Wendepunkt, Zäsur
5 Bilanz ziehen

1. What has changed in your lives, your daily routines, your timetable, the way you spend your spare time, the time you hang out with friends, your sports activities, etc.?
2. Draw up two lists: what do you miss from your former life? What have you gained?
3. What kind of people have you met in your new surroundings? What's the influence they have on you?
4. Has the fact that you are now earning money changed your behaviour or your habits? In what way?

Discuss your experience in class.

4.2 A beginner's experience

Evelyn has put a few thoughts down in her diary. See what you think.

Track 14

©rocketclips-fotolia.com

After a few weeks in the office, I realise that businesses are like very complex machines, full of moving parts[1] that need to be kept going. If one division[2] doesn't carry its weight[3], all the others will suffer. Having worked in an office job for a little while now, I'm beginning to get a feel for how the company works. All the different departments interact[4]. If you take one away, production, sales, accounting[5], personnel[6], legal[7], the machinery of the company will begin to stutter[8] and stop running.

In my job, especially at my entry level[9], I'm starting to realise how the decisions of my boss influence the employees, the way they work, the way they think ...

1 bewegliches Teil
2 Abteilung
3 voll mitziehen
4 zusammenwirken
5 Rechnungswesen
6 Personalwesen
7 Rechtsabteilung
8 stottern
9 Eingangsstufe

[10] in welchem Umfang
[11] ein bedeutender Teil
[12] effizient, effektiv
[13] sich hinziehen
[14] es geht vor allem um Verhandlung
[15] Liefertermin
[16] Gehalt
[17] Frist einhalten
[18] schmollen
[19] wirkungsvoll kommunizieren
[20] Bildung von Netzwerken
[21] sich ständig wiederholen
[22] Ausgewogenheit

I could never have imagined to what extent[10] meetings are a major part[11] of the business world. Some of them are quick and efficient[12], others drag on[13] for hours. I never realised that business is all about negotiating[14]: with customers about goods, prices, delivery dates[15], with staff about working hours, salaries[16], project work, meeting deadlines[17], etc.

And I've noticed that dealing with people is not easy. The routines I practised at home, with friends or in school didn't get me very far. Sulking[18] doesn't help. I had to make an effort to be friendly and polite, help others, dress properly, communicate effectively[19], etc.

I've become aware that networking[20] can make life a lot easier. It's true what some people say: "It's not what you know, it's who you know." When I have a problem to solve, knowing the right people makes my tasks a lot easier. In our big office it wasn't too difficult to become friendly with people from different departments. I just say "Hello!" when I pass their desks, talk to the people in the kitchen or in the cafeteria.

So, all in all, I'm positive about things. I know I'm learning a lot as I go along. I'm beginning to organise my life a bit better – my work by seeing what others are doing and how they're doing it and following their good examples – stealing with my eyes, as some people put it. Some work is really very boring and repetitive[21], but someone's got to do it, I reckon. Other things are very challenging indeed. In the end, I think it's the balance[22] that counts. And it comes down to my own attitude to work. So, I just get on with it. And some day, I'll move on and somebody else will do my work.

Evelyn's experience and yours

1 Re-read the text and change these statements if necessary.

1. There is nothing as complex as businesses.
2. The departments are permanently in contact with each other.
3. When one department stalls[1] the others get into full swing.
4. Like everybody else, Evelyn is strongly influenced by her boss.
5. It's difficult to keep meetings short.
6. Dealing with people and finding solutions to problems is a key part of any business activity.
7. Politeness does pay off[2].
8. Getting to know people is not as easy as one might think.
9. Evelyn's attitude to work is somewhat sceptical[3].

[1] zum Stillstand kommen
[2] sich auszahlen
[3] skeptisch

2 Say why you agree/disagree with Evelyn's statements.

- Businesses are like machines.
- The different departments interact.
- Meetings are an important part of business activities.
- It's not really difficult to make new friends.
- Networking makes life easier.

3 What is the situation like in your company? – What are the main activities that you notice in your team?

4.3 Organising my day

What is your working day like?

Draw a table as suggested below and enter your activities in a normal working week, including your breaks[1] (morning, lunch, afternoon).

[1] Pause

	Monday	Tuesday	Wednesday	Thursday	Friday
Time	Tasks	Tasks	Tasks	Tasks	Tasks
8.00 – 9.00	Arrive at work, collect & distribute the mail, team meeting, start up my computer				
9.00 – 10.00	Help … with her chart, check and answer my mails, filing, …				
10.00 – 10.15	Coffee break				
10.15 – 11.00	Continue filing, copy and paste[1] texts and graphics for my boss				
11.00 – 12.30	Help prepare a mailing list[2]				
12.30 – 13.15	Lunch break				
etc.	…				

[1] *hier*: einfügen
[2] Versandliste

Looking at your activities at work

1 Use a highlighter to mark in your chart the activities which occur[1] regularly: every day, once a week, less often. Say which they are.

2 Comment on your activities. Say whether you like/dislike them and give reasons for your attitude.
You may wish to use phrases such as the following:
- I very much like … because …/I like … most, because it means I can …
- I'm (not) very keen on …, simply because …
- I really hate/dislike …
- I can't see why I should always …
- I still can't get used to …
- I never thought I would warm up to[2] the idea of …
- Meetings are interesting/boring, because …
- I'm not a tidy person really. But seeing the mess in the kitchen every day, I …
- Having to clear things away may be a bore[3], but …
- Now that I know why … has got to be done, I just get on with it.
- I love doing …

[1] vorkommen
[2] sich erwärmen für
[3] langweilig sein

3 Explain to the other members of your group what a typical working day is like in your company.

4.4 How about filing[1]?

Track 15

[1] Ablage machen
[2] Paketauslieferung
[3] speichern
[4] Intranet
[5] beschleunigen
[6] erheblich, mächtig
[7] im Bruchteil einer Sekunde
[8] Kundennummer
[9] Vereinbarung aufsetzen
[10] Rundschreiben
[11] Protokoll schreiben
[12] Informationen bereitstellen/geben
[13] seine Berechtigung erhalten
[14] als Nachweis
[15] aufgrund gesetzlicher Vorschriften
[16] Unterlagen aufbewahren
[17] Handwerker
[18] Ablagesystem
[19] Zahlensystem
[20] Hängeregistratur
[21] aufstapeln
[22] Regalschrank
[23] hervorholen, auffinden
[24] Kodierung
[25] Klammer, Halterung
[26] Teiler
[27] unmittelbar verfügbar sein
[28] Rollcontainer
[29] Problem angehen
[30] Aktenlagerung

In our age of electronic communication, paper documents are a thing of the past. That may be true when you think about electronic tickets, online shopping, online banking and logistics even (e.g. parcel delivery[2]).

In the office, things are quite different. It is true that a lot of information is available and stored[3] online on the company's/institution's intranet[4] only. And this certainly helps to speed up[5] things no end[6], because staff have a customer's details available on their screen in a split second[7]. They just need the customer account number[8].

But when it comes to drawing up agreements[9], sending out invoices or circulars[10], drawing up minutes[11] of meetings, providing information[12] of whatever sort, the printed document comes into its own[13] again. Many documents need to be kept for reference purposes[14] or for legal reasons, because by law[15] private individuals and businesses have to keep certain records[16] for longer periods of time. Did you know that private people need to keep craftsmen's[17] invoices for two years?

Of course, companies everywhere in the world have set up their own filing systems[18], and some may even operate several systems side by side depending on the requirements of the different departments. Such systems can be arranged alphabetically, by subject, by project, by customer name or number (ID number) or by geographical area. Thus, the alphabet, a numerical system[19] and/or the postal code are frequently used to organise the filing system.

©mnirat-fotolia.com

The type of system often depends on national traditions: in German-speaking countries, file folders in wall units are the preferred method; hanging files[20] in desks or filing cabinets are often found in Britain, France or the U.S.A.; folders stacked up[21] in filing shelves[22] are common in Britain, the U.S.A. or Germany. Whichever method is used, in the day-to-day work routine it is important to be able to retrieve[23] the files quickly.

And the file itself demands some form of organisation as well: chronological order of documents, colour coding[24], fasteners[25] (paper clips) or dividers[26] for specific kinds of documents. Obviously, quite a few files need to be at hand[27] all the time (mostly kept on or in desks or in roller containers[28]), while others are only used once in a while. This needs to be taken into consideration when the issue[29] of file storage[30] is addressed[29].

Few people like the task of filing. And yet, everybody is pleased when they find things quickly and don't have to search around for documents for hours on end.

Filing and beyond

Answer these questions, please.

1 Where, in your experience, has electronic communication replaced paper documents?

2 Where and how have you, as a customer, benefited from data being available online?

©mnirat-fotolia.com

3 Can you name documents that your company/institution keeps in paper form?

4 For which kind of services does your company/institution have customer identification numbers? How often do you use these services?

5 How does your company/institution store files and where are they kept?

6 What do you think of the systems for storing data and files that you have seen in your company/institution?

1 "We have been promised the paperless office. But we seem to be forever printing out things." Discuss and explain why we print out things.

2 Find reasons why most people are still very keen to have a printed copy in front of them when working on a project. Share your experiences and your views with your classmates.

4.5 Organising my desk

©thodonal-fotolia.com

©Photographee.eu-fotolia.com

©sergign-fotolia.com

Workplaces can be different. Deal with the questions below.

1 What does your desk look like?

2 How do you leave your desk when you finish work in the afternoon?

3 What would you seriously like your desk to look like? Don't forget that some people can work very well and are most creative[1] with a very untidy desk. Others need everything cleared away[2] to be able to concentrate. Share your views.

[1] kreativ, schöpferisch
[2] beiseite räumen, wegräumen

Track 16

Evelyn has some ideas

Filing systems, once established, are there to stay[1]. And for good reason. With time they may be expanded[2], but their basic structure will remain what it has always been. This is different with my workplace. This is my "kingdom[3]", so to speak. I myself am responsible for organising my immediate work environment so that I've got things close at hand[4] when I need them. I know my routines best, and that makes me work efficiently.

On my first day in the office, I needed to sit at my desk for a few minutes and figure out[5] where I'll instinctively look or reach for things. Some people pick up the phone with their right hand, others with their left hand. What do you do when you need to take notes when telephoning? I don't like to move the receiver[6] from my right ear to my left ear.

I have a roller container to the right of my workstation[7]. When I first organised my desk, I didn't have anything in it. In the past, when I needed some writing utensils[8] (pencil, biro, rubber, highlighter, paper clips or my stapler[9], etc.), the top right-hand drawer[10] was the place where I would look first. So naturally, I put all these things in that drawer. For me, it was the natural home for these items.

I keep the second drawer for the files and any other documents I'm currently[11] working on. I keep the files that I don't need immediately in a filing cabinet further away from my workstation. Some colleagues even have a file holder[12] and in and out trays[13] on their desks. But I don't like that idea very much. And I use the larger bottom drawer for my personal belongings, my bag, hankies[14], some snacks, lunch box[15], etc.

I know everyone will do this differently. And what works for me may not work for somebody else. But taking a few minutes to sit down and reach for equipment, supplies and files certainly helped me organise my work processes. This is an arrangement that keeps my desk nice and tidy. And that pleases my boss. But I don't know where to put my coffee mug[16]. Any ideas??

1 dauerhaft bleiben
2 erweitern
3 „Königreich"
4 in Reichweite
5 herausfinden
6 (Telefon-)Hörer
7 Arbeitsplatz
8 Schreibutensilien
9 Heftapparat
10 Schublade
11 gegenwärtig, gerade (jetzt)
12 Aktenablage
13 (Post)Ein- und Ausgangskorb
14 Taschentuch
15 Brotdose
16 Kaffeetasse

Would you agree with these statements? Say why or why not.

1 The desk is a workstation that reflects a person's sense of order.
2 Writing utensils etc. can be put anywhere.
3 It doesn't matter in which hand you hold the receiver of the phone.
4 I don't like roller containers. We have lockers where we keep our private things.
5 Workstations should be tidied up every night.
6 Documents get lost or forgotten in the in trays.

What kind of worker are you?

How did you arrange your workplace? State the reasons for the arrangements that you made for yourself.

Be honest! What do you keep in the bottom drawer of your desk?

Complete the text below. There is something missing in every third word.

When we receive a document from a colleague or customer it's tempting[1] to just put it away i___ a pile[2] o___ your desk or draw___ for the ti___ being, because w___ want to ha___ a closer lo___ later. That sou___ familiar. After a whi___, many such docu___ build up, lead___ to a lo___ of clutter[3]. It___ highly unlikely th___ you'll ever fi___ time to g___ back and g___ all of that inform___ organised, especially consider___ that you're usu___ under pressure[4] wi___ other things.

You can spe___ hours of prec___ time searching fo___ documents that you___ filed away somew___, because it's ea___ to forget whe___ you put th___. Or you ev___ forget that y___ got the docu___ in the fir___ place. So, get bet___ at managing your ti___.

1 verführerisch
2 Haufen, Stapel
3 Durcheinander, Unordnung
4 unter Druck stehen

Revision

Simple present and present progressive

A few simple rules:

The **simple present** is used

- for actions that occur regularly and to express habits (note the signal words: *always, usually, sometimes, normally, every …, often, never*).
- for general statements *(The dollar is a leading currency.)*.
- to express the time of a future event (timetable)
  Examples: *The train leaves at 7.30 hrs./The meeting is at 10 o'clock tomorrow.*
- with verbs that express mental processes (e.g. *doubt, hear, mean, remember, think, believe, wish*):
  Examples: *I wish they could see us now./I think working in an office is fun./I remember you were ill last month.*

The **present progressive** is used

- for actions taking place at the time of speaking *(I'm preparing the room for the meeting tomorrow.)*.
- to refer to arrangements made for the future *(We are sending goods to China next week.)*.
- for repeated events which are only temporary *(She's helping me with the filing today.)*.
- for present time actions indicating change *(House prices are rising like never before.)*.

Put the verbs in brackets into the proper form.

1 I usually (to start) work at 7.30 in the morning.
2 When I (to arrive), my colleague normally (to sit) at her desk already.
3 I often (to go) to lunch with an office junior from another department.
4 I (not to think) we (to make) any progress with putting all these files away today.
5 We can't go away on holiday this summer, so we (to stay) at home.
6 Our company (to manufacture) screws[1] for the car industry.
7 I (to write) an e-mail just now.
8 Short weekend trips (to become) more and more popular.
9 We (to believe) that we (to see) a gradual decline in the number of bookshops.

1 Schraube

Express these ideas in English.

Example: Er wartet gerade auf einen Anruf. – *He is waiting for a phone call.*

1. Er denkt, dass es regnet.
2. Die Schwester liest gerade ein spannendes Buch.
3. Sie macht nie eine Kaffeepause.
4. Der Flieger kommt morgen um 18.25 Uhr in Manchester an.
5. Sie arbeiten diese Woche länger, weil sie am Freitag einen Tag frei *(a day off)* haben wollen.
6. Sie meint, wir vergessen oft die Interessen der Kunden.
7. Wir hören nicht genau hin, wenn die Chefin etwas erklärt.
8. Sie macht jetzt den Tee für alle.
9. Wenn er das Büro verlässt, arbeiten die anderen noch.
10. Normalerweise gehen sie dienstags ins Kino; aber morgen schreiben sie einen Test, und deswegen bleiben sie heute zu Hause.

4.6 Written communication[1]

Communicating is one of the key activities in the daily office routine. For written communication, businesses use purposefully designed[2] stationery[3]. In Germany, the DIN standards mean that the information printed on company stationery and, to some extent[4], also the layout of business letters are very similar.

[1] Schriftverkehr
[2] speziell entwickelt
[3] Firmenbriefpapier
[4] bis zu einem gewissen Grade

Note

There is a difference between *stationery* and *stationary*. *Stationery* is the term for writing utensils (esp. writing paper and envelopes), whereas *stationary* is used for something that is not moving, e.g. a car/bus.

Describe company stationery.

Find out from your partner which layout her/his company uses (type and arrangement of the information, design, colours, etc.). Where can this kind of information be found? Are there any differences in layout? Which are they?

Use expressions such as the following:

- at the top/bottom
- in the top/bottom right-/left-hand corner
- on the right/left
- in the centre
- number in the commercial register[1]
- bank account number[2]
- left-justified[3]
- justified text[4]

[1] Handelsregister
[2] Kontonummer
[3] linksbündig
[4] Blocksatz

©Redshinestudio-fotolia.com

4.6.1 Sample letter[1]

Layout and organisation of a business letter (American style).

Letterhead[1] (sender's name, address & contact data)	J. STEPHENS MARKETING LTD 385 West 47th Street New York NY 10012 Tel (0173)4844 85891 Fax (0173)4844 85881 Mail info@jstephensmarketing.com
Date (reference initials[2])	July 22nd, 20.. JB/QC
Addressee's address	Mable Park Inc., 217 Fisher Street, Fairhaven, Mass. 02719.
Subject line[3]	Request for[4] tourist information
Salutation[5]	Dear Ms. Littlebrook:
Text of the letter	Thank you for your enquiry[6] about tourist information for organized tours to New York. We are able to offer a wide range[7] of exciting tours of New York. The enclosed brochure[8] will give a good overview of our activities. It also contains[9] some indications[10] of more specialized trips. We are able to make all the necessary arrangements[11] for your groups, including hotel bookings, visits, boat trips, theater tickets, etc. If you wish, we have highly experienced tour guides[12] to accompany your groups. If you require more information, please contact us. Our prices obviously vary depending on the services required. We would suggest[13] that you get in touch[14] so that we can discuss your needs[15]. We look forward to hearing from you.
Complimentary close[16]	Yours truly,
Signature **Name, function** (department, telephone & fax numbers, office hours etc.) **Enclosure**[17] (if any)	J. Stephens jr. (Managing Director) Encl. Brochures Price-list

1 Musterbrief

1 Briefkopf
2 Bezugszeichen
3 Betreffzeile
4 Bitte um
5 Anrede
6 Anfrage (nach)
7 umfassendes Angebot
8 Broschüre
9 enthalten
10 Hinweis
11 Vorkehrungen treffen
12 Touristenführer/in
13 vorschlagen, anregen
14 Kontakt aufnehmen
15 Anforderungen
16 höfliche Schlussformel
17 Anlage

Compare the layout above with examples of letters from German companies that you have seen. What differences do you see?

4.6.2 British and American usage

When communicating with business partners abroad, you will be told to use the conventions[1] or DIN standards that apply[2] in your company. And yet, it's good to know about a few details that are commonly[3] found in English-speaking countries. The most important refer to[4] forms of addressing your partner, closing a letter, writing the date, to mention but the most important. Use these conventions when writing to your partners abroad.

1 Standard
2 gelten
3 allgemein, häufig
4 sich beziehen auf

British usage

<table>
<tr><th></th><th>Salutation</th><th>Complimentary close</th><th>Date*</th></tr>
<tr><td>You do not know your partner</td><td>Dear Madam; Dear Sir
Dear Sir or Madam
Dear Sirs</td><td>Yours faithfully</td><td rowspan="4">21 October 20..
October 21st, 20..
21 Oct. 20..
Oct. 21st, 20..
Note: For convenience, choose the form in line 1. The short forms below should only be used in informal communication (e.g. memos):
21/10/20.. or
21-10-20..</td></tr>
<tr><td>You know your partner</td><td>Dear Mr Kingsley
Dear Ms Beecham</td><td>Yours sincerely</td></tr>
<tr><td>In circulars</td><td>Dear Customer/Client</td><td>Yours sincerely/ faithfully</td></tr>
<tr><td>You know your partner very well</td><td>Dear Robert
Dear Laura</td><td>Yours
(With) Best wishes
(With) Kind regards</td></tr>
</table>

American usage

<table>
<tr><th></th><th>Salutation</th><th>Complimentary close</th><th>Date*</th></tr>
<tr><td>You do not know your partner</td><td>Gentlemen: ...
Ladies and Gentlemen: ...</td><td rowspan="3">Yours sincerely,
Yours (very) truly,
Sincerely yours,
(Very) Truly yours,</td><td rowspan="4">October 21st, 20..
Oct. 21st, 20..
Note: The short forms below should only be used in informal communication (e.g. memos):
10/21/20.. or
10-21-20..</td></tr>
<tr><td>You know your partner</td><td>Dear Mr Kingsley: ...
Dear Ms Beecham: ...</td></tr>
<tr><td>In circulars</td><td>Dear Customer/Client: ...</td></tr>
<tr><td>You know your partner very well</td><td>Dear Robert: ...
Dear Laura: ...</td><td>Yours,
(With) Best wishes,
(With) Kind regards,</td></tr>
</table>

Make sure you know the proper German phrases.

Note

In formal written communication, *Ms* is now commonly used to address females regardless of whether a person is young, single or married.

Info

Punctuation[1]

GB It is common practice now **NOT** to use punctuation in the address, in the date, after the salutation and after the complimentary close. If, however, a comma is used after the salutation, there **MUST** also be a comma after the complimentary close. The short forms for the date (e.g. 5th, 21st, etc.) are no longer used.

US Punctuation in the address (commas after every line, full stop after the last line) is fairly common[2] still; this applies to the address section and the closing section of the letter as well. After the salutation, a colon (:) must be used.

Note: Contrary to German practice, the first word in the text of the letter/e-mail is always capitalised in English-speaking countries.

1 Zeichensetzung
2 sehr gebräuchlich, allgemein üblich

Info (cont.'d)

Postal code[1]

The British postal code seems very complex. The first 3 or 4 digits indicate a larger postal area (one or two letter(s)) and a postal district within this area (one- or two-digit figure). The code is usually put after the name of the town/city or county. If the county name ends on "-shire", this is often abbreviated[2] to just "s" (*Yorkshire* = *Yorks*). The county name is not needed for mail to big cities. There is a special code system for London.

The American five-digit ZIP code is always preceded[3] by the short form for the state, e.g. *NY* for *New York*, *CA* for *California*, *TX* for *Texas* or *FL* for *Florida*.

In all countries, the address is now organised in a block form (see the sample letter) starting with the name of the recipient and ending with the postcode in GB or the ZIP code in the US. For mail going abroad, the name of the country is written in the last line of the address. Sometimes it is printed/written in capitals.

The postal codes are always clearly stated in the sender's address; so copy them with great care.

[1] Postleitzahl
[2] abkürzen
[3] vorangehen

Please write the address, date (use today's date), salutation, complimentary close in a suitable manner and put the address details in the proper order.

1	2	3	4
GB	New York	Manchester	Laurence Kirk
LE4 5HO	U.S.A.	Gianna Levi	Waterson Inc.
Leicester	NY 10027	M1 9QP	Atlanta
James Peterson	Tomkins Ltd	47 Salford Street	37 Stone Road
Leics.	78 Canal Street	GB	GA 30344
15 Ashley Drive	(name unknown)		(very well known)

4.6.3 E-mails

Up to now, you've probably used the e-mail as a form of texting or mobile messaging[1] between yourself and friends and family. In business, e-mails are closer to business letters. Being a fast form of communication, they often replace the traditional letter or a telephone call even. In contrast to a phone message, the e-maill allows the partner to read and react at her/his convenience[2]. It can also serve as a kind of memo for arrangements made in more complex telephone discussions.

There are only few requirements of form[3] and style. For outside communication[4], use *Dear Mr* or *Ms* if you know the name of your partner. If you do not know the name, use such forms as *Hello*, *Good morning/afternoon*. Sometimes the name is added, e.g. *Hello Ms Simpson*. On a more informal level and in inter-office[5] communication, the first name is used. In the US, the informal form *Hi* may be found.

[1] Nachrichtenaustausch
[2] nach Belieben, wann es ihm/ihr passt
[3] formale Anforderungen
[4] Kommunikation mit Außenstehenden
[5] bürointern

The CC function (referring back to the traditional carbon copy[1]) makes it possible to inform a larger group of recipients[2] at the same time.

For the complimentary close use: *Best wishes* or *Kind regards*. In external mails print your full name, job title, department, telephone and fax numbers at the end. As people in other countries often do not know whether a first name is for a female or a male, it is helpful to add (*Ms*) or (*Mr*) after your name.

[1] Durchschlag
[2] Empfänger/in

Dealing with e-mails

1 What is the practice for using e-mails in your company/business?
2 What are the rules that you have been told to observe when writing internal or external e-mails?
3 What is your personal practice?
4 How often and when do you check your mailbox?
5 What do your more senior colleagues do?

Discuss the information collected from the answers to these questions in class and decide on a list of best practice.

Info

Some basic rules and points to consider

- Having to go through e-mails is very costly in terms of time and energy. And time is money.
- Use e-mails to communicate relevant[1] and meaningful information.
- Use the CC or "Reply to all"-function only when really necessary.
- Choose a meaningful subject line. This allows the recipient to prioritise[2] their replies or actions.
- Keep the text short. Use paragraphs to break up your text.
- Get to the point quickly and be concise[3].
- Avoid slang and abbreviations, except for inter-office mails.
- Be professional. Avoid emoticons or any other personal or critical comment.
- Inter-office communication often is very direct. But be respectful to your seniors[4].
- A less formal approach is often used with close business contacts.
- Do not send overlong[5] attachments[6].
- Do not clutter up[7] the recipient's mailbox.
- Make sure your language, spelling and punctuation are correct.
- Check your text before pressing the "send" button.

[1] wichtig
[2] nach Wichtigkeit ordnen
[3] präzise
[4] Vorgesetzte, ältere Mitarbeiter(innen)/Kollegen/Kolleginnen
[5] übermäßig lang
[6] Anhang
[7] zumüllen

E-mails can be a pest.

1 What are your priorities[1]? Decide which of the points above are
a) important, b) not so important, c) irrelevant[2].

2 From your experience with e-mails, which points would you add or drop?

3 Rephrase the points above using *you must, you mustn't, you should, you shouldn't*.

[1] Priorität
[2] nebensächlich

Decide where in an e-mail you can use these phrases.

Phrase	Beginning	Middle	End
As regards the problem of …			
As requested I'm sending you … as an attachment.			
As yet I have not been able to discuss the problem of …			
Do not hesitate to get in touch if …			
I do hope that you will be happy about this decision.			
I just wanted to let you know …			
I look forward to hearing from you.			
I will come back to you with more information as soon as …			
I will write to you in more detail as soon as I'm back in the office.			
I'll keep you informed of any new developments.			
I'm very sorry about this and will do my best to …			
Let me know what you think about this idea.			
Please accept my apologies[1] for …			
Thank you for your speedy reply.			
Thank you for your understanding.			
This is to inform you that …			
Tomorrow's meeting has been cancelled[2].			
We would like to ask you if you could send …			
You will be pleased to know …			

[1] Entschuldigung
[2] stornieren, absagen

How would you express the statements above in German?

Complete the text of the e-mail below with some of these words/phrases.

• assistant • conference • documents • equipment • furthermore • ideas • inform • list • meeting • office • prepare • reasons • service • second • tables • weeks •

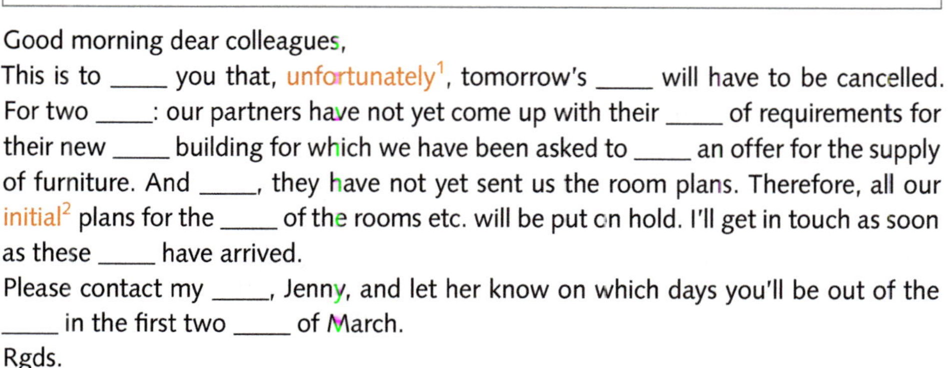

Good morning dear colleagues,
This is to _____ you that, unfortunately[1], tomorrow's _____ will have to be cancelled. For two _____: our partners have not yet come up with their _____ of requirements for their new _____ building for which we have been asked to _____ an offer for the supply of furniture. And _____, they have not yet sent us the room plans. Therefore, all our initial[2] plans for the _____ of the rooms etc. will be put on hold. I'll get in touch as soon as these _____ have arrived.
Please contact my _____, Jenny, and let her know on which days you'll be out of the _____ in the first two _____ of March.
Rgds.
Sue

[1] leider
[2] ursprünglich, anfänglich

Decide what these phrases mean and find another way of expressing these ideas.

1 to come up with sth.
2 to put on hold
3 to get in touch
4 to be out of the office

Write an e-mail for your boss.

Wegen mehrerer dringender Termine *(urgent appointments)* in der kommenden Woche kann Ihr Chef/Ihre Chefin nicht wie geplant an der Marketing-Konferenz in Glasgow teilnehmen. Da er/sie sehr beschäftigt ist, sollen Sie in ihrem/seinem Namen *(on her/his behalf)* eine Mail an die Veranstalter *(organiser)* (Ms Jessie Bennett und Mr Roger Bowie) schreiben. Bitten Sie um Entschuldigung und Verständnis *(understanding)*. Schreiben Sie eine höfliche Absage.

And finally – how does it work at work?

What is your reaction to these statements?

The bottom drawer of my roller container is the revolving door[1] to my supply of snacks.

I'm always very busy when the boss comes round.

My office chair is ideal for a power nap[2].

There's somebody who keeps stealing my Coke from the fridge. But who is this office thief[3]?

I just stare at my screen, but it looks like I'm concentrating on my work.

The kitchen is an ideal place for having a chat[4] with colleagues about colleagues.

My coffee mug is my best workmate[5].

I'm sending an e-mail to my colleague next to me to ask her/him about having lunch together.

I hate those people who stand around the coffee machine just gossiping[6].

1 Drehtür
2 Kurzschlaf
3 Bürodieb
4 ein Pläuschchen halten
5 Kollege/Kollegin
6 tratschen

Unit 5 Getting supplies

5.1 Where do companies shop?

1 In your company/institution, have you been asked to order office supplies[1]? If so, explain to your classmates how you went about it or what you had to do. What kind of products did you have to get?

2 If you do not use the usual buying channels[2], how and where can you find out about potential[3] suppliers[4]?

3 Does your company purchase supplies from wholesalers[5] or from retailers[6]?

1 Büromaterial
2 Einkaufs-, Bezugsquelle
3 möglich, in Frage kommend
4 Lieferant
5 Großhändler
6 Einzelhändler

Celia, a German trainee on an exchange visit, recently joined CIss (Creative IT Support Services) Inc. to do a two-month internship as an office junior. CIss Inc. will soon be relocating[1] to new premises[2] in downtown[3] Manhattan, 37 Canal Street, New York, NY 10002-6339. Her head of department, Doreen Chang, asks her to check out[4] suppliers of office equipment[5].

Track 17

1 umziehen
2 Geschäfts-, Büroräume
3 *hier*: Zentrum
4 etw. heraussuchen, sich schlau machen
5 Büroausstattung

Listen to this conversation.

Doreen: Celia, I'd just like to have a word with you. Or are you busy right now?

Celia: No, I'm not. I don't have anything urgent to do. So? What can I do?

Doreen: Well, we'll need to get started with planning our move[1] to our new offices. And one important thing on the agenda[2] is getting new office equipment. We'll be needing desks and chairs for everybody, or at least most people. Then roller containers, filing cabinets, furniture and equipment for the breakroom and all sorts of[3] other things on top[4].

Celia: And how about the technical equipment[5], light fittings[6]? And PCs and printers, photocopiers etc.? Or do we take all that with us?

Doreen: Well, I've already been given the green light[7] to replace all our current technical equipment.

Celia: That sounds super. Everything new and modern!! Wow.

1 *hier*: Umzug
2 *hier*: anstehen
3 alle möglichen
4 außerdem, dazu, zusätzlich
5 technische Ausstattung, Geräte
6 Beleuchtungskörper
7 grünes Licht geben, Zustimmung bekommen

8 Angebot
9 etwas Ordentliches für unser Geld
10 entwerfen
11 Katalog
12 vorgehen, verfahren
13 sich dran/an die Arbeit machen

Doreen: You're right. But, what's more urgent now, we need to get in offers[8] from office equipment suppliers and make sure we get good value for money[9]. And this is where you come in.

Celia: What do you mean? I don't have to …

©Robert Kneschke-fotolia.com

Doreen: No, not quite. First, I want you to check things out on the internet and find out what office equipment suppliers there are here in New York. And, as a second step, I want you to draft[10] an e-mail asking them to send us their catalogs[11] and all that. And once we've got an idea of what there is on the market, we can decide how we want to proceed[12].

Celia: OK. I'll get going[13] then.

Doreen: Right, you do that.

Which questions would you ask to get these answers?

©virtua73-fotolia.com

1 Celia has nothing urgent to do.
2 Doreen wants to discuss the move to new offices.
3 We need new desks and chairs, filing cabinets, etc.
4 They will also look at new furniture for the breakroom.
5 We can replace all our technical equipment.
6 I want you to find out where we can get office supplies.
7 I have to draft an e-mail asking the suppliers to send us catalogs.
8 Once they've got an idea of what there is.

5.2 Making enquiries

5.2.1 Enquiry for office furniture

1 zusätzlich zu
2 Gelbe Seiten (= Branchenbuch mit Anschriften von Firmen)
3 Anfrage
4 vorschlagen, sich ausdenken
5 außer (+ Dat.)

Track 18

It does not take Celia very long to put together a list of potential suppliers. In addition to[1] the internet, she also used the Yellow Pages[2] for New York. Celia discusses her lists with Doreen. And Doreen had also asked her to draft an e-mail enquiry[3].

Do you have an idea which search words Celia may have used for her internet research?

And this is what Celia came up with[4], a text that can be used for both the companies listed on the net (A) and also for those in the Yellow Pages (B), except for[5] the first paragraph.

Ladies and Gentlemen:

A Searching the internet to find experienced suppliers of high-end[1] office furniture, we visited your website and were attracted[2] by the variety[3] and quality of the designs[4] you displayed[5] there.

©poligonchik-fotolia.com

[The first sentence could also read as follows:]

B We have been searching in the Yellow Pages to find reliable suppliers of high-class[6] office furniture and also enquired with[7] some of our business partners, who recommended[8] your firm.

Our company, a medium-sized[9] provider of IT support services[10] here in Manhattan, will be relocating to new premises in the near future. That is why we intend to replace all our office furniture and equipment.

In order to get more detailed information about the products that you distribute[11] and their designs, we would kindly ask you to send us your illustrated[12] catalog. Of course, we would also appreciate[13] being given some indication of the prices for your product lines[14]. Please send your literature[15] to the address indicated below[16].

Once we have obtained an overview of the market offer[17], we will contact you again to discuss further details.

Of course, we would let you have the customary references[18] once we have decided to place our order with[19] you.

We thank you in advance for your kind attention to our enquiry[20] and look forward to hearing from you at your earliest convenience[21].

Yours sincerely,

Doreen Chang,

Head of Department,
Clss Inc.

Our address:
XXXXX

[1] hochwertig
[2] *hier*: beeindruckt
[3] Vielfalt
[4] Modell, Gestaltung
[5] zeigen, ausstellen
[6] hochwertig
[7] nachfragen bei
[8] empfehlen
[9] mittelgroß, mittelständisch
[10] IT-Dienstleister, Anbieter von IT-Dienstleistungen
[11] vertreiben, verkaufen
[12] bebildert
[13] sich freuen (, wenn …)
[14] Produktlinie, Sortiment
[15] Prospektmaterial
[16] unten angegeben
[17] Angebot im Markt
[18] (branchen-)übliche Referenz
[19] jdm. einen Auftrag erteilen
[20] für die Bearbeitung der Anfrage danken
[21] sobald wie möglich, umgehend

Work with the text.

1 In the text, find the following sections:
- information about your business
- polite ending
- references
- source of supplier's address
- your specific requirements

2 This is an American-style e-mail. Find at least five reasons.

Learn about the language and style of enquiries.

1 Decide in which of the sections 1–5 the **Useful phrases** below can be used and then arrange them in a suitable order for an enquiry.

Sections: (1) source of information about supplier and product
(2) information about yourself as a potential customer
(3) requirements
(4) request for information
(5) polite ending

Useful phrases

- A business partner recommended your company as a reliable supplier of …
- An early reply would be (much) appreciated.
- As one of the leading companies in a very competitive[1] market …
- At the recent … fair you displayed/showed …
- If your prices and terms are competitive, we can promise large orders at regular intervals.
- In our fast-growing business we produce/make/manufacture[2] …
- Kindly/Please also let us know your terms and conditions[3].
- Kindly let us have/send us some samples[4] for testing purposes[5].
- Our company is a wholesaler/specialist retailer of …
- Please send us your catalogue and current price-list[6].
- We look forward to receiving your (early) reply.
- We noticed your advertisement for … in the … magazine/edition of the … Journal.
- We would also be pleased to learn what discounts[7] you are prepared to grant.
- Your offer for … would be much appreciated.

[1] umkämpft, wettbewerbsintensiv
[2] herstellen, produzieren
[3] allgemeine Geschäftsbedingungen
[4] Muster, Probe
[5] für Prüfzwecke
[6] derzeit gültige Preisliste
[7] Rabatt, Nachlass

Note

If you write on behalf of[1] a company/department, always use "we". The pronoun "I" should only be used if the request[2] is for the writer her- or himself. But avoid using "we" too often. In an enquiry you often need to ask for information about prices, discounts, terms and conditions. For reasons of style, do not ask direct questions. Instead, use phrases similar to the ones in the box above to state what you need.

[1] für, im Auftrag von
[2] Anfrage, Bitte

2 Doreen is really happy with the text, but asks Celia to make it somewhat less formal. Use the phrases below to rewrite Celia's draft[1] mail.

[1] (Roh-)Entwurf

are planning	moving to new offices
as soon as possible	sell
best regards	show
for an early reply	soon
for suppliers of good-quality furniture (2x)	we checked the internet
Hello, good morning	we looked up the Yellow Pages
in the near future	what is available in the market
like to get some idea of the prices you charge	your brochure(s) and price list(s)

5.2.2 Write an e-mail enquiry.

Alina, an office junior at Wilkens Lebensmittel-Großhandel GmbH & Co KG, has been asked to draft an enquiry to potential British suppliers of biscuits, shortbread[1] and tartlets[2]. She has completed the text, but some terms and phrases are still missing.

[1] Butterkeks
[2] Törtchen

Please fill the gaps in the e-mail below with expressions from this list. Note: there are more terms and phrases than you need. Pay attention to the grammar.

agricultural fair[1]	to display	market potential[2]	promising[3]
broad range	general terms and conditions	market research[4]	sample
comprehensive[5]	to grant a discount	market share[6]	trade reference
current price-list	to indicate	marketing campaign[7]	wholesale company[8]

[1] Landwirtschaftsmesse
[2] Marktpotenzial
[3] vielversprechend
[4] Marktforschung
[5] umfassend
[6] Marktanteil
[7] Vermarktungskampagne
[8] Großhandelsunternehmen

Hello and good morning,

In January we visited your stand at the (1) ____ *(Landwirtschaftsmesse)* in Berlin and were impressed by the (2) ____ *(umfassendes Angebot)* and the quality of the products your company (3) ____ *(ausstellen)* there.

Our (4) ____ *(Marktforschungen)* has shown that the demand for British-made biscuits, shortbread, tartlets etc. has been growing over the past few years. And we are optimistic about the future (5) ____ *(Marktpotential)* here, especially after a nationwide (6) ____ *(Werbefeldzug)*. But to begin with, we would like to test and develop our regional market here in Lower Saxony.

We are a (7) ____ *(Großhandelsunternehmen)* and distribute food throughout Lower Saxony and also in Hamburg and Bremen. Over the years we have been very successful in increasing our (8) ____ *(Marktanteil)*.

If you are interested in cooperating with us, we would be pleased to receive your (9) ____ *(umfassend)* catalogue and (10) ____ *(derzeit gültige Preisliste)*. Please also let us know what your (11) ____ *(allgemeine Geschäftsbedingungen)* are and what kind of (12) ____ *(Nachlässe/Rabatte)* you are prepared to ____ *(gewähren)*.

Of course, we are willing to supply the usual (13) ____ *(Handelsauskünfte)*.
Our postal address is (14) ____ *(angegeben)* below.
We look forward to hearing from you soon.

Best wishes,

©derkien-fotolia.com

Write an e-mail from notes.

Situation: Sie machen eine Ausbildung als Bürokauffrau/-kaufmann bei der Firma Bürosysteme Franz GmbH. Wegen der wachsenden Nachfrage in ihrer Region sollen jetzt auch Hängeregistraturen *(hanging filing system)* in das Verkaufsprogramm *(product range)* aufgenommen *(include)* werden.

Task: Entwerfen Sie einen englischen Text für eine Anfrage an verschiedene britische Lieferanten. Bitten Sie um Zusendung eines Katalogs und einer gültigen Preisliste. Außerdem bitten Sie um Informationen über Rabatte bei der Abnahme von größeren Mengen *(discount for bulk orders)*.

©Maxim_Kazmin-fotolia.com

Note

The word ***wear*** is used for items of clothing and shoes ***(underwear, outerwear, swimwear, ladieswear, footwear)***. The word ***ware*** is used for other goods ***(kitchenware, glassware, hardware, chinaware)***.

Politeness creates goodwill

Being polite goes a long way to bringing success. This is particularly true when you ask someone to do something for you. Learn to use these phrases:

- Please send/let us/me have …
- We would be pleased/grateful[1] to receive information on/details of …
- Kindly inform us about …/send us information about …/let us know …
- It would be nice/very kind if you could/would …
- We would (also) like to know whether/what/when …
- We would (very much) appreciate being given/receiving information about …
- We would (kindly) ask you to …
- Your early reply would be much appreciated.
- Would you be so kind to …?
- Could I perhaps ask you …?

And don't forget: In Britain people say "please" and "thank you" much more often than people in Germany do.

1 dankbar

5.2.3 Make a telephone enquiry.

Study your role cards carefully and use the language of a polite telephone conversation.

Role A: You work as an office junior in the purchasing department[1] of a chain store[2] for sportswear. Your company wants to expand its range by adding sports equipment for children. Your boss has asked you to get information from a selected[3] list of suppliers. Ask your partner for catalogues and price-lists. All information should be sent to: Nothing but Sports Ltd., Purchasing Department, Halesowen Business Park, 32 Park Row, Halesowen B63 8BQ.

You will find the text for Role B on p. 203.

1 Einkaufsabteilung
2 Filialkette
3 ausgewählt

5.3 Making an offer

Track 19

The mails Celia sent out to a large number of prospective[1] suppliers resulted in[2] several useful offers. Here are just two of them.

Note: Both texts are American-style letters.

© S. Wessels

1 möglich, in Frage kommend
2 *hier*: erbringen

5.3.1 Letter 1

Clss Inc.,
37 Canal Street,
New York, NY 10002-6339.

Miller Office Furniture
1115 Broadway
New York, NY 10010
Tel 212-633-2400
Fax 212-633-2401

Sept. 23rd, 20..

Offer of office furniture

Dear Ms Chang:

We refer to your enquiry of Sept. 21st for office furniture and are pleased to send you our comprehensive catalog and price-list under separate cover[1].

As you will see, we distribute furniture from the most renowned[2] office furniture manufacturers[3] in the country. There is a high demand for[4] these kinds of products because of their excellent[5] modern designs and good workmanship[6].

Our prices are quoted net[7]. Delivery[8] may take up to ten weeks from the date of your order[9]. For orders exceeding[10] $25,000 in value, we are able to grant[11] a volume discount[12] of 5 percent. Payment in full within a fortnight[13] of receipt of our invoice[14] is subject to[15] a cash discount[16] of 2 percent.

We are confident[17] that our huge range of items[18] and color combinations will allow you plenty of scope[19] to furnish[20] your new offices according to your needs and taste.

If you have any further queries[21], please do not hesitate to contact us.

We look forward to hearing from you at your convenience[22].

Yours sincerely,

Laureen J Baxter,

Head of Sales,
Miller Office Furniture.

1 mit getrennter Post
2 namhaft, renommiert
3 Hersteller
4 große Nachfrage nach
5 ausgezeichnet
6 Verarbeitung
7 unsere Preise sind Nettopreise
8 (Aus-)Lieferung
9 Termin/Datum der Auftragserteilung
10 übersteigen
11 gewähren
12 Mengenrabatt
13 vollständige Bezahlung innerhalb von zwei Wochen
14 Rechnungserhalt
15 unterliegen
16 Barzahlungsrabatt, Skonto
17 zuversichtlich
18 Sortiment
19 viele Möglichkeiten
20 einrichten, möblieren
21 weitere Fragen
22 bei Gelegenheit, wenn Sie mögen

Please answer these questions.

1 What does the letter refer to?
2 Why do you think the catalog is sent under separate cover?
3 How does Laureen "praise[1]" her company?
4 Why is there a high demand for this kind of office furniture?
5 How long is the delivery going to take?
6 When is the customer entitled to a 5 per cent discount?
7 What does the customer have to do to get the 2 per cent discount?
8 What is the 2 per cent discount called?
9 What should the prospective customer do if there are any problems?

©Wessels

1 herausstellen, anpreisen

In which sections of Letter 1 do you find information about the following?

1 complimentary close
2 contact
3 discounts
4 information sent
5 product quality
6 terms and conditions

5.3.2 Letter 2

Track 20

[1] in der Anlage, beigefügt
[2] meistverkauft
[3] Auswahl
[4] feststellen
[5] kundenspezifische/individuelle Lösung
[6] vorschlagen
[7] vorlegen, unterbreiten
[8] Gesamtpaket, umfassende Lösung
[9] berücksichtigen
[10] Ausstellungsraum
[11] abschließend bearbeiten
[12] zustimmen
[13] Einbau/Montage vornehmen
[14] *hier*: abgebildet
[15] *hier*: einzeln, als Einzelstücke
[16] langjährige Erfahrung

Dear Ms Chang:

Thank you very much for contacting us and especially for your interest in our products and services. We are pleased to send you enclosed[1] a number of brochures about some of the best-selling[2] lines from the vast selection[3] of office furniture that we supply.

Normally we assess[4] our customers' needs first before making an offer. From our brochures and the price-lists you will see the prices for individual pieces of office furniture. But many of our customers prefer bespoke solutions[5] for furnishing their offices.

Therefore, we would propose[6] that you have a good look at what is available. We would then recommend that one of our sales agents comes to see you. They will discuss your ideas and your requirements before submitting[7] an all-in solution[8] that takes into account[9] your specific needs. Of course, you are also very welcome to have a look at the furniture displayed in our showrooms[10].

Once our offer has been finalised[11] and approved[12] by you, it will take about ten weeks to manufacture the furniture and complete the fitting[13]. After all, we want you and your staff to be comfortable and relaxed in your new offices.

But we are also very happy to supply any of the items illustrated[14] in our brochures separately[15], so that you can arrange the furnishing and fitting yourself.

We are sure that with our long-standing experience[16] we can help you to find the best possible solutions for your needs. But whatever you decide to do, talk to us first.

We look forward to hearing from you soon.

Yours truly,

Ben Wilder,

Head of Sales,
Office Empire Inc.

©Christian Hillebrand-fotolia.com

Work with the letter.

1 Please answer these questions.

1 How does Ben send his information package?
2 What is the information in the brochures about?
3 What is Ben's policy with regard to dealing with prospective customers?
4 What kind of solutions are the customers looking for?
5 Do you think it's a good idea to help customers with planning the layout of their offices? State why or why not.
6 Why, in your opinion, does Ben not mention terms and conditions?
7 Why do you think the production and fitting take ten weeks?
8 Why does Ben not seem so keen on the idea of do-it-yourself?
9 Why does Ben mention his company's long-standing experience?

2 In Letter 2, find English equivalents for these terms.

berücksichtigen	feststellen	herstellen	Montage
Dienstleistungen	Geschäftsräume	maßgeschneidert	umfassende Lösung
endgültig festlegen	große Auswahl	langjährig	zustimmen

Try to get the message.

Ms Chang does not have the time to read all the letters that the potential suppliers have sent. Therefore Celia prepares notes listing the main points made. She also briefly comments on the "tone" of the letters. Do this for Letters 1 and 2.

Choosing a supplier is not easy.

1 Please find reasons for selecting a particular supplier. Which of these two proposals would you prefer? Discuss your views in class.

2 It is Doreen's job to make a final decision. Can you imagine what kind of points she will have to consider? Copy the list below in your exercise book and number the points according to their priority. Discuss your results in class and give reasons for your choice.

• budget[1] available • colour schemes • delivery period[2] • design • discounts • distances from windows and doors • fitting costs[3] • layout of the office and planned seating arrangements	• practicability[4] • prices • quality and finishing[5] of the furniture • quantities (of desks, chairs, cabinets, technical equipment etc.) • reputation[6] and experience of supplier • sizes of the items of furniture • space available • specific needs for storage[7] and filing

1 Etat(-mittel)
2 Lieferfrist
3 Montage-, Einbaukosten
4 Umsetzbarkeit, Durchführbarkeit
5 Endbearbeitung
6 (guter) Ruf
7 Archivierung, Lagerung

5.3.3 Phoning a potential supplier

Role play

Doreen Chang has seen Celia's shortlist of interesting offers and decides to follow up some of them. She asks Celia to share in some of the telephoning. It is her task to phone Ben Wilder to make an appointment for Doreen to discuss the project in some detail (what is on offer, designs, prices, colour schemes, possible layout, etc.).

Think of what you can say/need to say to play Celia's role. Act out this dialogue with a classmate.

Reception/Ben Wilder	**Celia**
This is Reception at Office Empire. You are speaking to Janet. What can I do for you?	Nennen Sie Ihren Nachnamen und sagen Sie, dass Sie Herrn Wilder sprechen möchten.
What did you say your name was?	Nennen Sie ihren vollen Namen. Sie rufen Im Auftrag von Frau Chang von der Firma Clss an.
And what are you phoning about?	Es geht um das Angebot von Herrn Wilder, das Sie vor einigen Tagen bekommen haben.
Yeah, OK. I'll put you through. Just a sec, please.	Sie bedanken sich.
Ben Wilder speaking. What can I do for you?	Sie nennen Ihren Namen. Sie rufen wegen des Angebots für Büromöbel an, das Ihre Firma vor ein paar Tagen bekommen hat.
Yes, I do remember now. That's the Clss company in Manhattan, isn't it?	Sie bestätigen das. Sie sagen, dass Ihre Chefin, Doreen Chang, gern einen Gesprächstermin vereinbaren würde (*arrange an appointment*), um einige Details zu besprechen.
Yes, of course. No problem at all. Which date would suit you best?	Frau Chang würde am liebsten (*to prefer*) am Montagnachmittag kommen.
Well, Monday is a bit difficult really. We have quite a few appointments already. And I really want our sales agent there as well. How about next week on Tuesday afternoon then?	Sie zögern etwas, stimmen dem vorgeschlagenen Tag zu und fragen dann nach der Uhrzeit.
OK. That's fine then. Shall we say at about two in the afternoon?	Sie finden das sehr gut. Aber Sie müssen das noch kurz mit Frau Chang abklären (*to check*) und rufen dann zurück, um den Termin zu bestätigen.
Good. I'll be waiting for your call then. Thank you and goodbye.	Verabschieden Sie sich freundlich.

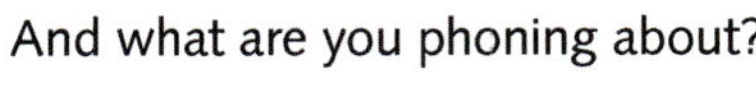

5.3.4 Write an e-mail from notes.

Situation: You are currently working as an office junior in the sales department of a Menden-based company. The person at Reception who took a phone call from a caller from Scotland has passed on this memo to your boss.

Memo

Von: *Empfang* An: *Verkaufsabt.*

Datum: *24 Sept. 20..* Zeit: *15.50 Uhr*

Anruf von: Brian McTaggert, United Scottish Technologies, 24 Morriston Trading Estate, Dundee DD4 0DB

- Anrufer interessiert am regelmäßigen Kauf von Mikrofiltern *(microfilters)* für Dieselmotoren in der Landwirtschaft
- Bittet um Zusendung von Prospektmaterial
- Fragt nach Rabatten für regelmäßige Bestellungen und Zahlungsmodalitäten *(terms of payment)*

Use the hand-written comments of the head of department to prepare a reply.

- *Bitte Antwort erstellen*
- *bei regelmäßiger Abnahme von 100 Stück/Monat Mengenrabatt (quantity discount) von 10 Prozent möglich*
- *unbedingt Handelsreferenz anfordern*

Revision

Simple past and present perfect

Both tenses refer to actions and events in the past. The simple past is used for actions that

- occurred once or several times: *I went to the client's goods depot last week. – She went to see her parents every month.*
  (**Note:** the adverbials of time refer to a definite time in the past: *yesterday, last year, a couple of days ago, early this morning*)
- follow one another: *First she got money from the bank. – And then she went shopping.*
  (**Note** the signal words: *then, after that* etc.)

The present perfect is used

- to talk about actions/events that are still relevant at the time of speaking, or have only just come to an end: *We have noted your interest in our products and are putting an information pack together. – I have just finished drafting the e-mail.*
  (Note the signal words: *already, not yet, ever, never, so far, just* etc.)
- to introduce past actions and events: *One of the candidates has been to the U.S. He only came back last month.*

Note: In German the present perfect is regularly used to talk about things that happened in the past.

Choose the right tenses to fill in the gaps.

1 I ___ (go) to see my boss this morning. But she ___ in her office (not to be).
2 When we ___ (to start) out on this project, we ___ (have) no idea where it would take us.
3 Our sales ___ (rise) steadily in the first quarter, but we ___ (not to see) much demand recently.
4 On Monday, I first ___ (visit) my colleague who is off ill; and then I ___ (have) an interview with my future employer.
5 They all ___ (seem) to like our new boss. But I ___ (not to meet) her yet.
6 I ___ (receive) the enquiry this morning, and I ___ (already to send) out an offer.
7 She ___ (not to recognise) me at first, but we soon ___ (be) on friendly terms again.
8 The computer screen suddenly ___ (go) blank. But we ___ (not to lose) any data, I think.
9 When you ___ (write) to us last week, we ___ (not to have) any catalogues to send you.
10 So far he ___ (study) the sales figures for July. Since then the number of orders ___ (continue) to rise.

5.4 Learning phrases

Written communication (letters and mails) in the business world often is highly standardised[1]. Set phrases are used regularly to "transport" certain ideas. Here are some examples:

Thank you for contacting us …
We refer to[2]/With reference to[3] …
Should/If you have any queries, please …
We look forward to hearing …

[1] normen, standardisieren
[2] Bezug nehmen auf
[3] verweisen auf

And there are many more. Go through the letters and e-mails in this unit and write out similar phrases. In each case try and think what you would say in German. You will no doubt find that in German, too, there are many set phrases. If you know them well, half your work is done already.

Info

Using capital letters

In English most words are written with small letters. *God* and the words referring to God (*He, Him, His*) and not to forget "*I*" are capitalised, as are the following word groups:

- Names of persons and also animals (***D**ouglas **S**tuart*)
- Days of the week, months, public holidays (***M**onday, **M**arch, **E**aster*)
- Geographical names and adjectives, names of streets, squares, buildings (*the **A**lps, the **S**cottish border, **D**owning **S**treet, **T**rafalgar **S**quare, the **E**mpire **S**tate **B**uilding*)

Info (cont'd)

- Foreign languages (***E**nglish, **T**urkish, **S**panish*)
- Titles and words indicating family relationships or professions (***Q**ueen **V**ictoria, Auntie **M**ae, **F**ather or **M**other,* when used on their own, ***J**udge Marsh*)
- Names of institutions, organisations, political parties, historic events, etc.

Using hyphens[1]

There are no hard and fast rules for the use of hyphens. The hyphen links words or small word groups closely together. Some of these combinations are fixed: *father-in-law, husband-to-be, day-to-day routine*. It is often up to the writer to make the close link clear to the reader. The hyphen should be used when two words of different word classes are linked together: *family-friendly holiday town* (noun and adjective), *built-up area* (participle and preposition), *top-secret letter* (noun and adjective), *one-off event* (numeral[2] and preposition). Hyphens are useful in word groups which qualify a noun. They can help avoid confusion[3] over the meaning of a longer phrase: *a record-breaking sales result*. Language development shows that hyphenated[4] noun groups tend to become proper compounds[5]: *baby-sitter → babysitter, bank-note → banknote*.

1 Bindestrich
2 Zahlwort
3 Verwirrung
4 mit Bindestrich
5 zusammengesetztes Wort

5.5 A difficult choice to make

Look at the photos below and also those in the first half of this Unit. Decide which office equipment you would prefer for your workplace. Think of the design, possible costs, colour schemes, etc. Give reasons for your choice.

©Wessels

©Wessels

©virtua73-fotolia.com

©fischer-cg.de-fotolia.com

Use phrases such as the following:

Beginning	Like/dislike/not sure	Organising your thoughts
• If I could decide, I would … • If I had enough money, I would … • In my opinion … • To begin with, I would say that … • Looking at the photos … • At first glance … • That's a very difficult decision to make, but … • Well, if you ask me like that, I would …	• I would prefer … • I('d) much rather like … • I think the … is super. • I very much like … • But I'm not (very) keen on … • I don't like … at all. • And, of course, one has to consider … • I would definitely choose another colour/design/ arrangement, because … • … looks very modern/ (rather) old-fashioned • There (also) is the question of … • I'm not really sure whether/what … • I can't really make up my mind …	• To begin with … • First one has to consider … • … for a start • And then (of course,) … • But we mustn't forget … • To conclude … • All in all, I would say … • It comes down to … • Finally, … • In the end …

Don't stumble over false friends. Decide which alternative is correct.

1 a *In my opinion* we should turn to another supplier.
b *In my meaning* we should turn to another supplier.

2 a I don't have the *actual* figures about our sales.
b I don't have the *latest* figures about our sales.

3 a Our company increased its *profit* last year.
b Our company increased its *win* last year

4 a My friend drives a very *economic* car.
b My friend drives a very *economical* car.

5 a Before coming to us, our new *chief* had worked in the sales department.
b Before coming to us, our new *boss* had worked in the sales department.

6 a I must *control* the number of parcels going out.
b I must *check* the number of parcels going out.

7 a I have my car *insured* with the XYZ company.
b I have my car *assured* with the XYZ company.

Use your online or printed dictionary to make sure you know the differences in the use of these words.

Unit 6 Handling orders

6.1 Let's get going!

Talk about and share your experiences with your classmates.

1 When you buy goods from home, how do you do it? Mention the steps that you normally follow.

2 What do the people in your company do when they need goods (for the office or for the production of goods)?

3 Describe what happens when an order comes in. If possible, describe the stages the order goes through before production or packing is started.

©Joachim Wendler-fotolia.com

Info

In firmly established business relations[1] ordering goods does not involve any written form of communication by means of an accompanying letter or e-mail. Businesses mostly use order forms[2] that are then sent online or by fax. With initial orders[3] it is a good idea to use a letter to confirm[4] the terms of business[5] (discounts, delivery, payment) laid down[6] in the offer. The same goes for orders transmitted[7] by phone – the written confirmation serves as proof[8] of the points agreed between the business partners. It is only when there are changes in the terms or when problems occur that written communication is useful.

1 *hier*: feste Kundenbeziehung
2 Bestellformular
3 Erstauftrag
4 bestätigen
5 Geschäftsbedingungen
6 niedergelegt
7 übermitteln, übersenden
8 als Nachweis dienen

6.2 Placing a new order

You are working for a German wholesaler of office supplies in Hamburg. Your company has been able to establish a fast-growing customer base in Britain. Although your British business partners use your German-language illustrated catalogues, most of them prefer to communicate in English.

Track 21

Read this letter from Jonathan Myers, a British customer.

Order for office supplies

Dear Mr Sailer,

Thank you for your letter of 24 May and for sending your catalogue No. 17, both of which we have just received. The demand for[1] some of the products you distribute is increasing fast. The attached[2] order reflects this rise in interest in office supplies made in Germany.

In view of the size of this order and also our steadily rising order volumes[3] in the recent past, we would like to ask you to reconsider[4] your quantity discount, currently at 20 per cent, especially as we can promise the same size of orders in future. In fact, we are firmly convinced[5] that the demand for German-made office supplies will continue to grow.

1 Nachfrage (nach)
2 beigefügt
3 Auftragsumfang
4 nochmals prüfen, überdenken
5 überzeugt

[6] sich bewusst sein
[7] *hier*: dauern bis zu
[8] angesichts, wegen
[9] keine Gebühr
[10] Verpackung
[11] hiermit
[12] Zahlung innerhalb von 14 Tagen nach Rechnungserhalt
[13] 30 Tage netto
[14] was ... betrifft, bezüglich

We understand[6] that delivery may take up to[7] a week and, in view of[8] the size of this order, there will be no charge[9] for transport and packing[10]. And we herewith[11] confirm the terms of payment which are: cash discount of 2 per cent for payment within a fortnight of receipt of invoice[12] or 30 days net[13].

We look forward to hearing from you with regard to[14] the quantity discount.

Yours sincerely,

Jonathan Myers

Buyer

Please complete these sentences with the information found in the letter.

[1] Bezug nehmen auf
[2] berechtigt sein zu, Anspruch haben auf

1 Reference is made[1] to ...
2 The ... is rising fast.
3 There is a growing interest in ...
4 ... please find our order.
5 Our order volumes have been going up ... and will ... to do so.
6 We would ... if you could grant us a higher ...
7 The goods ... within a week of receipt of order.
8 ... are free of charge.
9 We hereby agree to ...
10 We are entitled to[2] a ... for payment within a ...

©phanuwatnandee-fotolia.com

Structure of a written order

[1] Geschäftsbeziehung

Although the letter above does not stand at the beginning of a business relationship[1], it has nearly all the parts that you find in a written order.

Decide which part of the letter refers to the following:

- Confirmation of the terms of payment (1)
- Discussion of discounts (2)
- Order being placed (3)
- Reply to an enquiry (4)

For your senior colleague, who does not know much English, say what the letter is about.

Discounts are an important element in price negotiations. And many companies grant a trade discount when selling goods to business customers.

1 When do you get a volume or quantity discount?
2 When can you expect to be granted a cash discount?
3 When do you think companies grant a fair discount[1]?
4 Who do you think is entitled to an employee discount[2]?
5 Can you hope to be granted a seasonal[3] discount because it's cold outside?
6 Why do you think some companies grant introductory discounts[4]?

[1] Messerabatt
[2] Personalrabatt
[3] saisonal, jahreszeitlich
[4] Einführungsrabatt

Letter plan						
Thank you (very much) for Referring to We refer to	your		letter offer quotation[1]		of (date).	
We	are pleased to would like to	place	the following order.			
	have enclosed		our order form for …			
Please find enclosed						
We	are aware[2] note understand	that	your (catalogue) prices the prices you quote[3] the prices stated in your letter	include a	cash trade[4] volume/quantity	discount[4] of … per cent.
As requested[5] As agreed We confirm that	payment will be made	by	credit/bank transfer[6]. cheque.			
		immediately on within a fortnight of	receipt of	the goods . your invoice[7].		
Kindly Please We would ask you to	confirm acknowledge[8]	(your) acceptance the receipt[9]	of this/our order.			
We thank you for your trouble and if	you have any questions/queries[10] regarding/concerning there are any problems with	our order	(please do) (please) do not hesitate to	contact get in touch with	me. us.	
We look forward to receiving our goods in due course.						

[1] Preisangebot, Kostenvoranschlag [2] sich bewusst sein [3] Preis nennen [4] Wiederverkaufs-, Handelsrabatt
[5] wie gewünscht, wunschgemäß [6] Banküberweisung [7] Rechnung [8] bestätigen [9] Empfang, Erhalt [10] Rückfragen

Use the phrases in the letter plan to write an order.

Situation: Schreiben Sie (mit heutigem Datum) eine Erstbestellung an Winterton Office Furniture Ltd, 225-229 Leeds Road, Bradford BD3 9PS. Sie nehmen Bezug auf das Angebot (Eingang vor 14 Tagen) und verweisen auf das beigefügte Auftragsformular. Bestätigen Sie die Liefer- und Zahlungsbedingungen. Die Lieferung soll in 4 Wochen nach Auftragserteilung erfolgen.

D – E

(Make sure you understand the phrases in the letter plan before starting your letter.)

6.3 Placing a telephone order

Leslie works as an office junior for the Glasgow-based retailer for textiles, Dixon's Textiles, which operates[1] stores in several towns in central Scotland. Her boss, Jim McLure, asks her to ring their regular supplier to place an order for various items of curtain cloths[2].

1 *hier*: betreiben
2 Vorhang-, Gardinenstoff

An order placed by phone

In the left column you find the utterances[1] of the supplier's agent[2]. Use the information on the right to conduct[3] Leslie's part of the telephone conversation[4].

1 Äußerung
2 *hier*: Sachbearbeiter/in
3 (Gespräch) führen
4 Telefongespräch

Supplier's agent	Leslie
Hello, this is Linda Ramsay of Wilson & Sons Furnishings[1]. How can I help you?	Say the time of day and your name. Also say who you are working for.
OK. What is it you require[2]?	You want to order curtain fabrics[4]. Mention the Spring catalogue No. 17.
Fine. I've got that. And what is it exactly that you want?	You want curtain fabrics with these catalogue numbers: 2 rolls of catalogue no. XYB 2014 4 rolls of no. PRT 1464 6 rolls of no. PRT 1278 3 rolls of no. ORT 8742 5 rolls of no. GHD 7190 1 roll each of nos. HDF 8630, HDG 9752, HDK 1895 and HDP 7593
OK. Let's just go through this again. I repeat what I noted down[3]. From the Spring catalogue No. 17 you wish to order the following items: 2 rolls of catalogue no. XYB 2014 4 rolls of no. PRT 1464 6 rolls of no. PRT 1278 3 rolls of no. ORT 8742 5 rolls of no. GHD 7190 1 roll each of nos. HDF 8630, HDG 9752, HDK 1895 and HDP 7593. Is that correct?	Say that that's OK.
And who do you say this is for?	Repeat the name of your company and say where it is based.
Fine. And have you got your customer number ready?	State your customer number: CT 74334.
Yes, I got you here on the screen. So we can deliver your order on Monday, 31 March. Is that OK for you?	Agree to the delivery date.
Good. We'll get your order ready straightaway. And the usual terms apply for payment.	Agree to the terms of payment.
OK. That's fine then. Thank you very much for your order. And cheerio for now.	Say "Goodbye".

1 *hier*: Möbel-, Einrichtungshaus
2 benötigen
3 aufschreiben, notieren
4 Gardinen-, Vorhangstoffe

Please summarise.

Leslie's boss wants to know what the telephone conversation was about. Just state the main points.

6.4 Order for office supplies

Copy the purchase order form[1] below into your workbook. Fill in the form.

Use the information below (2 addresses and 12 items of office supplies). Select 8 items for your order. Note: the items and the addresses are arranged in alphabetical order, but something went wrong with the order of information about the items.

- 2-hole[2] paper punch[3], 15 pcs, $12.47/piece, P 1004
- Buyer: Henderson Business Consulting, 455 East 87th Street, Manhattan, New York, NY 10028; today's date, 7 working days from order date
- Correction tape[4], 50 pcs, L 4329, $4.99/piece
- Desktop stapler, $8.79/piece, S 1071,15 pcs
- Easy close envelopes[5] (white), 1000 (10 boxes), $11.39/box, size DL, E 9531
- File holders[6] (colored), C 0231, 500 (5 boxes), $8.99/box, letter size
- Hanging file holders, letter size, 500 (10 boxes), $20.99/box, A 2653
- Monthly calendars, $11.69/piece, 20 pcs, Z 431
- Padded mailers[7], E 9841, $8,69/box, 250 pcs (10 boxes)
- Printing paper (40 boxes @ 2500 sheets), B 9400, $69.99/box
- Self-sealing[8] envelopes, size C5, 2500 pcs, (5 boxes)/box, $441.99, E 9006, (white)
- Seller: Queens Office Supplies Inc., 221 Denton Ave, New Hyde Park, NY 11040,
- Tape dispenser[9], T 0045, 15 pcs, $5.49/piece
- Weekly appointments book[10], 30 pcs, (black), $28.99/piece, Z 234

1 Bestellformular
2 Loch
3 Lochapparat, Locher
4 Korrekturband
5 (Brief-)Umschlag
6 Aktenmappe, -ordner
7 gefütterte Versandtasche
8 selbstklebend
9 Klebebandspender
10 Terminkalender

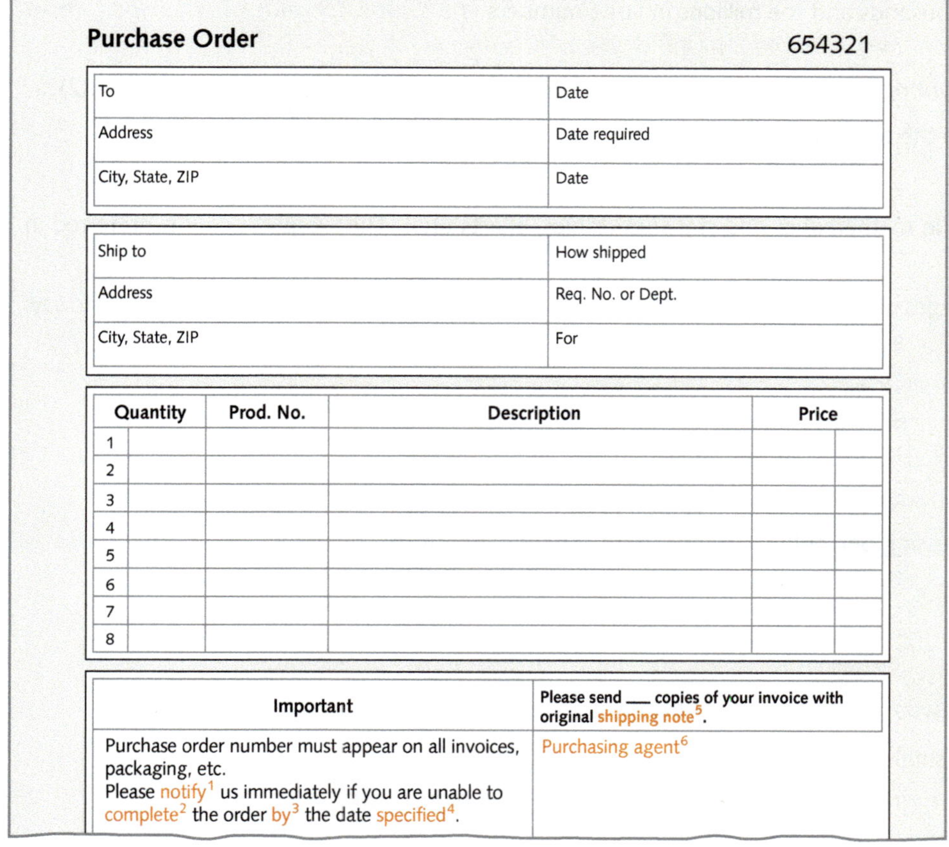

Purchase Order 654321

To	Date
Address	Date required
City, State, ZIP	Date

Ship to	How shipped
Address	Req. No. or Dept.
City, State, ZIP	For

	Quantity	Prod. No.	Description	Price	
1					
2					
3					
4					
5					
6					
7					
8					

Important	Please send ___ copies of your invoice with original shipping note[5].
Purchase order number must appear on all invoices, packaging, etc. Please notify[1] us immediately if you are unable to complete[2] the order by[3] the date specified[4].	Purchasing agent[6]

1 in Kenntnis setzen, informieren
2 *hier*: ausführen
3 *hier*: bis zu
4 angegeben
5 Lieferschein
6 Sachbearbeiter/in Einkauf

Write an e-mail.

As an office assistant, write an accompanying mail to the buyer to which you attach the purchase order on p. 75. You want the goods to be delivered free of charge to the office address within two working days. You expect to be granted the usual business discount[1] of 10 per cent plus a quantity discount of 5 per cent.

[1] Firmenrabatt

Revision

Using numbers (numerals)

Of course, you know how to use numbers. There are cardinal numbers: *one, two, three* and so on. And there are ordinal numbers: *the first, the second, the third* and so on.

In texts, the numbers from one (1) to twelve (12) are usually written as words; after that you use the numerals 13, 14, etc.). This also goes for ordinal numbers.

Remember: In English and American usage 2,000,000,000 (= two thousand million) is *2 billion* (German: *2 Milliarden*). The German *Billion* is *trillion* in English. The English abbreviations are: *45m = 45 million* or *45bn = 45 billion*.

Always use the plural form to indicate a quantity of more than one of something (*miles, metres, litres, kilos, dollars, pounds, euros* etc.). But *thousand, million, billion* do not have a plural when combined with a number.

Examples: *1.1 mls (= one point one miles)* or *1.5 kms (= one point five kilometres)* or *£ 5.4m (five point four million pounds)*

Punctuation

When writing numbers, use a full stop for the decimals *(1.3 kilometres = one point three kilometres)*. And use a comma to separate the thousands and the millions in large numbers *(1,345,005,455 euros= one billion, three hundred and forty-five million, five thousand four hundred and fifty-five euros)*.

A hyphen (-) is used when writing out two-digit *(zweistellig)* numbers: *forty-seven* (= 47), *eighty-two* (= 82).

The word ***and*** is used before the tens: 125 = *one/a hundred and twenty-five*

Percentages

The percentage sign is used in mathematics and statistics (tables, charts etc.). The word *per cent* is preferred in texts: *The rate of increase is 1.7 per cent.* Or: *The price rose by 2.1 percentage points.*

When talking about percentages of people, English speakers often avoid mathematical language. They prefer to say:

one in three meaning *a/one third (= 33 per cent)*
one in four meaning *a/one quarter (= 25 per cent)*
one in five meaning *a/one fifth (= 20 per cent)*
one in six meaning *a/one sixth (about 16 per cent)*
one in seven meaning *a/one seventh (about 14 per cent)*

Of course, this way of expressing percentages seems more concrete; and it can be varied: *two in five, three in seven, three in ten.*

Fractions

Fractions are said as follows:

$\frac{1}{2}$ = *a/one half;* $\frac{2}{3}$ = *two thirds;* $\frac{3}{4}$ = *three quarters;* $\frac{7}{8}$ = *seven eighths*

Decimals are usually said in single digits as follows:

0.725 = *nought point seven two five* or *zero point seven two five [US]* or just *point seven two five*

Practise using numbers.

1 Write the numbers 1 to 12 as cardinal and as ordinal numbers. Pay attention to the changes in spelling.

2 Write down the cardinal and ordinal numbers from 20 to 90.

3 Please use full sentences to say the dates for the following:
New Year's Day — Christmas Day — Your date of birth
The birthday of your best friend — The first day of your training
The first and last day of your last or your next holiday
The day when you last changed department in your company/institution

4 Try and work out the mathematical percentages for the following:
three in ten — three in five — one in twenty — three in eight — four fifths

Ask your neighbour to write down these numbers.

13	15	47	58	94
328	789	1,066	23,515	618,792
2,361,047	€4,444,833	£13,989,506	$8.375bn	1.750 kms

6.5 Chasing up[1] a fax order

Track 22

Julia, a 17-year-old girl from Nordhorn, is in her second year of training to become an office management assistant. With an EU grant[2] (Leonardo da Vinci exchange programme) she is able to spend part of her office training in Britain. She is now working in the general administration department[3] of McCallum Engineering plc in Leicester. Her senior colleague had given her an order list[4] for various items of office supplies to fax to their usual supplier. She has not heard from Leicester Office Supplies Ltd for a couple of[5] days. And the goods have not arrived either[5]. Therefore Julia phones in the early afternoon to enquire whether the items ordered could possibly be supplied on the same day.

[1] nachjagen, verfolgen
[2] Stipendium, Zuschuss
[3] Verwaltungsabteilung
[4] Auftrags-, Bestellliste
[5] ein paar, einige
[6] auch nicht

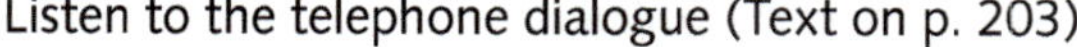

Listen to the telephone dialogue (Text on p. 203).

Please listen to the dialogue again and then answer these questions.

1 What's the situation? Why does Julia phone Leicester Office Supplies Ltd?
2 Who did Julia send the fax to?
3 What were the items listed in the fax?
4 Why is Brian angry?
5 When is Leicester Office Supplies Ltd closing?
6 Are all the items mentioned in the fax immediately available?
7 What does Brian say he'll do?

Get it right.

Julia's English is not very good really. Go to p. 203. Rewrite her part of the dialogue and use some of the phrases below. They are listed in alphabetical order. Before you start on this task, listen to the dialogue again.

Useful phrases

- As far as I know there's only one fax number.
- I appreciate everything you've done for us.
- I sent you a fax a couple of days ago. And so far, I haven't had a reply.
- Oh, I'm sure you'll try your very best. You know we're completely out of toner and print cartridges and can't print anything any more.
- Thanks ever so much.
- That's very good of you. Thank you very much indeed.
- That's very kind of you. You're being very helpful.
- That sounds like our fax.
- We haven't got any other number.
- We need the office equipment ASAP[1] (as soon as possible).
- We really need the things right away, because we are completely out of stock.
- Well, obviously the sooner the better. If you could supply the goods today or tomorrow morning at the latest, that would really be great.
- When do you think you'll be able to deliver the goods?
- Yes, that must be it.

[1] schnellstmöglich, sofort

Translate these phrases into idiomatic German.

Idiomatic expressions

Decide which phrase in *Column A* below comes closest to the expression in *Column B*. In Column B there are more phrases than you need.

A	B
not to stock sth.	as long as the goods are available
stocks are running low	everything is sold out
to apologise for sth.	not to sell a particular type of good
to appreciate sth.	there is little time to do sth.
to be completely out of stock	to ask so. to send goods
to be in short supply	to be very difficult to get
to be very short notice	to be very grateful for sth.
to be very urgent	to bring goods to the customer
to check sth. out	to find out about sth.
to deliver goods	to have available for sale
to place an order	to have very few things left
while stocks last	to know sth. well
	to need to get sth. done as soon as possible
	to say you are sorry for sth.

6.6 Paying for goods and services

1 How do you yourself pay when you buy goods or services? Think of food, clothes, petrol, clubs, your car insurance, online shopping etc.?

2 What payment methods have you observed in shops, cafes etc.?

3 When on holiday in other countries, how do you pay? And how do local people pay?

©Andrey Popov-fotolia.com

Track 23

Terms of payment

In our everyday shopping activities, we are used to receiving the goods after having paid the bill either in cash or by bank card[1] (electronic cash[2]). When we buy large and more expensive items (furniture, car, etc.), we are often asked to make a down-payment[3] and pay the remainder[4] when the goods are delivered and handed over[5]. When we shop online, the suppliers of goods or services (e.g. airline tickets) expect us to pay upfront[6], which means at the time of ordering the goods or booking tickets or a flight. In this case, the suppliers can be sure of getting their money; and the buyers have to trust[7] the suppliers to "deliver" whatever they may have bought. Sometimes, and this is increasingly rare in everyday transactions, we are allowed to pay when the goods are delivered to our home.

Of course, in most cases the buyers have the right to return[8] the goods if they don't like them or if they are sub-standard[9] or faulty[10]. So, up to a point, one can say that there are built-in[11] "safety elements[12]" in our purchasing transactions[13]. And this goes for[14] the buyer as well as for the seller.

All of this comes down to the question: to what extent[15] can the buyer rely on[16] the seller to sell their goods and services as offered? And, on the other hand, to what extent can the seller rely on the buyer to pay when asked to do so?

©russell102-fotolia.com

The same way of thinking[17] can be found in the business world. Only here, the terms of the transaction are laid down in a contract of purchase[18], i.e. the order and the general terms and conditions, which set out[19] the rights and obligations[20] of both the buyer and the seller. And obviously, the higher the value of the goods sold, the more the seller wants to be sure that the amount of money due[21] is actually[22] paid.

1 Bank(kunden)karte
2 elektronisches Geld
3 Anzahlung
4 Rest(-betrag)
5 übergeben
6 im Voraus bezahlen
7 darauf vertrauen, dass
8 zurückschicken, -geben
9 von minderer Qualität
10 fehlerhaft
11 eingebaut
12 Sicherheitselement
13 Einkauf, Kauftransaktion
14 das gilt für
15 Umfang
16 sich verlassen auf
17 Denkweise, „Denke"
18 Kaufvertrag
19 darlegen
20 Verpflichtung, Pflicht
21 fälliger Geldbetrag
22 tatsächlich

Please answer these questions.

1 When are customers expected to make a down-payment?

2 Why do customers often have to pay upfront when they buy online?

3 Name three reasons for returning goods.

4 Why are purchasing transactions often based on trust?

5 Why can a purchasing contract be useful?

©Stillfx-fotolia.com

Find out about the different methods of payment used in private and in business transactions.

Our payment methods are changing. What, if any, are the advantages of electronic cash over banknotes and coins? – Discuss and consider aspects such as convenience[1], the time required, the risk of theft[2], etc.

1 Bequemlichkeit

2 Diebstahl

Method	Time of payment	Goods available to buyer	Risk to seller	Risk to buyer	Comments
Cash with order (CWO)[1]	When placing the order (payment upfront)	Upon delivery	None	Buyer relies on seller to supply the quality & quantity of goods as ordered	• May apply to new customers • Special reasons, e.g. seller must purchase expensive materials before starting to manufacture[2] goods to buyer's specifications[3] • Very common in online transactions
Cash/ Payment in advance (CIA/PIA)[4]	Before shipment[5] (payment upfront)	After payment	None	Buyer relies on seller to supply the quality & quantity of goods as ordered	• Special reasons, e.g. seller must purchase expensive materials before starting to manufacture goods to buyer's specifications • Seller wants to "play safe[6]"
Cash on delivery (COD)[7]	When goods are handed over to the buyer	Upon payment	None	None	• Payment is made to shipping company[8] by cheque or electronic means[9] • Often used in online transactions • Common form in everyday purchasing activities

1 Zahlung bei Auftragserteilung
2 herstellen, produzieren
3 Angaben des Käufers
4 gegen Vorkasse
5 Versand, Transport
6 „auf Numero sicher" gehen
7 gegen/per Nachnahme
8 Transportunternehmen
9 elektronisch

Method	Time of payment	Goods available to buyer	Risk to seller	Risk to buyer	Comments
Letter of credit (L/C)[10]	After shipment of goods and handing over of documents (invoice, bill of lading [B/L][11], etc.)	After payment	Payment against documents; payment is assured[12] when documents match[13] the terms agreed in the L/C	Shipment is assured; the importer must trust the exporter's reliability[14]	• Complex step-by-step[15] transaction in international business directly involving banks in the buyer's and the seller's countries • Protects the interests of both the buyer and the seller
Payment by bank transfer[16]	After receipt of invoice	After receipt of goods	Buyer might not pay (and keep the goods); claiming[17] the goods back[17] is not easy	None	Standard form of payment in business transactions
Open account[18]	After receipt of invoice (monthly, quarterly)	Payment at regular intervals[19] to reduce administration costs[20]	Relies on buyer to pay as agreed; involves trust	None	Common for partners with frequent and regular transactions

[10] Akkreditiv, Kreditbrief
[11] Konnossement
[12] übereinstimmen mit
[13] *hier*: gewährleisten
[14] Zuverlässigkeit
[15] Schritt für Schritt
[16] *hier*: Zahlung per Überweisung
[17] zurückfordern, zurückverlangen
[18] laufendes Konto, Kontokorrentkonto
[19] in regelmäßigen Abständen
[20] Verwaltungskosten

Study the table and answer the following questions.

1 Which method of payment is frequently used for new customers?
2 Which method of payment helps to reduce administrative costs and why?
3 Why is "Cash on delivery" more or less risk-free for both the buyer and the seller?
4 Which is the preferred method of payment for online transactions and why?
5 Which methods of payment allow the customer to get the goods before paying?
6 Which method of payment is the riskiest for the seller? State why this is so.

Decide how and when payment must/can be made.

What does the buyer have to do if the supplier states the following terms in her/his offer (*Column A*)? Choose from the list in *Column B*.

[1] abziehen

A Terms of payment	B Action
2% cash discount for prompt payment	Make payment immediately after receipt of the invoice
Cash only	Make payment in advance
Cash terms only	Make payment when the invoice has arrived
Net 30	Make payment when placing the order
Payable net cash	Make payment within 30 days
Payment on receipt of invoice/ Prompt payment	Make payment within 30 days without any deduction
CIA/PIA	Make payment without any deduction
CWO	Pay by cheque
	Pay cash
	Pay early and deduct[1] a small percentage from the invoice amount
	Pay electronically (bank card, credit card, PayPal)

6.7 Changing the terms – Reply

Track 24

Mr Sailer has weighed up[1] the pros and cons of Mr Myers' request for a bigger volume discount. He needs to word his arguments carefully. On the one hand, he wants to develop the British market further; and the business with Mr Myers' company has been growing very nicely over the past couple of years. On the other hand, he has to bear in mind[2] the general pricing structure[3]. There are many customers with a much larger annual turnover. And this is what he comes up with.

[1] abwägen
[2] daran denken, nicht vergessen dürfen
[3] Preisstruktur

Dear Mr Myers,

Thank you very much for your letter of 25 May 20.. We are pleased to note[1] that the demand for our goods in your country is on the increase. And quite obviously, we will do everything we can to help you develop your business with German office materials even further. So, do not hesitate to let us know if and when we can assist you with your marketing campaigns.

We have given your suggestion[2] of allowing you a larger volume discount very careful thought[3]. At 20 per cent, the volume discount that you have been granted is at the upper end of our range. To accommodate you[4] and show goodwill[5], we can promise[6] you an increased volume discount of 22 per cent. In addition, we have decided to change the terms of payment in your favour[7]. We would be prepared to extend[8] the time allowed for payment[9]. But we will leave the cash discount unchanged at 2 per cent. So, starting with this order, payment is due[10] within 30 days of receipt of invoice.

We hope that you will be satisfied with these new terms and look forward to an increase in the volume of our business activities.

Your orders will always have our best attention[11] and be executed[12] promptly.

We look forward to hearing from you in the near future.

Yours sincerely,

Thomas Sailer

[1] feststellen
[2] Vorschlag, Anregung
[3] sorgfältig prüfen
[4] jdm. entgegenkommen
[5] Wohlwollen, Kulanz
[6] versprechen
[7] zu jds. Gunsten
[8] verlängern
[9] Zahlungsfrist
[10] fällig
[11] sorgfältig bearbeiten
[12] *hier:* ausführen

Look at the letter on pp. 71/72 again and say what has changed.

Please mediate.

Obviously Mr Sailer has had some expert[1] help with writing this letter. What do you think Mr Sailer may have asked his expert to write? Just state the main points of the letter in German.

[1] Spezialist/in, Experte/in *hier:* fachmännisch
[2] Möglichkeit, Alternative

In class, discuss what other options[2] Mr Sailer could have had.

Test your language skills.

Find out which of the alternatives (in **Columns B, C** or **D**) come closest to the meaning of the words and phrases used in the letter on p. 82 **(Column A)**. Note: sometimes there is more than one correct solution.

Column A	Column B	Column C	Column D
Used in the text	**Alternative 1**	**Alternative 2**	**Alternative 3**
note	experience	learn	read
be on the increase	be enlarging	be growing	be rising
help	assist	encourage	lend a hand[1]
let us know	inform us	say to us	tell us
suggestion	demand	proposal	requirement[2]
grant a discount	agree to a discount	allow[3] a discount	offer a discount
to accommodate so.	to meet so.	to come to so.	to come towards so.
in addition	furthermore	on top of that[4]	next to that
raise	grow	increase	upgrade[5]
satisfied	happy	lucky	relaxed
volume	amount	quantity	mass
materials	stuff	matters	goods

1 helfen
2 Erfordernis
3 gewähren
4 darüber hinaus, ferner
5 aufwerten, höherstufen

Write an e-mail.

For your company, Rosemount Inc., you have just placed an urgent telephone order for a range of household supplies. Write an e-mail to your partner, Emily Priscoe of Angus Home Supplies Corp, and confirm the arrangements made on the phone earlier this morning. Use the following points:

- Refer to phone call
- Order is placed for a variety of[1] household items (as per attached order form)
- Delivery to be made within seven days at the latest[2]
- Usual volume discount of 25 per cent on list prices
- Payment on receipt of invoice (usual terms apply)
- Usual friendly close

1 verschiedene
2 spätestens

Unit 7 From manufacturer to customer

7.1 Let's get going!

Talk about and share your experience.

©Adkasai-fotolia.com

1 When you, as a private person, have chosen the goods that you want to buy, what happens next? What do you do? What do the staff in shops normally do?

2 Do you note any differences between buying goods (petrol, clothing, cosmetics, IT products, etc.) and buying services (apps, car insurance, bank products, etc.) for example? If so, describe what they are in your experience.

3 Try and describe what happens in your company when goods or services are sold.

7.2 Transport problems

Track 25

©canaran-fotolia.com

OfficeTech Incorporated[1] is a manufacturer of office equipment based in Pittsburgh/Pennsylvania. They have completed an order for steel filing cabinets placed by Office Village Corp., a large wholesaler of office supplies operating from Newark in New Jersey. The order is for a customer in Montreal/Canada.The goods are to be shipped[2] by the manufacturer.

[1] *etwa:* GmbH od. AG
[2] versenden, zum Transport aufgeben; transportieren

Listen to this telephone call.

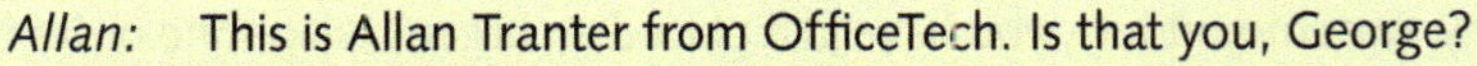

Allan: This is Allan Tranter from OfficeTech. Is that you, George?

George: Oh, hello Allan. Yes, it's me alright. Is anything the matter?

Allan: Yes, I'm afraid so. And to come straight to the point because I haven't got much time to talk just now. We're having some problems with your order for filing cabinets.

George: Hmn.

Allan: Well, you know, the consignment[1] is ready for shipment[2] to your customer in Montreal. But I'm afraid our haulier[3] has let us down[4].

George: What?? Really??? That's rather unfortunate[5]. What's the problem then?

Allan: Well, the point is that one of the haulier's trucks broke down[6]. And the repair is likely to take a couple of days. All their other trucks are on the road with tight[7] delivery schedules[8]. And that's why the haulier is having problems with rescheduling[9] his deliveries.

George: And what exactly does that mean for us?

[1] Sendung, Partie
[2] versandfertig
[3] Spediteur, Transportunternehmer
[4] jdn. „hängen"/im Stich lassen
[5] unglücklich, schlecht
[6] *hier:* liegen bleiben
[7] dicht, eng
[8] Liefer-, Belieferungsplan
[9] umorganisieren, umplanen

Allan: Well, as I said, the haulier has no other transport capacity[10] available[11]. We either have to try and get another haulier to do the job, which, at such short notice[12], might be very difficult and costly[13] as well. Or else we'll just have to wait till that truck is repaired. What do you think?

George: Now, that's very annoying[14] indeed. You see, we made a very firm promise[15] to our customer as regards the delivery date. And in fact, we might be held responsible[16] if the goods don't arrive as agreed. So, I don't think there is going to be any hope for much understanding there.

Allan: That doesn't sound good at all.

George: It certainly doesn't. I would say the best thing to do is to look for another haulier who is willing and able to move the goods at very short notice. Could you do that perhaps?? And also find out about the costs? If that fails[17], I'll just have to persuade[18] our customer to accept a delay in delivery[19]. And that won't be easy, I can tell you.

Allan: OK then, I'll try my very best. I'll let you know as quickly as possible.

George: OK, you do that. And bye for now.

[10] Transportkapazität
[11] verfügbar, zur Verfügung
[12] kurzfristig
[13] teuer, kostspielig
[14] ärgerlich
[15] fest versprechen, feste Zusage machen
[16] verantwortlich machen
[17] wenn das nicht klappt/funktioniert
[18] überzeugen
[19] Lieferverzug

Dealing with the text

1 Answer these questions.

1 Why does Allan come straight to the point?
2 What's the problem with the consignment of steel filing cabinets?
3 Why can the haulier not reschedule the deliveries?
4 Finding another haulier is difficult, Allan says. Why?
5 Why is the situation difficult for George?
6 What are the options that George is talking about?

2 Find terms in the text that could be replaced by the following.

carrier	fix	plan
change the delivery plans	inform you	ready for dispatch[2]
expensive	lorry	ship[3] goods
find	other freight capacity[1]	so quickly

[1] Fracht-, Transportkapazität
[2] versandbereit, -fertig
[3] versenden, verschiffen

3 Write down useful phrases from the dialogue and make sure what you would say in German.

4 You are Allan. Write a brief memo stating the main points of the telephone conversation.

With a partner, write and act out a telephone conversation.

You work for a company that provides[1] hospitals and surgeries[2] with medical supplies[3] for the treatment[4] of patients. Call the goods-in department[5] of the Royal Victoria Hospital and inform your partner that the weekly delivery[6] will be made two days late. The reason is that, due to the illness of a couple of drivers, the delivery schedules had to be reorganised. The other drivers will be working longer hours[7]. You hope that things will be back to normal within a fortnight. Ask for their understanding. Your name is Colin Soames from MedSupplies Ltd. and your partner in the Royal Victoria Hospital is Fiona McInnes.

1 beliefern/versorgen mit
2 Arztpraxis
3 Medizinbedarf, Sanitätsartikel
4 Behandlung
5 Wareneingang(-sabteilung)
6 *hier*: An-, Belieferung
7 länger arbeiten, Überstunden machen

Start by writing out the dialogue as outlined above. Use the pattern below for your telephone conversation.

Colin Soames		Fiona McInnes
	←	Accept the call. Say your name etc.
Say your name. Explain the situation.	→	
	←	Ask for the details to be repeated.
Repeat the (technical) details.	→	
	←	Say that you understood the new delivery arrangements.
Say you are sorry for the situation. Explain that the drivers are working extra hours.	→	
	←	Say that you understand the situation.
Offer help if some goods are needed urgently.	→	
	←	Say thank you and express the hope that things will be back to normal soon.
Say thank you for understanding the difficult situation.		

©Picture-Factory-fotolia.com

You may find some of these words and phrases helpful.

Colin Soames	Fiona McInnes
delay[1] in the shipment[2] of … to phone/call about to change the routes[3] and delivery times[4] to make special arrangements to offer one's apologies[5] to thank for so.'s understanding	to be rather unfortunate[6] to insist on[7] deliveries being made as promised to be able to cope[8] to call in a case of emergency[9] to appreciate[10] the efforts[11] made to inform customers

1 Verzögerung, Verzug
2 Versand, Belieferung
3 *hier*: Streckenführung, -plan
4 Lieferzeit
5 sich entschuldigen
6 *hier*: nicht gut
7 bestehen auf
8 klar-, zurechtkommen
9 Notfall(-situation)
10 zu schätzen wissen
11 Anstrengung

7.3 Dispatching[1] goods

[1] Versand (von)

7.3.1 Yet more paperwork?!?

Read the "to do" list and decide which of the points listed involve paperwork.

	Things to do	Requires[1] paperwork	Requires general attention[2]	Chronological order
1	Check and file the delivery notes[3].			
2	Check that the vehicles only carry the goods to be delivered. Check the packaging[4] of the goods.			
3	Do not dispatch[5] damaged[6] goods.			
4	Ensure[7] that the packing lists[8], delivery notes, invoices are correct.			
5	Ensure that the vehicle is clean and that you are satisfied[9] with the appearance[10] of the driver. (Leaving a good impression[11] with the customer is very important.)			
6	Inform the customer about the dispatch date[12], the name of the carrier[13] (if necessary) and the expected date of arrival of the consignment (advice of dispatch[14]).			
7	Keep a record[15] of the goods dispatched.			
8	Make sure the drivers can prove that delivery has been made (customer's signature[16] on the delivery note).			
9	Carefully check the correctness of the information on the documents[17]: customer's name, address and number, order number[18], the number of items/ packages sent, delivery address[19].			

[1] erfordern, verlangen
[2] Aufmerksamkeit verlangen/ erfordern
[3] Lieferschein
[4] Verpackung
[5] versenden
[6] schadhaft, beschädigt
[7] sicherstellen
[8] Pack-, Versandliste
[9] zufrieden
[10] Aussehen, Erscheinungsbild
[11] einen guten Eindruck machen
[12] Versandtermin
[13] Spediteur, Transportunternehmen
[14] Versandanzeige
[15] *hier*: Nachweis
[16] Unterschrift
[17] *hier*: Unterlage
[18] Auftragsnummer
[19] Lieferanschrift

What could the chronological order be? Develop a flow chart.

7.3.2 Shipping terms

Use your (online) dictionary to find out what these phrases mean in German.

carriage forward (C/F) carriage paid (C/P) deadweight (dwt) duty forward duty paid	exclusive of freight free at the receiving/arrival station freight collect freight paid freight prepaid	gross weight (gr. wt.) inclusive of freight franco domicile net weight (nt. wt.)

Decide which of the terms and phrases listed in the box on p. 87 can be used in these situations. Sometimes there are several correct solutions.

1 Our prices include all transport costs.
2 The buyer will be responsible for paying customs duties[1].
3 This item weighs 75 kilograms without packaging.
4 Our prices are all-inclusive[2].
5 The carrier will charge for transport.
6 The carrying weight[3] of this ship is 16,000 tons.
7 Our prices do not include transport charges[4].
8 These prices include transport charges to your premises.
9 The carriage[5] of the goods has been paid in advance.

[1] Zollgebühren
[2] alles eingerechnet
[3] Tragegewicht
[4] Transportgebühren, -kosten
[5] Transport, Beförderung

Note

Use the preposition *by* to indicate the means[1] and the mode of transport[2], e.g. *by lorry/truck/ship, by road/air/rail/inland waterway*, etc.

[1] Transportmittel
[2] Verkehrsträger, Transportart

7.4 Advice of dispatch

Having been informed by Allan Tranter of OfficeTech Incorporated that the steel filing cabinets will be ready for shipment in a few days, George Hamilton of Office Village Corp. writes a short note to the cutomer in Montreal to pass on this information.

Fill in the gaps.

Use the details below to complete the advice of dispatch. There are more phrases than you need.

• 27 April • at your premises • consignment • contract of sale[1] • doing business • • freight charges[2] • from our manufacturer • haulage company • in good order[4] • • order of 24 March • separate post • wholesaler •

[1] Kaufvertrag
[2] Frachtkosten
[3] (Straßen-)Transportunternehmen
[4] in gutem Zustand

20 April 20..

Dear Ms Johnson:

We refer to your _____ (1), order number PT 7891, and are pleased to advise[1] you that the _____ (2) of steel filing cabinets will be shipped to you by Dowling Hauliers Inc. of Newark, New Jersey. They will pick up[2] the goods _____ (3), OfficeTech Incorporated, at their works[3] in Pittsburgh on _____ (4). The consignment should arrive _____ (5) on 29 April. As agreed in our _____ (6) there will be no _____ (7). And the invoice will be sent by _____ (8).

We trust[4] that you will find the cabinets _____ (9).

Thank you very much for your order and we look forward to _____ (10) with you again in future.

Yours truly,

[1] informieren, in Kenntnis setzen
[2] *hier*: abholen
[3] Fabrik, Werk
[4] hoffen, davon ausgehen

7.5 Receiving goods

Track 26

The receipt of shipment[1] must be clearly documented[2] to keep track of[3] the goods received[4] and to provide the necessary information for the accounting department[5] which is responsible for making payment to the supplier. Such documentation[6] is also very useful to clear up any discrepancies[7] or to solve[8] problems when claims[9] have to be made. And here is a list of activities involved with the receipt of goods[10].

©imtmphoto-fotolia.com

- Assisting with the physical movement of goods[11] from the goods-in area[12] to the warehouse[13]
- Checking the purchase order number[14]
- Checking the consignment for the correct quantity[15]
- Checking the quality of the materials against the specifications[16] as stated in the order
- Checking the shipment for any visible[17] damage[18]
- Comparing the product numbers with the catalogue numbers in the order list
- Comparing the quantities received with those stated in the packing list or on the delivery slip[19]
- Counting the packages and the number of items
- Doing spot checks[20] to find defective[21] materials
- Entering the delivery notes into the company computer system
- Informing the relevant[22] department of any damaged goods received
- Passing on the documents to the accounts department[23]
- Physical inspection[24] of the goods
- Recording[25] the date (and time) of delivery
- Recording the name of the shipper[26]
- Rejecting[27] damaged or incorrect[28] goods and sending out a request for replacements[29]
- Updating[30] of goods received record[31]
- Weighing[32] packages

[1] Sendungsannahme
[2] dokumentieren, erfassen
[3] nachverfolgen
[4] Wareneingang, eingegangene Ware
[5] Buchhaltung, Abteilung Rechnungswesen
[6] *hier*: Unterlagen, Belege
[7] Abweichung, Unstimmigkeit
[8] lösen
[9] Forderung, Anspruch
[10] Warenannahme
[11] Warenbewegung
[12] Warenannahme(-bereich)
[13] Waren-, Materiallager
[14] Bestellnummer
[15] Menge
[16] Angabe, Spezifikation
[17] sichtbar
[18] Beschädigung, Schaden
[19] Lieferschein
[20] Stichprobenkontrolle
[21] fehlerhaft, mangelhaft
[22] *hier*: zuständig
[23] Buchhaltung(-sabteilung)
[24] genaue/eingehende Untersuchung
[25] erfassen
[26] Spediteur
[27] ablehnen, zurückweisen
[28] falsch
[29] Ersatz(-lieferung)
[30] auf den neuesten Stand bringen, aktualisieren
[31] Nachweis der Warenannahme
[32] (ab)wiegen

Describe the work in the goods-in department.

1 Decide which items in the list above do **not** involve paperwork.

2 Decide on the proper sequence[1] of these activities.

3 Use the information in the bullet points above to describe your first week in the goods-in department. If your company/business does not have such a department, describe the routines used in your office for receiving goods. Start as follows:

1 (Ab-)Folge

1 ent-, ausladen
2 einlagern, auf Lager nehmen
3 genaue Prüfung

On Monday I began working in the goods-in department. Half way through the morning we had several lorries with goods that had to be unloaded[1]. The goods then had to be put into storage[2]. My boss asked me to help with …

4 Write an internal e-mail to the person responsible in the purchasing department informing her/him that the consignment of electric DIY tools arrived today. On closer inspection[3] you found that order number OXK 415 (item 5 on the order list) was missing. Suggest that he/she contacts the supplier.

7.6 Incoterms® 2020

1 Handelsbedingungen
2 im Einzelnen festlegen
3 Partei des Verkaufsvertrages
4 Abfertigung zur Ein- und Ausfuhr
5 *hier*: Transportweg
6 übergehen von … auf

The Incoterms (short for: International Commercial Terms) are standard sets of terms and conditions of trading[1]. They are commonly used in international trade and specify[2] the rights and obligations of the two parties to the sales contract[3], the buyer and the seller, with regard to transport, import and export clearance[4] and the point in the journey[5] of the goods when the risk passes from[6] the seller to[6] the buyer. They were created by the International Chamber of Commerce (ICC) as long ago as 1936 and were last updated in 2020 (now: Incoterms 2020).

Incoterms® 2020

1		Freight to collect terms						Freight prepaid terms				
2	Group	Any mode or modes of transport[1]		Sea and inland waterway transport[2]				Any mode or modes of transport				
3		EXW	FCA	FAS	FOB	CFR	CIF	CPT	CIP	DAP	DPU	DDP
4	Incoterm Ex works (place)	Ex works (place)	Free carrier[3] (place)	Free alongside[4] ship (port)	Free on board (port)	Cost & freight[5] (port)	Cost, insurance & freight (port)	Carriage[6] paid to (place)	Carriage & insurance paid to (place)	Delivered at[7] place (place)	Delivered at place unloaded[8] (place)	Delivered duty paid[9] (place)
5	Transfer of risk	At buyer's disposal[10]	On buyer's transport	Alongside ship	On board vessel[11]	On board vessel	On board vessel	At carrier	At carrier	At named[12] place	At named place unloaded	At named place
6	Obligations & charges											
7	Export packaging[13]	Seller	Seller	Seller	Seller	Seller	Seller	Seller	Seller	Seller	Seller	Seller
8	Loading charges[14]	Buyer	Seller	Seller	Seller	Seller	Seller	Seller	Seller	Seller	Seller	Seller
9	Delivery to port[15]/ place	Buyer	Seller	Seller	Seller	Seller	Seller	Seller	Seller	Seller	Seller	Seller
10	Export duty[16], taxes & customs clearance[17]	Buyer	Seller	Seller	Seller	Seller	Seller	Seller	Seller	Seller	Seller	Seller
11	Origin terminal charges[18]	Buyer	Buyer	Seller	Seller	Seller	Seller	Seller	Seller	Seller	Seller	Seller
12	Loading on carriage[19]	Buyer	Buyer	Buyer	Seller	Seller	Seller	Seller	Seller	Seller	Seller	Seller
13	Carriage charges[20]	Buyer	Buyer	Buyer	Buyer	Seller	Seller	Seller	Seller	Seller	Seller	Seller
14	Insurance	Negotiable[21]					Seller	Negotiable	Seller	Negotiable		
15	Destination terminal charges[22]	Buyer	Buyer	Buyer	Buyer	Buyer	Buyer	Seller	Seller	Seller	Seller	Seller
16	Delivery to destination[23]	Buyer	Buyer	Buyer	Buyer	Buyer	Buyer	Buyer	Buyer	Seller	Seller	Seller
17	Unloading at destination	Buyer	Buyer	Buyer	Buyer	Buyer	Buyer	Buyer	Buyer	Buyer	Seller	Buyer
18	Import duty, taxes & customs clearance[24]	Buyer	Buyer	Buyer	Buyer	Buyer	Buyer	Buyer	Buyer	Buyer	Buyer	Seller

1 Transportart 2 Binnenschifffahrt 3 Frachtführer, Beförderer 4 längsseits 5 Frachtgebühren 6 Fracht-, Transport(kosten) 7 angeliefert in 8 entladen 9 verzollt 10 nach Wahl des Käufers 11 Schiff 12 angegeben 13 Verpackung 14 Verladekosten 15 Hafen 16 Ausfuhrabgaben 17 Ausfuhrabfertigung 18 Abfertigungsgebühren am Abgangsort 19 Verladung auf Transportmittel 20 Transportkosten 21 verhandelbar 22 Gebühren am Zielort 23 Lieferung an den Bestimmungsort 24 Verzollung

Study the chart on p. 90 and then answer these questions.

1 Which terms apply to any kind of transport?

2 Which terms apply to sea or waterway transport only?

3 Which term is the "cheapest" as regards the costs and work involved for the seller?

4 Which term in transport by water is "expensive" for the buyer?

5 Which term for any mode of transport is the most "expensive" for the seller?

6 Under which term do the buyer's obligations and charges begin "on board vessel"?

7 Which terms hold the buyer responsible for unloading at the final destination?

8 Who is responsible for obtaining and paying insurance for the goods?

9 Under which terms is the buyer responsible for loading the goods?

10 Under which terms is the seller responsible for unloading?

11 In which cases is the seller responsible for customs clearance?

12 Under the CIF term the buyer's responsibility begins only when the goods have arrived at a terminal in the country of destination. Under which terms do the buyer's responsibilities begin in the country of origin?

Revision

Adverbs

General: You know that adjectives are used to qualify nouns, e.g. *early payment*. Adverbs add to the meaning of verbs; they say how something happens (manner – *fast, slowly*), when (time – *then, now, tomorrow*), where (place – *here, there, in town*), how often (frequency – *(very) rarely, often, seldom*) and also to what extent (degree – *fully, entirely*). Adverbs are also used to qualify adjectives *(fairly new, rather old)*, other adverbs *(very seldom, more slowly)*, prepositional phrases *(even at weekends)* and even complete phrases *(I haven't seen it yet.)*.

Forms: Many adverbs are formed by adding *"-ly"* to the adjective *(high – highly)*. Adverbs can also have the comparative and superlative forms *(more frequently, most frequently)*. Sometimes the forms of the adjective and the adverb are the same *(early, fast)*.

Note other forms of the adverb (adverbial phrases): *in a way, as a matter of fact, indeed, in that case, in town, yesterday evening, etc.*

Adverbs are also used for comparisons: *as … as, not as/so … as, than, the … the …, … and …*

Examples: *This year's sales were **as** high **as** last year's.*
*This year our sales did **not** rise **as** fast **as** last year.*
*This machine turns out more items **than** the old one.*
***The** lower the price, **the** more people will be attracted to buy.*
*The prices for fruit and vegetables are going up **and** up.*

Position: Usually adverbs are found before the word they qualify. If the adverb qualifies the verb and the verb has two or more parts, then the adverb is put after the first part. Other preferred positions are at the beginning or the end of the sentence (adverbs of time and place). Remember to put the adverb of place **before** the adverb of time. *I'll meet you at the station at 8.30 tonight.*

In the text below, try to identify the adverbs.

Nowadays, many people order goods online. And often enough they are out working all day and not at home to receive the goods when the parcel[1] is delivered. Ideally, if there is a problem, you should send the goods back with the driver of the delivery van[2] straightaway. When this is not possible, it is wise to act quickly, although, usually, you can return the goods at a later date. If the goods are returned immediately, however, the seller cannot say that the damage was caused[3] by you. The seller must react quickly to prove[4] that the goods were in good order and condition[5] and adequately[6] packed for the journey. Of course, unless you want your money back, you have the right to ask for the faulty goods to be replaced as speedily[7] as possible.

1 Päckchen, Paket
2 Lieferwagen
3 verursachen
4 be-, nachweisen
5 in gutem/einwandfreiem Zustand
6 angemessen, gut
7 schnell

Choose the right position for the adverbs in the sentences below. Use the words in brackets. Sometimes there are several possibilities.

1 How ___ have I told you that you must work ___? (more thoroughly, often)
2 ___ we've ___ had difficulties with this supplier. (in the past, never)
3 ___, I'll fax you a copy ___ ___. (first thing, of course, tomorrow morning)
4 I'll meet you ___ ___ ___ ___. (at noon, for lunch, in the pub, in Baker Street)
5 Have you ___ done something about the consignment that was reported missing[1] ___? (already, this morning)
6 The electrician's invoice has ___ been lying ___ ___ ___. (already, for more than two weeks, now, on his desk)
7 ___, we were able to solve this transport problem ___. (fortunately, quite quickly)
8 ___ faster you get this job[2] done ___ better for the team ___. (as a whole, the … the …)
9 I'm not ___ sure ___ that this supplier is ___ reliable ___ the previous[3] one. (anymore, as … as, even)
10 ___ you are right. We should work ___ to satisfy[4] our ___ demanding[5] customers. (harder, in a way, very)

1 als fehlend melden
2 Aufgabe, (Arbeits-)Auftrag
3 vorherig
4 zufriedenstellen
5 anspruchsvoll, schwierig

7.7 Invoicing[1]

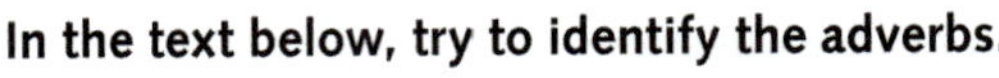

1 Rechnungsstellung

Invoices generally contain a number of items of information such as the following:

• 30 days net • a fortnight • 2% cash discount • customer number • (date of) order • reference/catalogue number[1] • invoice item[2] • invoice number • net price overall[3] • number of units per item[4]	• order number • percentage rate[5] of value added tax[6] (VAT) and amount • price for the total number of units ordered per item • price per item[7] • product description[8] • sub-total[9] • time of payment • total amount payable[10]

1 Bezugsnummer, Kennziffer
2 Rechnungsposten
3 Nettopreis insgesamt
4 Stückzahl pro Bestellnummer
5 Prozentsatz
6 Mehrwertsteuer
7 Preis pro Position/Stück
8 Produktbezeichnung
9 Zwischensumme
10 zu zahlender Gesamtbetrag

Study this invoice.

A winegrower[1] from Rhineland-Palatinate sent this invoice to a wholesaler based in Newcastle/GB. Identify[2] and/or fill in the missing items from the list on p. 92.

[1] Winzer, Weinbauer
[2] genau bestimmen

WEINGUT PETER STOLLEIS
Carl-Theodor-Hof

Weinbau in der Familie
seit 1668

Weingut Peter Stolleis • Kurpfalzstraße 99 • 67435 Gimmeldingen-Mussbach

Newcastle Wine Merchants
107 Westgate Road
Newcastle upon Tyne NE4 6XD
GREAT BRITAIN

25 October 20..
① ... 1045/20..
② ... 102879

Invoice

Your ③ ... of ... 20..
④ No: ...

⑤	⑥	⑦	⑧	⑨	⑩
1	192	0516	Riesling	€5.60	€1,075.20
2	216	0518	Silvaner	€5.20	€1,123.20
3	240	0523	Müller-Thurgau	€5.50	€1,320.00
4	168	0544	Weißer Burgunder	€6.50	€1,092.00
5	120	0616	Riesling-Sekt	€10.30	€1,236.00
6	192	0564	Dornfelder	€6.60	€1,267.20
7	216	0575	Spätburgunder	€5.80	€1,252.80
8	240	0582	Landwein	€4.40	€1,056.00
				⑪ ...	**€9,422.40**
				⑫ ... @ 19 %	€1790.26
				⑬ ...	**€11,212.66**

⑭ ... for payment within ⑮ ... of receipt of invoice or ⑯ ... net.
All goods remain our property[1] until they have been paid in full[2].
Thank you for your order and we hope to be of service again[3] in the near future[4].

[1] Eigentum
[2] vollständig bezahlen
[3] *hier*: wieder beliefern
[4] bald

Telefon (0 63 21) 6 60 71
Telefax (0 63 21) 6 03 48
E-Mail: weingut@stolleis.com
Internet: www.stolleis.com

Es gelten unsere Allgemeinen Geschäftsbedingungen.
Gerichtsstand und Erfüllungsort: Neustadt/Weinstraße

Sparkasse Rhein-Haardt IBAN: DE59 5465 1240 0001 9695 18 BIC: MALADE51DKH
Volksbank Kur- und Rheinpfalz eG IBAN: DE02 5479 0000 0000 1570 07 BIC: GENODE61SPE
HypoVereinsbank Neustadt IBAN: DE04 5462 0093 6600 1911 34 BIC: HYVEDEMM620

Look at the invoice of a British manufacturer of automobile parts.

MOTMAN LTD

Invoice

Customer No.	Payer No.	Supplier Code	Date	Invoice No.
30087	**30087**	**BFFJG**	**14-08-20XX**	**334069**

Payer
JLR LTD China
LR payables
PO Box 6816
Coventry
CV3 8QH

Delivery address
JLR Export Centre
Unit 8
Griffin Business Park
Walmer Way
Chelmsley Wood
B37 1UX

Our reference

Delivery Method
Your Forwarder

Order No.
7991148

Your reference

Delivery Terms
EXW

Delivery Note No.
9457975

Delivery Date	Due Date[1]	Payment Terms
14-08-20XX	**15-08-20XX**	**60 DAYS NET**

Currency[2]	Our VAT Reg. No.
EUR	**GB773605604**

Interest[3] will be debited with 1.25 % per month

Line	Your Item No. Item Number Description	Quantity	Price Your Order No. Customs Sta No.	Price Qty	Amount
250	**D24SJ177087** Pan Head 8.8 DEP Screws with head, hexagon[4] Class 8.8	4250 PCS	395.48	1000	**1,680.79**

Exchange rate[5] 0.7304 — 245.53 GBP

Total	**1,680.79**
VAT 20.0 %	**336.16**
Invoice Total	**2,016.96**
To Pay	**2,016.95**

Gross weight (kg)	Net weight (kg)
205	170

MOTMAN — Reg.No/VAT No. — Bank
Address — Tel./Fax/Mail — Swift Code
IBAN

[1] Fälligkeitstermin
[2] Währung
[3] Zinsen
[4] Flachkopfschraube, sechskant
[5] Wechselkurs

Study this invoice and find the following information.

customer number delivery date description of the goods exchange rate interest to be paid number of delivery note number of invoice	order number payer number place of delivery price of the goods sent price per 1,000 items quantity of pieces sent rate of VAT	terms of delivery terms of payment total amount to be paid VAT registration number weight of the goods sent

7.8 How to pay for goods and services

©Francois Doisnel-fotolia.com

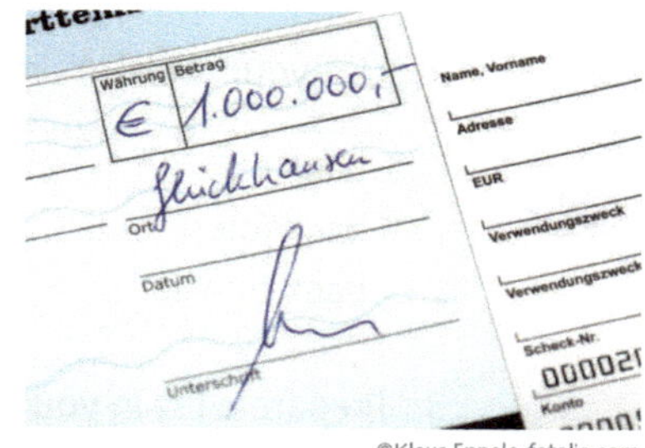

©Klaus Eppele-fotolia.com

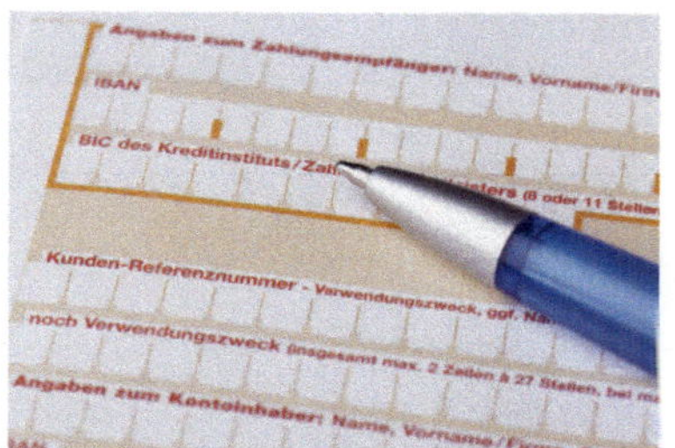

©Lena Balk-fotolia.com

©sidmay-fotolia.com

©Gina Sanders-fotolia.com

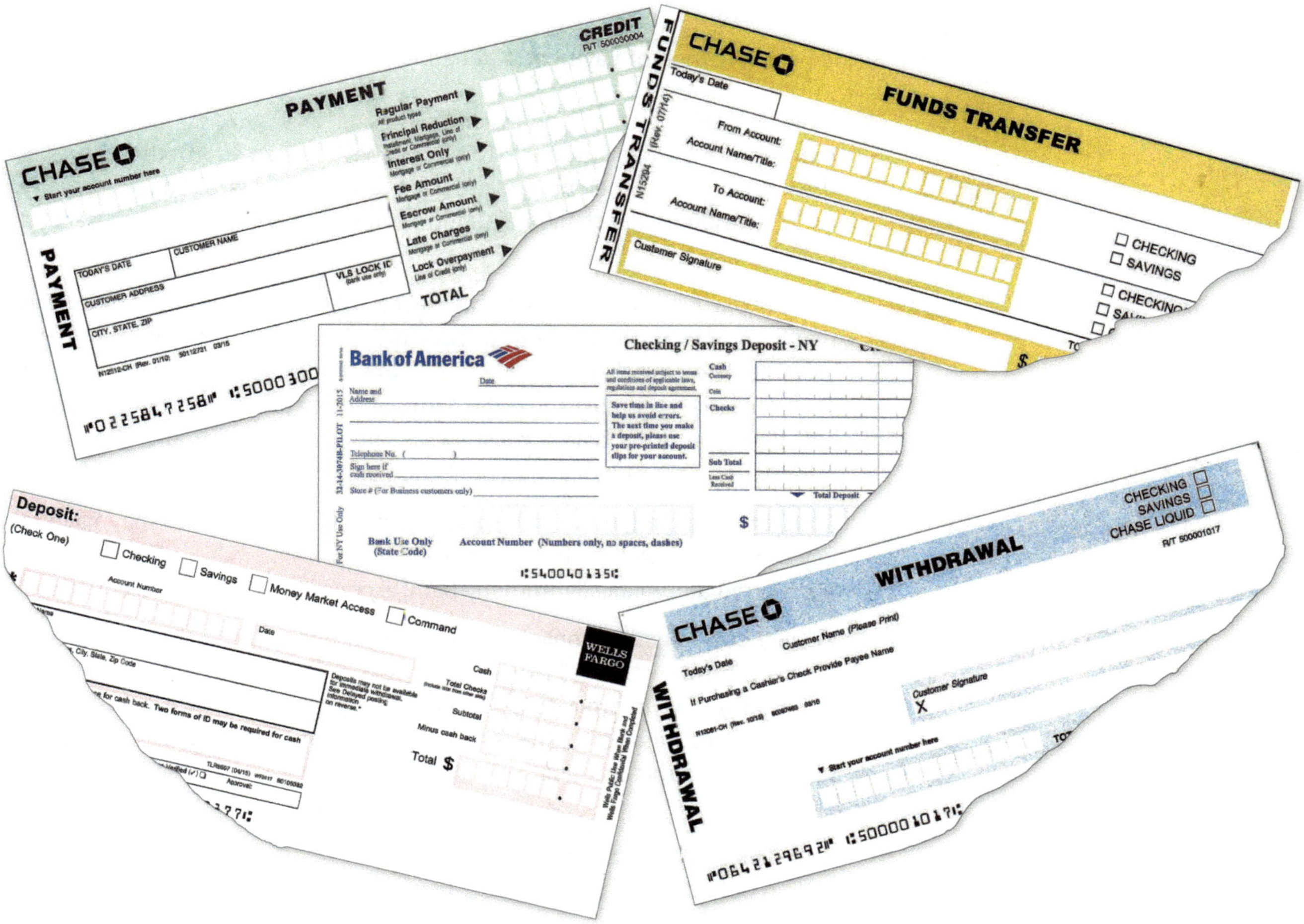

Decide how best to pay.

1 erkennen
2 Entsprechung

1 Which of the payment instruments on p. 95 do you recognise[1]?

2 Use your (online) dictionary to find the German equivalents[2] for these terms.

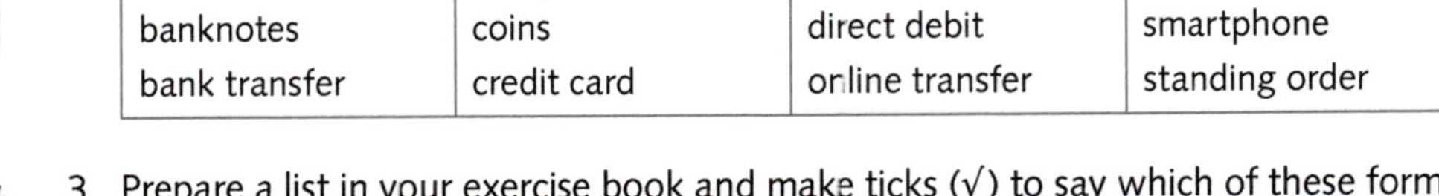

bank card	cheque	debit card	PayPal
banknotes	coins	direct debit	smartphone
bank transfer	credit card	online transfer	standing order

3 Prepare a list in your exercise book and make ticks (√) to say which of these forms of payment you or your family use - often, regularly or only every now and again.

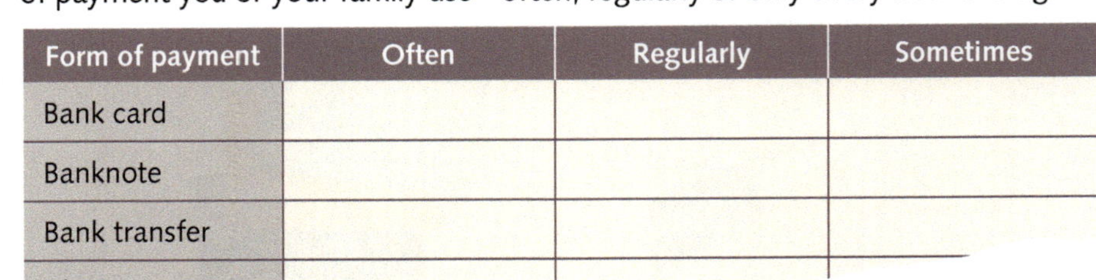

Form of payment	Often	Regularly	Sometimes
Bank card			
Banknote			
Bank transfer			
Cheque			

For each form of payment say where and for which reason you decide to pay in this way.

DIGITAL+
Track 27

4 Decide which method of payment is described in each of these explanations.

1 I give the seller/payee[1] permission to get her[2]/his bank to withdraw[3] the money from my bank account. To do so, I have to sign a form that the seller then passes on to[4] her/his bank. Such transactions can be made regularly, and the amounts can change. This form can also be used for one transaction only.

2 I hand over a piece of paper to the payee, who then presents it to her/his bank. The amount is paid out in cash or transferred[5] to the payee's bank account. The payee's bank will obtain[6] the money from my bank account. This piece of paper must show the name of the payee, the amount in words and figures and the date. I must sign it, of course. And it also shows the information about my bank account (number and sort code[7]).

3 I put a plastic card into a little machine or hold it against it. I may have to key in my PIN[8] and/or, in some cases, sign a cash receipt[9]. The money is transferred automatically from my bank account to the seller's account.

4 When I buy something online, this is the best possible and cheapest way of paying for my purchases[10]. I just need to set up[11] an electronic account and put money in it. In order to pay I press a button[12], give my e-mail address and enter my password. The rest is done automatically. I can also receive payments into this account.

5 I instruct[13] my bank to transfer a certain sum of money regularly at a fixed date. The bank needs the account data[14] (IBAN[15], BIC[16]) of the payee. For a certain period of time (say a year), the amount does not change.

1 Zahlungsempfänger/in
2 jdn. bitten/veranlassen etw. zu tun
3 abheben
4 weiterreichen/-leiten an
5 überweisen
6 erhalten, bekommen
7 Bankleitzahl
8 Geheimzahl
9 Kassenquittung, -bon
10 (Ein-)Kauf
11 einrichten
12 Knopf, Taste
13 beauftragen
14 Kontendaten
15 Internationale Bankkontennummer
16 Bankleitzahl

6 I use my computer to transfer the money to the payee. I just fill in an online form with the account details of the seller, the IBAN and the BIC, the amount, a reference[17] to the transaction (e.g. customer number, invoice number and date) and the date on which the transfer is to be made. I need to authorise[18] the transfer with my TAN[19].

7 I use a multi-part[20] transfer form[21] which I get from my bank. I fill in the account details of the seller/payee, the IBAN and the BIC, the amount and the reason for payment. I also need to give my name and bank account number. And finally[22], I have to enter[23] the date, sign the form and leave it with my bank which will process[24] it. This form of payment can also be used in online banking[25].

8 I use a plastic card. And I have to sign a receipt[26]. If I use it to pay for online purchases, I have to enter the card number, the period of validity[27] and the reference number on the back. The money is withdrawn from my account once a month. In some cases I get a statement[28] of my purchases and can decide when to make the transfer; in this case I may have to pay interest[29].

[17] Hinweis, Verweis
[18] bevollmächtigen, autorisieren
[19] Transaktionsnummer
[20] mehrteilig
[21] Überweisungsformular
[22] schließlich, zuletzt
[23] eingeben
[24] ver-, bearbeiten
[25] Online-Banking
[26] Quittung
[27] Gültigkeitsdauer
[28] *hier*: Aufstellung, Liste
[29] Zinsen

5 Decide which method of payment is the best for yourself or for a business to pay for goods purchased or for services received. In most cases there may be several solutions.

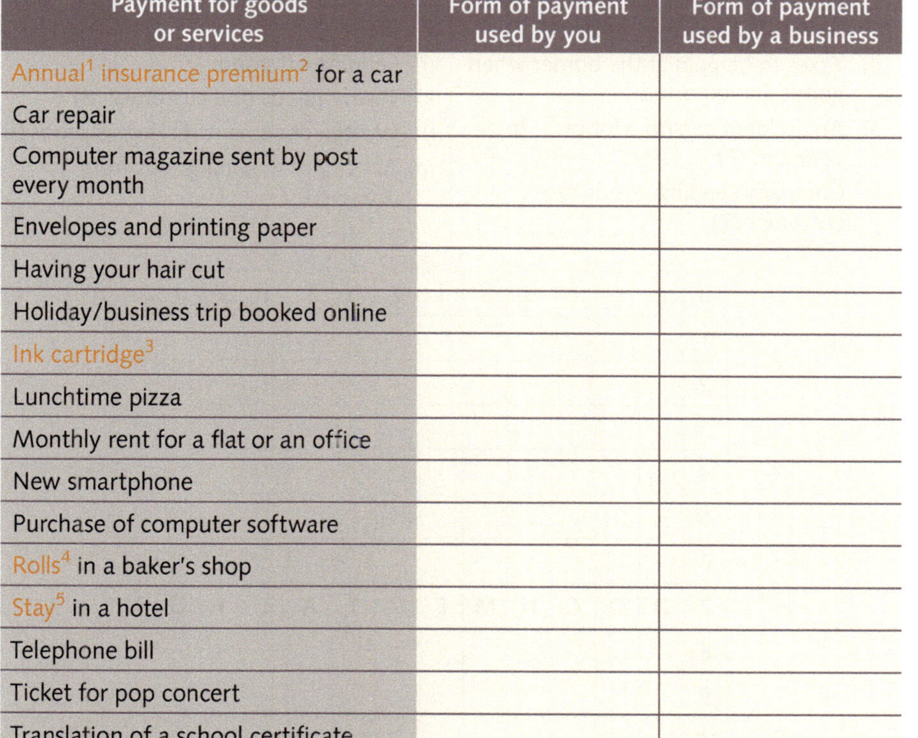

Payment for goods or services	Form of payment used by you	Form of payment used by a business
Annual[1] insurance premium[2] for a car		
Car repair		
Computer magazine sent by post every month		
Envelopes and printing paper		
Having your hair cut		
Holiday/business trip booked online		
Ink cartridge[3]		
Lunchtime pizza		
Monthly rent for a flat or an office		
New smartphone		
Purchase of computer software		
Rolls[4] in a baker's shop		
Stay[5] in a hotel		
Telephone bill		
Ticket for pop concert		
Translation of a school certificate		
Winter coat		

[1] (all)jährlich
[2] Versicherungsprämie
[3] Tintenpatrone
[4] Brötchen
[5] Aufenthalt

Compare your answers in class and explain the reasons for your solutions.

7.9 Looking ahead

Some people are talking about doing away with money altogether[1]. They want to get rid of[2] all paper money (banknotes) and coins as well. They think that paying by electronic means (smartphone, debit card, credit card, direct debit) will be much easier and quicker for many people, especially shopkeepers[3], but banks as well. Nobody has to count money anymore at the end of the day. And shopkeepers do not have to carry large sums of money (the day's takings[4]) to the bank. And we don't have to worry that there will be someone out there who just wants to steal our purse[5] or wallet[6]. A life without cash – how wonderful!?!?

1 gänzlich, vollständig
2 loswerden, abschaffen
3 Ladenbesitzer, Geschäftsinhaber
4 Tageseinnahmen, -losung
5 Geldbörse
6 Brieftasche, Portemonnaie

What do you think life without banknotes and coins would be like for us, for businesses? Exchange your ideas.

Revise your vocabulary.

Fill in the puzzle below with words that fit these definitions. The number of letters needed is shown in brackets and for each word one letter is shown in line 7 across.

a) If the train is late, there is a … (5)
b) Office at the border where goods are checked (7)
c) Piece of paper showing that something has been received (7)
d) Taxes to be paid at the border when goods are imported (4)
e) An accident can do a lot of … to your car. (6)
f) Company sending goods to a customer (7)
g) Your name below the text of a letter (9)
h) What you pay for the transport of goods (7)
i) Company transporting goods for payment (7)
j) Sending off goods (8)
k) Taking goods to a customer (8)
l) Written document serving as proof (6)
m) Activity of moving goods from A to B (9)

0	a	b	c	d	e	f	g	h	i	j	k	l	m
1													
2													
3													
4													
5													
6													
7	**D**	**O**	**C**	**U**	**M**	**E**	**N**	**T**	**A**	**T**	**I**	**O**	**N**
8													
9													
10													
11													
12													

Unit 8 How to deal with complaints

8.1 Let's get going!

Can you remember when you, a member of your family or a friend complained[1] about something that went wrong?

- What was the reason for the complaint[2]? The purchase of faulty goods or poor service?
- Who did you complain to?
- How did that person react?
- How was the problem finally solved? Describe your experience.

©Gstudio Group-fotolia.com

1 sich beschweren
2 Beschwerde, Mängelrüge

Exchange your experiences in class.

What strategies for solving problems did you notice?

Which of these do/don't you like? State your reasons.

8.2 A sympathetic way of handling a complaint

Track 28

Nobody likes making complaints and nobody likes receiving them. And, in actual fact[1], one can say that the vast majority of business transactions[2], whether with private customers or with business customers, are completed without any problems. And yet, complaints do occur. Making a complaint and solving a complaint require some thought about what one wants to achieve and how to go about it[3].

The story of the British supermarket chain Sainsbury's shows how a complaint can be used as a great opportunity[4] to do something out of the ordinary[5] and help build a positive image.

1 tatsächlich
2 Geschäftsvorgang
3 etw. machen
4 Gelegenheit, Möglichkeit
5 außergewöhnlich

Sainsbury's takes advice from a 3-year old

Lily Robinson (who, when it happened a few years ago, was three and a half years old) was somewhat confused by[1] the name of a type of bread her mother used to buy[2] at Sainsbury's, a product they called "Tiger bread". She thought the top[3] of the loaf[4] didn't look like a tiger at all and that, in fact, it looked more like a giraffe. With the help of her parents she wrote in to the retail company[5] saying:

1 verwirrt wegen
2 oft gekauft haben
3 Oberseite
4 Brot(-laib)
5 Einzelhandelsunternehmen

> Dear Sainsssssssssssssssbbbbbbbbbbbbuuuuuuuuuuuuryyyys,
>
> Why is the tiger bread called tiger bread? – It should be called giraffe bread.
>
> Love from Lily Robinson, age 3 1/2

[1] Kundendienst-mitarbeiter/in

Track 29

Lily was surprised to receive a letter back from the customer support manager[1], Chris King, which read as follows:

[1] Fleck(en)
[2] Streifen
[3] gestreift
[4] Geschenkgutschein
[5] Süßigkeiten

Dear Lily

Thank you so much for your letter. I think renaming tiger bread giraffe bread is a brilliant idea – it looks much more like the blotches[1] on a giraffe than the stripes[2] on a tiger, doesn't it?

It is called tiger bread because the first baker who made it a loooong time ago thought it looked stripey[3] like a tiger. Maybe they were a bit silly.

I really liked reading your letter, so I thought I would send you a little present. I've put a £3 gift card[4] in with this letter. If you ask your mum or dad to take you to Sainsbury's, you could use it to buy some of your own tiger bread (and maybe, if mum and dad say it's OK, you can get some sweeties[5] too). Please tell an adult to wait 48 hours before using this card.

I'm glad you wrote in to us and hope you like spending our gift card. See you in store soon.

Yours sincerely

Chris King (age 27 & 1/3)
Customer Manager

Enclosed: £3 gift card

©siankoo-fotolia.com

[1] viel berichten
[2] nachgeben

The story was well publicised[1] in the British press and widely discussed in the social media as well, and, eventually, Sainsbury's gave in to[2] popular demand and renamed the loaf "giraffe bread". This change was advertised as follows:

[1] Rezept

Thanks to a clever suggestion from one of our customers, we've changed the name of our tiger bread to giraffe bread. Don't worry. The recipe[1] hasn't changed and the bread still tastes as great as ever.

Mediate.
Imagine you read this story on the internet. Tell your German friend what happened.

1 Chris King uses Lily's letter as a kind of model for his answer. How does he do it?

2 Chris's letter also is a clever piece of marketing. Find examples and comment.

[1] Gutschein

Have you had any experience with gift cards or vouchers[1] when you, your family and/or your friends made a complaint and wanted your money back? If so, share your experience with your classmates.

8.3 Can a customer complaint be a gift?

Track 30

Complaints are not problems to be avoided. On the contrary[1], they are gifts[2] to be welcomed and important for several reasons:

- You don't know how to improve your products or services if you don't know what's wrong.
- Customer complaints can give you ideas for new products and services.
- Complaints give you valuable[3] information about what's important to people, what they're willing to spend money on[4].

Complaints also tell you that the customers still want to do business with you; they still care about[5] the relationship with[6] your company and they want you to fix the problem[7]. However, many customers don't complain; they just take their business elsewhere[8], because they've given up hope of getting what they need from you.

The problem is: most business people think that customer complaints are bad and that no complaints means there are no problems. But how should you handle[9] complaints when they **do** occur? Just as we thank someone who gives us a birthday gift, you should thank someone who brings you a complaint. They have given you something valuable and useful, something that can help make your business stronger and more profitable[10]. Complaints are a sign that your customers want you to make a change so that the business relationship[11] can continue. If they stop talking to you, that's when you should worry.

Treating[12] complaints as gifts involves a step-by-step process:

1) Thank the person for her/his complaint. Tell her/him how much you appreciate her/his taking the time to tell you about her/his problem.
2) Tell them why you're thanking them: you care about your relationship; and the complaint gives you an opportunity to address something that isn't working[13] as it should.
3) Apologise for whatever makes the customer unhappy. Note: you don't need to say that it's your fault; simply say, "I'm sorry you're having this problem."
4) Promise to do whatever you can to solve the problem.
5) Ask for more information so that you can fully understand your customer's problem.
6) Take steps to correct the problem. Focus on[14] things that are within your control[15]. If something is out of your control[16], explain that. If it is something that really has nothing to do with you, say that you will follow this up[17].
7) And most important: give some feedback[18] to your customer. Feedback shows that you care.

Make sure to learn from the situation. Complaints can provide ideas for new products or services, as well as make you aware of weak points in your organisation.

And what is most important, always emphasise[19] what you can do, rather than[20] what you can't. Look for what is possible, rather than telling your customer what is impossible. Pointing out what you can't do simply makes both you and your customer more frustrated[21].

None of us like to hear negative feedback. But feedback is the breakfast of champions.

(Shortened and adapted from "A Customer Complaint Is a Gift" (http://www.huffingtonpost.com/evanne-schmarder/...)

1 im Gegenteil
2 Geschenk
3 wertvoll
4 Geld ausgeben für etw.
5 *hier*: sich Gedanken machen wegen, wichtig sein
6 Beziehung zu
7 Problem lösen
8 woanders hingehen
9 *hier*: umgehen mit
10 gewinnbringend, profitabel
11 Geschäftsbeziehung
12 behandeln
13 funktionieren
14 sich konzentrieren auf
15 *hier*: beeinflussen können
16 nicht beeinflussen können
17 (einer Sache) nachgehen
18 sich zurückmelden, Rückmeldung geben
19 hervorheben, betonen
20 (an)statt
21 unzufrieden, frustriert

©ibreakstock-fotolia.com

Work with the text.

1 Decide whether these statements have been made in the text. If not, rephrase the statement.

1 Businesses try to avoid complaints.
2 Complaints are very important for the development of new products and services.
3 Customers always complain, because they want to continue to do business with you.
4 When they have reason to complain, many customers turn away.
5 A complaint can be a valuable gift.
6 Having to deal with lots of complaints reduces profits.
7 A complaint leads to a change in the business relationship.
8 Always apologise. That makes the customer happy.
9 Getting detailed information from a customer can help solve the problem.
10 There will be a lot of frustration if you are not helpful.

Satisfied?? - Tell others!!
Dissatisfied?? - Tell us!!
Here!

2 Decide which of the phrases in Box A can be used to replace those found in the text (Box B).

Box A (Synonymous phrases)		Box B (Phrases from the text)	
1	apologise	A	are an indication
2	appreciate	B	be grateful to
3	can't be done	C	concentrate on
4	emphasise	D	deal with
5	fix	E	develop … further
6	focus on	F	give
7	follow up	G	is impossible
8	handle	H	look into
9	improve	I	point out
10	take their business elsewhere	J	reply
11	tell you	K	say you are sorry
12	thank	L	solve
		M	turn to another supplier
		N	value highly

3 In the text you find recommendations[1] for dealing with complaints. Decide which of the points made below can be linked to any of the recommendations 1–7.

a) Act quickly to solve the problem.
b) Ask for further details.
c) Ask the customer how you can solve the problem.
d) Confirm the solution[2] agreed on.
e) Follow up the problem.
f) Inform the customer about the result of your investigation[3].
g) Listen carefully and don't interrupt[4] the customer.
h) Offer your sincere apologies.
i) Offer a solution.
j) Put yourself in the customer's shoes.
k) Thank the customer for drawing your attention to[5] a problem.
l) Thank the customer for giving you the opportunity to put things right.

[1] Empfehlung
[2] Lösung
[3] Untersuchung, Nachforschung
[4] unterbrechen
[5] (jdn.) aufmerksam machen auf

8.4 Learning to be polite

Decide which of these sentences would possibly be used by a customer making a complaint and which by a customer services manager.

No.	Phrases	Angry customer	Customer services manager
1	I can fully understand why you feel disappointed.		
2	I can let you have this item at a much reduced price if you decide to keep it.		
3	I sincerely apologise for the inconvenience[1] caused.		
4	I think there is something wrong with the goods we received today.		
5	I'll look into this straightaway and will come back to you[2] as soon as possible.		
6	I'm afraid there must be something wrong with the invoice.		
7	I'm really very sorry you were disappointed with the way your order was executed.		
8	I'm sorry, but I think I have reason to complain about a delay in delivery. The goods arrived two weeks late.		
9	I'm wondering whether there may have been a mistake with the quantities and the colours of the cloths.		
10	It was only when we unpacked the goods that we noted that somebody had got the order numbers wrong.		
11	Much to our regret[3] we have to inform you that we were sent sub-standard[4] goods.		
12	Please let us have suitable[5] substitutes[6] if your Silverstone china sets[7] are no longer in stock.		
13	Thank you very much for your understanding.		
14	Unfortunately, we noted that the goods are not of the quality that we ordered.		
15	We are prepared to grant you a reduction of 50 euros on your next order.		
16	We are very sorry about this and will certainly do our best to meet[8] your expectations.		
17	We have been promised delivery by 30th August.		
18	We would ask you to accept our sincere apologies.		

1 Unannehmlichkeit
2 sich wieder melden
3 sehr zu unserem Bedauern
4 minderwertig
5 geeignet
6 Ersatz(-ware)
7 Porzellanservice
8 *hier*: entsprechen, erfüllen

Mediate.

How would you express the ideas in the box above in German? Do not attempt a word-for-word translation.

8.5 A very angry customer

Track 31

The wholesaler for Continental European wines and spirits in Newcastle/GB was not very happy about the consignment received from a winegrower from the Rhineland-Palatinate. Listen to what the problem is and how Herr Freyer of Paulig Weinbau and Paul Williams of Newcastle Wine Merchants, both employees in their businesses, solve it.

Freyer: Paulig Weinbau. Guten Morgen. Mein Name ist Freyer. Was kann ich für Sie tun?

Williams: Hmm, this is Paul Williams from Newcastle Wine Merchants. Can I talk to someone who speaks English, please?

Freyer: I think I can understand what you say if you speak slowly and clearly. Who is it?

Williams: I'm from Newcastle Wine Merchants.

Freyer: Oh, yes?? Newcastle in England? Is that right?

Williams: Yes, Newcastle Wine Merchants in England.

Freyer: OK. And what can I do for you?

Williams: I'm phoning about a problem with your consignment which we received yesterday.

Freyer: Oh, I'm sorry to hear that. What's wrong?

Williams: When the goods arrived yesterday morning, I noticed there was some damage to the plastic wrapping[1] of the transport pallets[2].

Freyer: Uh-huh.

Williams: And it seems that something is wrong with the quantities.

Freyer: Uhm. And what is wrong??

Williams: Well. We ordered 20 cases[3] of Sekt, and there were only 18. And then we wanted 18 cases of Silvaner. But there were only 16. Or did you send the wrong quantities?

Freyer: I'm very sorry about that. But I really can't understand what happened. We checked every item on the packing list very carefully and also the number of cases. The wines are packed in cases of twelve bottles each, and the Sekt is packed in cases of 6 bottles. So, you should have received 20 cases of Sekt and 18 cases of Silvaner.

Williams: But as I said, we didn't.

Freyer: OK. I'm really sorry about that. Let me just check[4] the quantities sent against[4] your invoice. Just a moment please. – ...

Freyer: Thank you for waiting. But I see the quantities on the delivery note and the invoice are both the same. Very strange!! I really don't understand that. We've never had this kind of problem. And actually, did you talk to the driver of the van??

Williams: Yes, of course I did. He said he didn't have anything to do with the loading of the van. And he certainly was very surprised when I pointed out the damage to the plastic wrapping. But what can we do in this situation?

[1] Plastikhülle
[2] Transportpalette
[3] Karton, Kiste
[4] abgleichen mit

Freyer: Mhm. Well, I think the best thing to do is that you deduct the items from the invoice amount[5]. Or we could send replacements for the missing cases. But that would be very costly, of course.

Williams: Well, I think in that case we'll just deduct the amount from your invoice.

Freyer: Yes, I think that's the best solution. I'll make a note of[6] that. So that's 12 bottles of Sekt and 24 bottles of Silvaner less than ordered. Is that right?

Williams: Yes, that's quite correct.

Freyer: OK. I'll send you a new invoice then. And I'll take it up with[7] our shipping agent. …

©minicel73-fotolia.com

[5] Rechnungsbetrag
[6] sich etw. notieren
[7] etw. mit jdm besprechen

Answer these questions.

1 In one sentence, state what the problem is that Mr Williams and Herr Freyer are talking about.
2 What is the problem at the beginning of the conversation?
3 Mr Williams mentions some damage. What was it?
4 And what is the second problem?
5 What does Herr Freyer want to check?
6 Why is Herr Freyer surprised?
7 Did the van driver do anything wrong? Say why or why not.
8 What is the solution that Herr Freyer and Mr Williams found in the end?

Choose phrases from the list below to replace some of those that Herr Freyer used. The list is not arranged in chronological order.

- And what exactly is that?
- Could you describe the damage, please?
- Could you just hold the line for a minute?
- Did you discuss this with the driver of the delivery van?
- I do apologise, but in the past we've never had a problem like this one.
- I would suggest the best solution is …
- I'm awfully sorry to hear that.
- Is that correct?
- Tell me what the problem is.
- This kind of problem has never occurred before.
- We made every effort to cross-check[1] the quantities sent with the packing list.
- Who is calling, please?
- Who is speaking, please?
- Would it be OK for you …?

"Do you know your customer rights???"

[1] genauestens prüfen

Describe the behaviour of the speakers.

How would you describe the behaviour and language of Mr Williams and Herr Freyer? Which of the adjectives in the lists below come closest to your impression? Before you start, listen to the dialogue again.

[1] sich entschuldigend
[2] schroff

Herr Freyer		Mr Williams	
angry	apologetic[1]	abrupt[2]	annoyed
difficult to deal with	helpful	business-like	easy to get on with
informal	matter-of-fact	fact-oriented	formal
polite	surprised	friendly	impatient
understanding	unfriendly	neutral	unwilling

Info

Experts say that there are four stages in the handling of complaints:

1 Listening and showing understanding

I see your point.
That's too bad.
I can appreciate that.
Thank you for pointing that out to us.
I do understand why you are so unhappy about …

2 Asking for details

Please tell me exactly what the problem is.
Just tell me what went wrong.
Could you perhaps describe the damage?
And tell me, how did this happen?
When did you first notice this?

3 Apologising and accepting responsibility

I'm so sorry for any inconvenience this may have caused you.
I'm really/so/terribly sorry about that.
Please accept my/our (sincere) apologies.
I apologise for the trouble this has caused you.

4 Promising to take action

I'll let my manager know how you feel (about this), and we'll try and find a solution.
I'll take this up with the manufacturer/our dispatch department[1].
We'll let you know as soon as possible.
In exchange we can offer you five per cent off your next purchase.
We'll credit your account with the sum of …
Let me straighten this out, and I'll get back to you later today.

[1] Versandabteilung

Find the parts in the telephone dialogue on pp. 104–105 that correspond to the stages 1 to 4.

Mediate.

Herr Freyer tells his boss about the telephone conversation. State what the problem was and what solution Mr Williams and Herr Freyer agreed on.

1 In the telephone conversation, Herr Freyer offers to change the invoice rather than sending another consignment with the missing bottles. What would you do in this situation? Exchange your views in class. Think of the extra freight costs and the cost of replacing the goods not received. Will Weinbau Paulig suffer a loss[1] as a result of this problem?

[1] Verlust erleiden

2 Herr Freyer was going to follow up the problem of the missing wine cases and the damage to the plastic wrapping of the transport pallet. What can he possibly do?

Write an e-mail.

Herr Freyer is asked by his boss to write an e-mail to Newcastle Wine Merchants. The boss has noted down the following:

- Neue Rechnung als Anhang beifügen
- Noch einmal Entschuldigung für die Minderlieferung *(short delivery)*, kein eigenes Verschulden *(our fault)*
- Dank für die Bestellung
- Hinweis auf neue Weinliste *(current wine list)* im Anhang
- Hoffnung auf weitere Aufträge

Revision

"if", "unless" ("if … not"), "whether"; "when"

"if" is used in conditional clauses to express a degree of possibility (real, hypothetical or impossible).

If the price is lower next week, we'll certainly place a large order.
If the customers showed more interest, we would consider buying larger quantities.
If we had known about this fantastic price, we would have bought this product immediately.

"unless" and ***"if … not"*** are often used in the same way.

Unless (wenn … nicht) *you replace/If you don't replace the faulty goods, we'll have to ask for our money back.*
I'll have to talk to our supplier, unless (es sei denn, dass … / außer …) *you have another idea.*

"whether" is used to express the possibility of an alternative.

I'm not sure whether the consignment was damaged when it arrived.

Note: "when" is used as a conjunction that refers to time (als, (dann) wenn). It is also used as an interrogative pronoun again referring to time (*wann?*). It must not be confused with the conditional *"if"* (wenn).

I'll talk to our representative when I next see him.
We had a very interesting conversation when I first met my new department head.
She couldn't remember when the parcel arrived.
When do you think can we expect a reply?

Decide which is the most suitable term to fill the gap *(if, when, if ... not, unless, whether)*.

1 We can grant you a reduction in price … you place your order before 1 October.
2 I'm not sure … Ms Simpson is in the office today.
3 We'll return the faulty goods immediately … you grant us a reduction of 20 per cent.
4 … I met her in the office this morning, she said she was in a big hurry.
5 … we bring our prices down just a little bit, we might attract more customers.
6 I'm not sure … I can help you with this problem.
7 Just let me know … Mr Jamieson calls back.
8 … I had known about this complaint earlier, we could have done something to avoid similar problems in future.
9 … you tell me what you have in mind, I can't do anything to reduce your workload.
10 As we've got a lot of work to do at the moment, I can't tell you … I'll be back home.

Sound-alikes. Try and read this tongue twister.

Whether the weather is hot
Or whether the weather is not,
We'll weather the weather,
Whatever the weather,
Whether we like it or not.

Make sure you understand the different meanings of *weather* and *whether*.

Translate the limerick.

8.6 Role play

As indicated[1] in the telephone conversation on pp. 104–105, Herr Freyer follows up this matter with the shipping agent[2]. At the same time Mr Williams also contacts the local delivery company[3] to find out more about this consignment.

[1] andeuten
[2] Spediteur, Versandbeauftragter
[3] Lieferfirma, Zustelldienst

Before you start the role play, read these phrases and decide which could be used for role A and which for role B.

©mediterranean-fotolia.com

- Could you please tell me your …
- I fully understand your situation/anger.
- I'll get back to you later.
- I'll try to find out who/what …
- I'm phoning/calling about …
- I'm really very surprised. And I know how you must feel.
- The driver was unable to give an explanation.
- The plastic wrapping of the consignment was severely/badly damaged.
- The whole thing is very/most annoying.
- There is little I can do (about it) at the moment.
- There's no need to get angry with me. I'm just trying to help you.
- There were some discrepancies between the quantities received and those indicated in the delivery note.

- We've never had an incident like this before.
- When can I expect to hear from you again?
- When checking the consignment we found/noticed ...

Role A: You are Mr Williams from Newcastle Wine Merchants (107 Westgate Road, Newcastle upon Tyne NE4 6XD). Phone the local delivery company. State what you are phoning about (Consignment no. ABP 364 received on 24 October) and then describe the damage. Try to find out in which condition the consignment was received upon arrival[1] in Newcastle. If any damage was noted, was it reported[2] to the on-carrier[3] from the seaport (Hull)? Make sure your partner understands that you would be very annoyed if any theft was not reported. You are not very happy about the outcome[4]. Show that you are angry.

[1] Ankunft
[2] anzeigen
[3] Weiterbeförderer
[4] Ergebnis

You will find the text for Role B on p. 204.

8.7 Satisfying customers is a must

Businesses/institutions do everything possible to ensure that their customers/clients are satisfied with the products and services they get. Although complaints do not occur very often and may in fact be helpful to address problems that may have been overlooked, they want to avoid such situations. They know very well that complaints are discussed among friends, and word gets round that ... This obviously may lead to a loss in the company's standing[1]. Therefore businesses and institutions make great efforts to avoid such incidents[2]. They train their staff to be polite, friendly and helpful. Furthermore, they look at issues such as product quality, adequate packing, meeting deadlines and delivery dates. And many have even made special arrangements for maintaining[3] an after-sales service[4].

[1] Ruf, Ansehen
[2] Vorfall, Vorkommnis
[3] aufrechterhalten
[4] Kundendienst

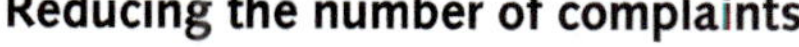

Reducing the number of complaints

Measures such as those listed below can help to reduce the number of complaints. Decide which person in a company could be responsible for implementing[1] these ideas. Choose from the following: *managing director, human resources manager, production manager, quality controller, customer services manager, sales staff.* Maybe you have some more ideas?!?

[1] umsetzen, realisieren

Discuss your reasons in class. Before you start, make sure you understand all the words and phrases.

Always ask for feedback from staff.	Involve staff in quality improvement[9] measures.
Check output[1] against targets[2].	Keep deadlines.
Check outgoing goods[3].	Listen to staff suggestions[10].
Create good working conditions.	Monitor[11] customer complaints.
Develop a quality assurance[4] concept.	Never sell sub-standard goods.
Ensure adequate packaging.	Offer a refund[12].
Explain quality objectives[5] to staff.	Provide a helpline service[13].
Get customer feedback.	Reduce the number of rejects[14].
Give customers a money-back guarantee[6].	Render[15] excellent service[15].
Improve our packaging.	Replace faulty or damaged products.
Improve products and processes.	Reward[16] hard-working employees.
Introduce a system for solving problems.	Only sell top-quality products.
Introduce random[7] quality checks[8].	Train staff regularly.

[1] (Produktions-)Ausstoß
[2] Ziel
[3] Warenausgang
[4] Qualitätssicherung
[5] Ziel(-setzung)
[6] Geldrückgabegarantie
[7] zufällig, Zufalls-
[8] Qualitätskontrolle
[9] Qualitätsverbesserung
[10] Mitarbeitervorschläge
[11] überwachen, kontrollieren
[12] Rückerstattung
[13] Notruf-, Hotline-Dienst
[14] Ausschuss(-stück)
[15] (Dienstleistung) erbringen
[16] belohnen

Discussing business policy

Use the ideas in the box on p. 109 to describe what your companies/institutions are doing to reduce the number of complaints. What is being done to improve the quality of products and processes, and to what extent are the staff and the top management involved? Also look at how customer complaints are handled. In small groups, share your experience at your place of work. Explain

(1) what happened in the past,

(2) what is happening now and

(3) what the plans are for the future.

Write down your thoughts and then present them in class.

You may wish to use some of these phrases:

(1) In the past we had regular seminars to discuss …
In staff meetings we talked about …
We shared our experience with …
Our boss explained to us how …
We learned how to deal with …
Quality improvement has always been …

©contrastwerkstatt-fotolia.com

(2) At the moment/Now/Currently/This year …
… is a topic in our weekly team meetings.
We regularly discuss … and share our experience with …
Our boss always presents the latest production statistics.
As a matter of routine[1] we spot-check[2] outgoing consignments[3].
We have trainings[4] in conflict management[5].
Customer satisfaction is one of our key priorities[6] …
Complaints procedures[7] always come up in our meetings.

[1] routine-, regelmäßig
[2] Stichproben machen
[3] abgehende Sendung
[4] Schulung
[5] Konfliktbewältigung
[6] oberste Priorität
[7] Beschwerdeverfahren

(3) My company/institution is going to introduce …
They are planning to …/There are plans to …
The management announced that they will …
We have been promised that there will be …
In future more attention will be paid to …
We aim/intend/want to reduce the number of …

Real life or not. Some odd complaints.

A customer complained to a hot dog seller[1]: "But this sausage is so hot I can't eat it." "But you asked for a hot dog, didn't you?" "Yes!" "Shall I do you a cold dog then?"

A diner[2] in a restaurant complained that the recommended wine was of very poor quality. Although he had consumed all but a glassful in the bottle, he insisted on a full refund.

A customer phones his gas supply company[3] to complain about the excellent service it provided and said that they should spend less money on training their service staff to work more efficiently. He asked that they reduce their gas prices instead.

[1] Würstchenverkäufer/in
[2] *hier*: Gast
[3] Gaslieferant

Have you come across any crazy complaints stories yourself? Tell them. If not, can you make one up yourself?

Unit 9 Customer acquisition[1]

[1] (Neu-)Kundengewinnung

©Charlie Edwards-shutterstock.com

9.1 Let's get going!

1 Look at the examples of print and store advertising[1] found in the USA and Britain.

- Have you seen similar kinds of offers? Describe them.
- Would such special offers persuade[2] you to buy the products? Say why or why not.
- Discuss your views and experiences in class.

[1] Werbung in Druckmedien und Geschäften
[2] überreden, überzeugen

2 Advertising[3] for products and services is part and parcel[4] of our daily lives, at home or when we are out and about. Share your experience with your classmates. Here are some ideas.

[3] Werbung
[4] fester Bestandteil

- What kinds of advertising do you come across every day?
- What products/services are advertised[5]?
- What attracts[6] you in the adverts that you see or hear?
- What adverts are there that you don't like? – Why not?
- Do adverts make you buy particular products? – Why? Why not?

Some vocabulary for your discussion

billboard, hoarding, leaflet, banner advertising, perimeter advertising (in sports grounds), print/media/online advertising, freebies, internet marketing, neon sign, poster, ad(vert), to advertise for, product launch, to place an ad(vert)

[5] bewerben, Werbung machen für
[6] locken, anziehen

Before you start, read the vocabulary in the box on the right and make sure you understand what the terms mean.

9.2 Purposes[1] and means[2] of advertising

[1] Zweck
[2] Mittel

Info

Track 32

Sales promotion[1] involves[2] a large variety of activities to approach[3] potential and/or existing customers[4]. This means that the advertisers[5] must make decisions about who they want to "talk" to, where, when, and above all, about what. Personal selling[6], that is selling by word of mouth[7] (indirectly: people talking to each other about products or services or directly: people being approached by sales representatives during visits or at fairs[8], for example), is just as important as non-personal selling by media contact[9] (printed information, the press, radio and television, online pop-ups, etc.) or by outdoor displays[10] (hoardings, shop windows, neon signs, logos or product names). The "sellers" are out to[11] make their products or services known to us, the potential customer, to create goodwill and above all to persuade us, the new or existing customer, to buy their products or services.

[1] Verkaufswerbung
[2] beinhalten
[3] ansprechen, zugehen auf
[4] bestehender Kunde
[5] Werbetreibende/r
[6] persönlicher Verkauf
[7] Mundpropaganda
[8] Messe, Verkaufsausstellung
[9] Medienkontakt
[10] Außenanzeige
[11] darauf aus sein, zu tun

1 Decide which of the terms in the box below belong to the categories:
a) customer information b) persuasion[1] to buy c) creation[2] of goodwill.
Some terms may fit more than one category.

Term	Customer information	Persuasion to buy	Creation of goodwill
commercial[3] (radio, tv)			
company image brochure[4]			
display stand[5]			
freesheet[6]/freebie			
give-away[7]			
hoarding			
mail circular[8]			
neon sign			
newspaper/magazine supplement[9]			
product demonstration[10]			
product tasting[11]			
sample			
stand-up display[12]			
travel brochure			
window display[13]			

[1] Überredung
[2] Schaffung
[3] Werbespot
[4] Imagebroschüre
[5] (Verkaufs-)Ständer
[6] Gratiszeitung
[7] Kunden-, Werbegeschenk
[8] Postwurfsendung
[9] Beilage
[10] Produktvorführung
[11] (Waren-)Verkostung
[12] (Werbe-)Aufsteller
[13] Schaufensterauslage

2 Describe and discuss with your classmates the sales promotion activities[1] that you have come across in the street, in shops, on weekly markets, on the internet or in the printed media[2].

[1] Verkaufsförderungsmaßnahme
[2] Druckmedium

3 State which of these advertising media your company/institution uses
1 regularly, 2 sometimes, 3 never.
Also say 1 what products they are used for,
2 in which location and
3 at what particular time.

Analyse the advert on the right.

1 Where do you think this advert was found?

2 Have a closer look at the language. What is there to catch the attention of potential customers?

3 Do some internet research. Find out about the processes that raw materials[1] need to go through to become finished goods[2] until they can finally be purchased by us, the customers.

4 How does Harbor Freight manage to cut costs? – In your answer refer to the supply chain[3] concept.

How Does Harbor Freight Sell GREAT QUALITY Tools at the LOWEST Prices?

We have invested millions of dollars in our own state-of-the-art[4] quality test labs[5] and millions more in our factories, so our tools[6] will go toe-to-toe[7] with the top professional brands. And we can sell them for a fraction[8] of the price because we cut out the middle man[9] and pass the savings on to you. It's just that simple! Come visit one of our 1300 stores nationwide.

1 Rohmaterial
2 Fertigwaren
3 Lieferkette
4 allerneuest, hochmodern
5 Labor für Qualitätsprüfung
6 *hier:* Werkzeug(-maschine)
7 in direkten Wettbewerb stehen/treten mit
8 Bruchteil
9 Zwischenhandel

9.3 advertising campaign[1]

Track 33

Jameson's Bakery[2] and Confectionery[3] of Edinburgh have decided to go abroad with their products (shortbread, oatcakes[4], fruit cakes, biscuits, chocolates, etc.) and get a foothold[5] in the German market. Sharon O'Connor, the product manager[6], and her team are engaged in[7] a brainstorming session to discuss possible advertising campaigns.

Sharon: So, our MD[8] wants us to come up with some useful ideas for a marketing campaign that reaches not only the buyers[9] in the big food retailing companies[10] but also the general public. Any bright ideas?

Robert: Sorry, Sharon, this is just a bit big for me. I think we need to think about two strategies first really, one for the buyers of the food retailers[11] and another for ordinary shoppers[12]. Each group needs a different approach, I think. As for me, it's not simply a question of one size fits all[13]. Don't you agree?

Sharon: That may very well be Perhaps I see what you're driving at[14]. But what do the others think?

Gina: I can't quite see the point Bob is trying to make. But it's obvious to me that we're talking about one big market which could also include Austria and most of Switzerland. So, language is going to play an important role, isn't it?

Sharon: Good point that, Gina. But that's something that, I think, we should look at later.

1 Werbekampagne
2 Bäckerei
3 Konditorei
4 Haferplätzchen
5 Fuß fassen
6 Produktleiter/in
7 dabei/beschäftigt sein
8 Geschäftsführer/in
9 Einkäufer/in
10 Lebensmitteleinzelhandelsunternehmen
11 Lebensmitteleinzelhändler
12 *hier*: einfache/r Kunde/in
13 eins passt für alle
14 auf etw. hinauswollen

Penny: If I may come in[15] here. Well, I feel that Bob's made a good point. The buyers, I'm sure, we need to talk to at trade fairs[16], maybe. I can think of the ANUGA in Cologne or the "Grüne Woche" – is it? – in Berlin, for example. And I'm sure there are many others. We'll just have to do some internet research.

Sharon: Good idea, Penny. Could you look into that[17], please? You know: dates, venues[18], costs, etc., and then report back to[19] us. It would be good if we could have this information a couple of days before our next meeting. Do you think you could do that?

Penny: No problem, I'll do that.

Sharon: Good. Thank you. Yes, Douglas? You wanted to …

Douglas: Yeah …, to come back to[20] Penny's idea. Do you really seriously want to consider attending fairs with all the expense[21] in terms of[22] travel, stand hire[23], staff, hotel costs and all that? Isn't that going over the top[24] a bit? After all, we're only a medium-sized company trying to sell low-cost[25] products with fairly small profit margins[26]. Wouldn't it be enough to send round parcels with samples and a convincing[27] circular to the big guys in the food retail chains[28] and then see what happens? Maybe follow that up with phone calls, etc.

Sharon: Hm. If you ask me, I'm not so sure. After all, Germany is a big market. And if you really want to get in, you must be prepared to spend some money upfront[29]. But I realise it's a bit of a gamble[30]. I'm with you there entirely. And yet, I certainly wouldn't want to throw out[31] Penny's idea at this stage.

Robert: Well, as for me, I also feel we should keep all our options open for the time being. And approaching buyers face-to-face[32] seems to me rather an effective[33] way of going about it.

Sharon: OK, let's do that then, if you all agree. Douglas, could you perhaps come up with some ideas of how best to approach the buyers by mail? We need to know about the costs of a mailshot[34] with parcels etc.

Douglas: Yeah, OK.

Sharon: And I think it might be a good idea to take up the point that Gina made. Austria and Switzerland might also come into the picture[35]. Could you take that into consideration[36] as well, Douglas?

©Boggy-fotolia.com

Douglas: Yeah, sure. No problem.

Sharon: Fine. Now, what we haven't talked about, of course, is the general public. Could I ask everyone here to do some serious thinking and come up with ideas how we can tackle[37] that, please? – And we'll talk about that next week then. Same time? Is that OK with you? …

[15] *hier*: mal einhaken
[16] Fachmesse
[17] einer Sache nachgehen
[18] Veranstaltungsort
[19] jdm. berichten
[20] wieder zurückkommen auf
[21] *hier*: Kosten, Ausgaben
[22] *hier*: für
[23] *hier*: Standmiete
[24] *hier*: übertreiben
[25] niedrigpreisig
[26] Gewinnspanne
[27] überzeugend
[28] Filialist
[29] im Voraus, zuerst einmal
[30] etw. riskant sein
[31] verwerfen
[32] direkt, persönlich
[33] wirkungsvoll
[34] (Post-)Wurfsendung
[35] ins Bild kommen
[36] berücksichtigen
[37] angehen, bewältigen

Work with the text.

1 Please answer these questions on the text.
   1 What is the problem discussed at the team meeting?
   2 Why does Robert think that two strategies are needed?
   3 Why does Gina think about Austria and Switzerland?
   4 What is Penny's suggestion?
   5 What is Penny's task for the next meeting?
   6 Why does Douglas think attending fairs is too expensive?
   7 What is Douglas's alternative?
   8 What is the job that Sharon asks Douglas to do?
   9 What is the point that has not been discussed?
   10 What does Sharon ask her team to do?

2 Look at the text again and find expressions that could come under these headings.

Agreeing	Disagreeing	Making suggestions	Giving instructions; things to do

List your answers in your workbook.

3 Write out other useful idiomatic expressions similar to the following:
... come up with ... ideas; – it's not simply a question of ...; – it's obvious to me ...

What it takes to win new customers.

1 Imagine you are Penny. Go on the internet and find out about the dates and venues of food-related fairs in Germany in the first and second half of the year (search words: *Lebensmittelmesse*; *Nahrungsmittelmesse*). Prepare a list of the dates, the locations and the products "shown".

2 In English, say why **or** why not a particular event could be useful for Jameson's Bakery and Confectionery. Work in groups.

3 It is Douglas's job to come up with ideas about contacting potential buyers by mail. Try to imagine the kind of activities involved. Prepare a list of things to do.

9.4 Minutes[1] of a meeting

Sharon O'Connor had asked Eva, the German intern[2] who is doing a six-month work placement at Jameson's Bakery and Confectionery, to write the minutes of the team-meeting.

To make sure she gets it right, Eva first writes down the main points in German (cf. Dialogue on pp. 113–114). Before you start, have a look at a copy of minutes in your company/institution and study the structure. Then write down your draft in German. Do not use full sentences.

[1] Protokoll
[2] Praktikant/in

Eva shows her English-language draft to Sharon for her to comment on and, maybe, make corrections. Here is the extract[1] concerning the planned activities in Germany.

[1] Auszug

Meeting of the marketing team
held on Tuesday, 2 March 20.., 8.30 to 9.30 am.

Chair[1]: Sharon O'Connor
Attendees[2]: Douglas, Gillian, Gina, Paul, Penny, Robert
Minutes taker[3] ①: Eva

Agenda: 1 Opening of the meeting
2 Review and adoption[4] of the agenda[5]
3 Reading and approval[6] of the minutes of the meeting of 26 Feb. 20..
...
5 Activities in Germany
...
8 Any other business[7] ②

...
Item[8] 5 Activities in Germany

Robert suggested ③ that different approaches should be used for the buyers in the big food retailing companies ④ and the general public. Gina pointed out ⑤ the need to think about the appropriate[9] language for a big market such as Germany and to possibly also consider ⑥ the Austrian and Swiss markets. This point is to be discussed in more detail ⑦ at a later stage. Penny agreed with Robert, but brought up[10] ⑧ the idea of thinking about trade fairs. Douglas remarked that, considering ⑨ the costs that attending ⑩ fairs involved[11], circulars and parcels with samples should be sent to the buyers in the grocery chains[12]. It was agreed that the options should be kept open for the time being[13] ⑪.

Action to be taken[14]:

Penny: to collect information about trade fairs (dates & venues) and the costs involved

Douglas: to assess the possibilities and costs of a mailshot for all the German-speaking countries.

This point will be taken up ⑫ at the next meeting.

The next meeting is scheduled[15] ⑬ for 9 March 20.. at 8.30 am.
Signed: Eva Approved ⑭: Sharon

[1] Vorsitz
[2] Anwesend(e)
[3] Protokollant/in
[4] *hier*: Verabschiedung
[5] Tagesordnung
[6] *hier*: Genehmigung
[7] Verschiedenes
[8] Tagesordnungspunkt
[9] angemessen, richtig
[10] (Gedanken) zur Sprache bringen
[11] *hier*: damit verbunden
[12] Lebensmittelkette
[13] vorläufig, bis auf Weiteres
[14] zu treffende Maßnahmen
[15] planen

Replace the terms and expressions in Eva's draft.

In the boxes below, find alternatives to replace items ① – ⑭ in Eva's minutes. There are more terms than you need.

AOB at the moment concerned criticised	discussed again food retailers going to in depth	in view of note taker planned put forward	recommended seen stressed think of

Note

The terms *minutes* and *notes* are nearly identical in meaning. The term *minutes* tends to be used for formal meetings.

9.5 Minutes writing: The dos and don'ts

In class, share your experience with reading or maybe writing minutes in your company/institution.

- How are they organised?
- What do they contain?
- What are the functions of the persons the minutes are sent to?
- What is the procedure[1] for writing, checking and circularising[2] the minutes?

[1] Verfahren
[2] verteilen, versenden

Info

Basically there are two types of minutes:

- Minutes that give an account[1] of every stage of the discussion (pros and cons) plus any decisions made and action points[2] (history/process log = *Verlaufsprotokoll*). The various points made by the participants plus the outcome of the discussion are expressed in indirect speech. The decision (i.e. the motion[3] to be adopted[4]/voted on[5]) is written out in full.
- Minutes that give only the decisions and action points (summary minutes; results log = *Ergebnisprotokoll*). Only the outcome of the discussion and the results of the vote (if any) are noted down.

In both types the following points need to be covered[6]:

- Date and time of meeting
- Names (and departments) of the participants (and of those who could not attend)
- Adoption of the agenda
- Approval[7] or correction of the minutes of the previous meeting
- Report/Information given by the chairperson[8]
- Decisions taken on each agenda item/point[9] and voting results (votes in favour[10] or against[11], abstentions[12])
- Action to be taken
- Date and time of next meeting
- Date of the minutes; name/signature of the minutes/note taker and of the chairperson/meeting leader

The minutes/notes need to be accurate, clear, objective and, above all, short. People's names are not normally mentioned. The same tense is used throughout. Very often the passive form is used.

[1] *hier*: informieren
[2] Aktionspunkt
[3] Antrag
[4] annehmen
[5] abstimmen über
[6] abdecken
[7] Zustimmung
[8] Vorsitzende/r
[9] Tagesordnungspunkt
[10] dafür
[11] dagegen
[12] Enthaltung

Read some tips for dealing with minutes/notes writing.

- Get a copy of the agenda before the meeting.
- Get the chairperson to read and correct the minutes before sending them out.
- Highlight[1] the actions required (name the persons/departments responsible).
- In your minutes, follow the order of the agenda.
- Pay attention to form and layout.
- Read the documents for the meeting beforehand[2].
- Sit next to the chairperson (to get clarification[3] on points you did not understand, if necessary).
- Study the minutes of earlier meetings to learn about the topics and especially also the language used.
- Take down the wording[4] of motions/decisions (and the voting results[5], if any).
- Turn your notes into minutes as soon as possible after the meeting.
- Don't try to take down every word. Get the key points of the discussion (arguments for and against, options discussed[6], solution).

[1] hervorheben
[2] vorher
[3] Erläuterung
[4] Wortlaut
[5] Abstimmungsergebnis
[6] diskutierte Alternativen

Put the tips into a meaningful order. Compare your results in class and explain your decision.

©Marzky Ragsac Jr.-fotolia.com

Useful phrases for writing minutes/notes

- It was said/argued/pointed out/stressed/recommended/agreed/decided that ...
- The discussion covered the following points: ...
- In the lively discussion the following points were raised: ...
- Among the points made/raised/discussed there were the following: ...
- Some of the participants/attendees/those attending proposed/suggested/criticised/noted/explained/argued/declared ...
- The agenda was / The minutes were approved without modification[1].
- There were 5 votes in favour, 2 against and/with 1 abstention.

Just be aware of some legal jargon:

- The motion (to do ...) was tabled and seconded. ≈ *Der Antrag (auf + Nomen; ... zu tun) wurde gestellt/eingebracht (und unterstützt).*
- The motion was carried by ... ≈ *Der Antrag wurde von ... angenommen.*
- The motion failed/was thrown out. ≈ *Der Antrag wurde abgelehnt.*

[1] Veränderung

Get some practice with the language of minutes.

1 Shorten and also rephrase the sentences 1–6 below. Use expressions from the Useful phrases above.

Example: *The sales manager asked for a decision to be taken to accept the strategy report prepared by the junior sales officer. Three of those attending agreed, one was against it and one didn't know.*

The motion to accept the strategy report was carried by 3 votes in favour, 1 against and 1 abstention.

1 The chairperson read out the minutes and, as there was nothing to criticise or change, the participants accepted them without change.
2 One of the attendees raised the point of brochures in English. Those who were at the meeting decided to change the agenda and to deal with that topic after Point 7.
3 The product manager, Dennis Laughton, reported about the progress that they had made with regard to the planned marketing activities in Denmark.
4 The participants discussed the plan for the marketing activities for next year at great length. Finally, they decided to accept the plan put forward by the marketing manager.
5 The attendees spent a long time talking about the advantages and disadvantages of selling a new and cheaper brand. In the end, they decided to continue their discussion at the next meeting.
6 The participants listened to the report of the chairperson and then talked about the situation in the regional markets. They also spoke about the changes in the differences in price in the various regions where the company was active. They didn't come to any conclusion and decided they needed to have more information.

"Have you got a sec perhaps?"

"Sorry, no. Not just now. It's taking me hours to write the minutes."

2 Sharon is quite happy with the language Eva used, but does not really like the way she did it. She wants the minutes to be shorter and snappier[1] and turned into a results log. Please rewrite Eva's text (p. 116) using some of the Useful phrases listed on p. 118.

[1] kürzer und knapper

9.6 Coming to a decision

Sharon and her team met again, and everyone had done their "homework". Read this oral report of the team meeting that Jonathan, another member of Sharon's team, gave to a friend during their lunch break.

Track 34

So, you know, we had this meeting again this morning. And then we talked about our marketing drive[1] in Germany. Penny reported that according to her internet research there were fairs all over Germany at most times of the year except in the holiday seasons and the pre-Christmas period. According to[2] her, the best choices seemed to be the fairs she had already mentioned in our meeting a week ago. She thought, however, that the costs of well over £10,000 for stand rent[3], fair booth construction[4], local staff, travel and accommodation[5], etc. for a five-day event were quite high, especially as it was uncertain how much business might develop from the contacts with potential buyers. ...

After that, the discussion quickly turned to Douglas's approach. He had worked hard to find out the names of the responsible[6] buyers in the big food retail companies in the German-speaking countries and of some important wholesalers as well. After some discussion, it was decided to send them all an e-mail plus attachments to draw their attention to our products. Penny proposed that they take up Douglas's and Robert's ideas to send round parcels with product samples and to follow that up with a series of phone calls.

[1] Marketingoffensive
[2] jdm. zufolge
[3] Standmiete
[4] Bau des Messestands
[5] Unterkunft
[6] *hier*: zuständig

… And you know, Paul suggested even that Sharon should travel to the Continent and talk to as many buyers as possible. And Gina pointed out that, obviously, a German-language information pack[7] should be prepared and texts translated into German. Gillian objected[8] that all these measures did not take the consumer[9] into account. According to her it was they who needed to be informed about our Scottish products and persuaded to buy Jameson's bakery and confectionery goods. Having discussed the pros and cons at great length, we all came to the conclusion that the main point was to get the buyers in the retail chains interested, because all of us were of the opinion that, once the goods were available in the shops, special marketing campaigns needed to be launched[10]. …

[7] Info(rmations)paket
[8] einwenden
[9] Verbraucher
[10] starten

Work with the text.

1 Make a short list of the points discussed by Sharon's team. Don't use more than five words per item.

2 Sharon asks Eva to write a memo of the outcome of the meeting. She wants to use it to discuss the matter with the managing director. Please prepare a draft.

3 Sharon and her team are keen to contact the buyers in the food retail chains. What could be the reasons?

4 What do you think can be the result of sending the buyers parcels with bakery and confectionery products?

5 In your experience, what kind of printed material could the information pack contain?

Revision

Reported speech

Reported speech is used when you tell someone else what another person said. In such a report, you may repeat the actual words or phrases that a person used – if you can remember them – or you state roughly what someone said.

In the introduction use so-called reporting words: *said, thought, remarked, stated, threatened, believed, complained, argued, observed* etc. These words are mostly used in the simple past.

Example: *Gillian said, "The measures don't take the consumer into account."* (direct speech)
Gillian said that the measures didn't take the consumer into account. (reported speech).

Note the most important changes when direct speech is transferred to reported speech:

1 The tenses are moved back one step (backshifting), i.e. present to past, present perfect to past perfect etc. *can* changes to *could*, *may* to *might* etc. But there is no change with the verb *must*.

2 The personal and possessive pronouns change from *I, you, we* to *he, she, they* or *my, our* to *her/his, their.*

3 Adverbials of time and place need to be adapted to the point of view of the reporting person.
Examples: *The trade fairs take place every year. – She reported that the trade fairs took place every year.*
I had a discussion with my boss yesterday. – He/She said that he/she had had a discussion with her/his boss the day before.
I am wondering whether our plan makes any sense. – He/She said he/she was wondering whether their plan made any sense. Or: *He/She was wondering whether their plan made any sense.*

4 Other changes may be necessary.
Example: *Can you write the minutes please, Eva? (Sharon asked) – Sharon asked whether I/she* (i.e. Eva) *could write the minutes.*

Practice using reported speech.

1 Change these sentences into reported speech.
   1 Our MD wants us to come up with some bright ideas. (She said …)
   2 I think we need to think of two strategies. (He observed …)
   3 I see what you're aiming at. (She stated …)
   4 It's obvious to me that we're talking about one big market. (He remarked …)
   5 We need to talk to the buyers at trade fairs. (She suggested …)
   6 Penny, could you look into these problems, please? (She asked Penny whether …)
   7 Wouldn't it be enough to send round parcels? (He wondered whether …)
   8 We need to know about the costs of a mailshot. (She pointed out …)

2 Look at Jonathan's report again (pp. 119–120), in particular at the sentences starting with phrases such as the following: *Penny reported that …; she thought that…; Penny proposed that …; etc.* and transform them into direct speech.
Example: *Penny said, "According to my internet research …"*

9.7 Developing and maintaining a customer base

Customer acquisition marks the beginning of a business relationship. This and developing such a contact to make it more permanent[1] are at the centre of marketing activities. Asking for feedback[2] and providing (technical) support[3] will go a long way to developing a lasting relationship. Depending on the size of a company/institution, several persons/departments are concerned with issues of customer relationship management[4] (CRM).

[1] dauerhaft
[2] Rückmeldung
[3] (techn.) Unterstützung
[4] Kundenbeziehungs-management

1 Decide which of the terms and phrases listed below refer to the activities of building and maintaining a customer base. Some apply to both activities. Tick the appropriate boxes and state reasons for your choice.

Terms	Developing a customer base	Maintaining a customer base
after-sales service		
circularisation[1] of households		
cold calls[2]		
customer care[3]		
customer loyalty[4]		
customer needs[5]		
feedback		
mailshots		
market research		
marketing mix		
pricing strategy[6]		
sales promotion[7]		
visits of sales representatives[8]		

[1] Verteilung von Werbematerial
[2] Telefonwerbung
[3] Kundenbetreuung
[4] Kundentreue
[5] Kundenbedürfnisse
[6] Preispolitik
[7] Verkaufsförderung
[8] Vertriebsmitarbeiter/in

2 Try to describe what kind of office work is connected with these terms (preparation, execution, listing of results). Start by drawing up a list in German and use your (online) dictionary to find the English equivalents[1]. Work in groups and share your results with all your classmates.

[1] Entsprechung

3 Describe at what stages and in which way you have been involved in any customer-related activities of your company/institution. Compare your activities with those of your classmates.

Tools for print advertising

Match the terms and definitions. There are more terms than you need. But first find out about the meaning of the terms.

Terms	Definitions
book	design of the packaging/container and labelling[1] of a product
booklet	large-format sheet of paper drawing attention to an event, often seen outdoors
catalogue	list of goods a customer wants to buy/a supplier has to send
flyer	list of products (often illustrated) sold by a company and arranged by product type with numbers, descriptions and prices
handbill	list of products saying what they cost, also mentioning reductions for larger quantities and how the goods can be ordered
handbook	printed advertisement, usually A4 format or smaller, distributed by hand to high street[2] shoppers and passers-by[3]
instruction manual	printed sheet of paper, folded and used to give information
leaflet	single sheet of any format giving information about events or products; both sides may be printed on
order list	small book giving useful information about a subject
poster	thin book usually with paper cover, often of a smaller size
price list	
product get-up	
recipe book	

[1] Etikettierung, Kennzeichnung
[2] Hauptgeschäftsstraße
[3] Passant/in

©gustavofrazao-fotolia.com

Give a definition of the terms not used.

In groups of three or four, describe where and when these printed materials can best be used. Think of the type of product, the need to attract attention, the information for the customer/user, the kind of wrapping[1]/container needed for the product, etc. Give examples and state the reasons for your choice. Use phrases such as the following:

[1] Verpackung

• … is useful/ideal to …	• … helps if you want to …
• … is ideally suited for …	• to attract attention
• … seems to be the best possible form/ means to/for …	• … is (very) informative
• I would (not) use … if I wanted to …	• … makes it easier to persuade/ convince …
• … could also be used if …	• … easy to recognise
	• … can be read/studied at home

9.8 A circular to buyers

After long discussions, Sharon and her team have finally opted for[1] the direct approach to buyers in the big supermarket chains and to major wholesalers. With the approval[2] of the MD, they now set about selecting[3] the right products for the parcels to be sent and also about writing a circular. Eva, nearly at the end of her six-month work placement and with greatly improved English language skills, prepared a first draft. She then made all the corrections that Sharon had recommended. And this is the final version.

Track 35

1 sich entscheiden für
2 Zustimmung
3 auswählen

Jameson's Bakery and Confectionery
85 Dalkeith Road, Edinburgh EH16 8BD

10 April 20..

Dear Buyer,

Bakery products and confectionery are all-important things in our lives. Following the highly successful launch[4] of our ranges in the Netherlands and Belgium, we would now like to explore the potentials[5] of the markets in the German-speaking countries.

As a major player[6] in the grocery market[7], you carry[8] a large range of bakery and confectionery goods in your outlets[9]. And, of course, you know your customers' tastes[10] and preferences[11].

Our products are somewhat special. Our range of oatcakes will please anybody looking for an alternative to bread at breakfast. They are also an absolutely ideal base for light refreshments[12] served at receptions or as part of a nice meal with friends. Our varieties of shortbread are an excellent[13] snack[14] to be enjoyed[15] during coffee or tea breaks. And our fruit cakes are not only delicious[16] and light, but also a very welcome addition[17] to any afternoon tea or coffee that people want to enjoy at leisure[18]. These are just some of the items in our broad range of products.

And need we say any more about our selections of exquisite[19] confectionery, all beautifully presented in a variety of boxes of different sizes? We are sure that your customers will enjoy such an addition to your bakery and confectionery ranges.

Have we made your mouth water? – Yes? – Well, anticipating[20] your interest, we have today dispatched a parcel to you with a representative[21] selection of the goods we produce. We hope you will try and enjoy our products.

In the parcel you will also find some literature in English and some of it in German which, we hope, will be of interest. Our product manager, Ms Sharon O'Connor, will phone you within the next two weeks to get your feedback and arrange a visit to negotiate the details of our future cooperation. But please feel free to phone us at any time to talk about any questions you might have. Or visit us on our website: www.jamesonbakery.com.

Have we whetted your appetite[22]? Then do contact us so that, together, we can whet the appetite of your customers.

Yours sincerely,

Sharon O'Connor (Ms)
Product Manager

4 Markteinführung
5 Potenzial
6 wichtiger Akteur
7 Lebensmittelmarkt
8 führen, listen
9 Laden
10 Geschmack
11 Vorliebe
12 kleine Stärkung, Häppchen
13 ausgezeichnet
14 Imbiss
15 genießen
16 köstlich
17 Ergänzung
18 in aller Ruhe
19 erlesen, fein
20 in Erwartung
21 repräsentativ
22 Appetit machen

Work with the text.

1 How does Sharon get the reader's attention?
2 How does Sharon praise the goods?
3 What kind of action is the reader expected to take?
4 Marketing experts say that advertising material should be based on the AIDA principle (A = attention, I = interest, D = desire and A = action). Find passages in the text that show the use of this principle.
5 The advice to sales letter writers is: a) Make it easy to read. b) Use short sentences. c) Write short paragraphs. Does the letter fulfil these requirements?
6 Find words and phrases in the text that can be replaced by the following:

• comments • discover • discuss • expecting • offer a wide variety • • ring • selection • start • superb • tasty • typical •

9.9 A buyer reacts

Only ten days after the circulars and parcels went out, Sharon receives this e-mail from one of the buyers.

©O_Schmidt-shutterstock.com

Sehr geehrte Frau O'Connor,

Vielen Dank für Ihren Rundbrief und das Paket, die wir vor einigen Tagen erhalten haben.

Inzwischen haben wir die Produkte probiert und auch von unseren Experten im Labor untersuchen lassen. Die Ergebnisse unserer Tests sind sehr positiv. Die Produkte schmecken außerordentlich gut und sind ansprechend verpackt. Wir können uns deshalb sehr gut vorstellen, dass sie nach einer gewissen Zeit der Markteinführung, die natürlich besonders beworben werden muss, von unseren Kunden gut aufgenommen werden.

Gern denken wir über eine Listung nach. Allerdings möchten wir zunächst noch zahlreiche weitere Details mit Ihnen besprechen. Dabei interessieren uns insbesondere Fragen der Preisgestaltung auf dem deutschen Markt, der Produktinformationen (auf Deutsch!!) und natürlich der Konditionen (Zahlungsbedingungen, Rabatte, Lieferzeiten etc.).

Wir würden uns freuen, bald von Ihnen zu hören und erwarten einen Terminvorschlag für ihren angekündigten Besuch.

Mit freundlichem Gruß

Frank Winter
(Einkäufer)

Mediate.

As her German is almost non-existent, Sharon asks Eva to tell her what the e-mail says. Give a summary in English of the main points of the e-mail. Before you start, make sure you know the English equivalents of the technical terms (ansprechend = *attractive(ly)*; Listung = *listing*; Produkt bewerben = *to advertise for a product*; Preisgestaltung = *pricing*).

Unit 10 Dealing with visitors

10.1 Let's get going!

1 In class, report about your experience with visits to your company/institution. What was the purpose of these visits? What do YOU do when you have visitors?

2 Do you know about the arrangements[1] that your company/institution makes when they receive visitors? If so, tell your classmates.

©bas121-fotolia.com

[1] *hier*: Vorbereitung

10.2 Gearing up to a visit from partners

Track 36

In a staff meeting[1], Donald Kemp, head[2] of the quality control department[3] at *Sweets and the like* in York, brings up the topic of the planned visit by a delegation of quality control officers[4] from the Romanian sister company[5] Ciocolată Anghel from Craiova/ Romania.

Donald: … And what I also wanted to say is that in four weeks' time we'll be welcoming guests from our sister company in Romania to our production plant here. They want to get a first-hand[6] insight[7] into our successful work of improving our quality standards. They'll be staying here for a couple of days. So, now it's our job to organise things for their visit. Well, Chris, you've done this before. Could you perhaps prepare a short introduction to our company, its history, products, etc., you know? And perhaps contact PR[8] to have some brochures and things ready.

Chris: Sure, no problem.

Donald: And Sarah, we need your specialist knowledge of all the quality regulations[9], you know, the EU stuff[10] and our food quality and also health and safety regulations[11]. Just put the key points together in a handout so that we can explain and discuss them if need be. And I want Jeremy to help you. Is that OK with you both?

Sarah and Jeremy: Yeah, that's fine.

Donald: And then there are the technical things. Alan, could you sort out[12] accommodation, transfer[13] from Manchester Airport, evening meals, lunch in the staff canteen[14], the usual hospitality[15], conference room, etc.?

Alan: Yeah, that's OK with me. As long as I know when, how many, and who will be attending[16] from our side.

[1] Mitarbeitertreffen
[2] Leiter/in
[3] Abt. Qualitätskontrolle
[4] Sach-, Mitarbeiter/in
[5] Schwestergesellschaft
[6] aus erster Hand
[7] Einblick
[8] Abt. Öffentlichkeitsarbeit
[9] Qualitätsvorschriften
[10] Kram, Zeug
[11] Arbeitsschutz-bestimmungen
[12] klären, erledigen
[13] Transfer, Fahrt
[14] Personalkantine
[15] Bewirtung
[16] dabei/anwesend sein

Donald: That's something I still need to clear up. But I'll let you know within the next couple of days.

Alan: OK, I'll get going then and finalise things as soon as I have all the necessary information from you.

Donald: Right. I think that's it, unless there are any questions. And yes, Jeremy, could you please help Alan with the telephoning and e-mailing whenever necessary.

Jeremy: Yes, I'll do that. But I have one question: Do our visitors speak English or do we need to start learning Romanian?

Donald: Trust you[17] to say that! Well, I assume[18] they all speak English well enough to understand. But note, everybody, don't make the language too difficult or technical. And it always goes down well[19] if you can say please and thank you in the other language. – So, I suggest we talk about the progress[20] made next week …

[17] typisch
[18] annehmen
[19] sich gut machen
[20] Fortschritt

Note

Some businesses operate as part of a larger ***group***. The controlling company is called the ***parent company [BE]*** or ***mother company [AE]***; the controlled companies are called ***subsidiaries [BE]*** or ***daughter companies [AE]***. Two subsidiaries of a group are then referred to as ***"sister companies"***. – One big family!! – Check the terms in italics in your (online) dictionary.

Work with the text.

1 List the tasks Donald gives his staff to do.

2 What does the term *hospitality* involve? – In your experience, what kind of hospitality do companies/institutions offer when they receive visitors?

3 Alan is responsible for seeing to[1] the "technical" arrangements. Try and think what that could mean. Prepare a "to do" list.

4 In your view, which facilities should be available in the conference room? Draw up a list.

5 Many companies have welcome packs[2] available for their visitors. What would you expect to find in them?

[1] sich kümmern um
[2] Begrüßungspaket, - mappe

Talk about your foreign-language experience.

1 Share your experience with meeting people in or from other countries. Did you try to say a few words in their language? Why? Why not? – Describe the reaction of the people you talked to in their language.

2 Do you know how to say *please, thank you, good morning* etc. in another language? Just for fun, draw up a list of the languages spoken by your classmates. Find out what people in their home countries say for the words mentioned here.
(By the way: In Romania people say *va rog* or *te rog* for "please" and *multçumesc* for "thank you". And *bună dimineaţa* means "good morning"; *domnule* means Mr and *doamnă* means Mrs).

10.3 The next step

Track 37

A few days later, Alan knows the number of visitors. He calls a couple of hotels in York to find out about the availability[1] of rooms and to negotiate[2] prices. Now listen to his telephone conversation with Juliet, the receptionist at the Beverly Hotel.

Juliet: Beverly Hotel. Good morning. My name is Juliet. What can I do for you?

Alan: This is Alan from *Sweets and the like* here in York. Could I speak to the receptionist, please?

Juliet: Well, that's me actually. How can I help you?

Alan: Sorry, I hadn't realised[3]. Well, I checked out your hotel on the internet. We'll be having visitors from Romania in about four weeks' time. And we need four single rooms and one double room. Could you perhaps let me know what your charges[4] are?

Juliet: No problem. As you may have seen on our website, we normally charge[5] £125 per night for single rooms and £145 for double rooms; and that includes a cooked breakfast and VAT, of course. There is £5 off[6] if you choose continental breakfast. And when did you say your guests are coming?

Alan: Well, they are due to[7] arrive on 25 October in the late afternoon and will be leaving on the 28th. So, that's three nights altogether.

Juliet: OK. Hold on a sec. Let me just check. … Yes, we still have enough rooms available for that period. Shall I book them for you, then?

©Brian Jackson-fotolia.com

Alan: No, no, not yet. I'd really like to know whether there are any reductions for company bookings[8].

Juliet: Well, our business rates[9] usually are about ten per cent lower, that is to say £115 and £130. There are higher reductions if your company has a standing arrangement[10] with us.

Alan: That sounds fine. I'll find out whether we have any such arrangement with your hotel. But I'd still like to compare your prices with those of other hotels. And by the way, how about internet access[11]?

Juliet: Well, all our rooms have internet access, of course. And that's free of charge[12].

Alan: Excellent. I think that's about it. Well, just one last thing. The rooms all have the usual three-star facilities, don't they?

Juliet: Yes, of course.

Alan: OK then. I'll let you know within the next couple of days.

Juliet: OK. I'll be hearing from you then. Thank you for calling and goodbye for now.

Alan: Thank you and goodbye.

1 Verfügbarkeit
2 aushandeln
3 das war mir nicht klar
4 *hier*: Preis
5 berechnen
6 der Preis reduziert sich um …
7 etw. tun sollen
8 Buchung für ein Unternehmen
9 Preis für Unternehmen
10 feste Vereinbarung
11 Internetzugang
12 kostenlos

Work with the text.

1 What do these figures stand for? 28 – 115 – 125 – 130 – 145 – 25

2 What do the prices include?

3 For how many nights does Alan need to book rooms?

4 For how many people does Alan need to find accommodation?

5 Why does Alan want to phone other hotels?

6 What category does the Beverly Hotel belong to?

Do some internet research.

1 Find out what hotels there are in York/GB in the three- and four-star categories.
- Make a list of the prices they charge for a three-day stay in single and in double rooms. Also list what is included in the price.
- Say why you would prefer a particular hotel. Use these categories: location, size, facilities, room interiors, priceworthiness[1].

[1] Preiswürdigkeit
[2] Tarif, Fahrpreis

2 Check out taxi services in York and report back with regard to the following: availability of cars, airport transfers, fares[2] (if possible), services, contact details.
Prepare a list with the information found on the internet. Work in groups and present your results in class.

Other countries – other eating and drinking habits

1 What do you reckon the difference is between a cooked (English/Scottish) and a continental breakfast? What are the ingredients[1] of a cooked breakfast? If you don't know, find out on the internet.

[1] *hier:* Bestandteil

2 Find out what the people do for breakfast in the countries where some of your classmates come from originally. – Share the information.

10.4 Getting things organised

1 Apart from the question of accommodation, Alan has to think about a lot of little things. After some brainstorming, he comes up with a "to do" list arranged alphabetically. Put the items in a sensible order and give reasons for your arrangement[1].

[1] Anordnung

No.	Things Alan has to do	When best to do them				
		At once	In week 1	In week 2	In week 4	Immediately before arrival
	Arrange meals in staff canteen					
	Arrange taxis					
	Ask taxi companies about fares					
	Book a conference room					

No.	Things Alan has to do	When best to do them				
		At once	In week 1	In week 2	In week 4	Immediately before arrival
	Check out bus routes and timetables[2]					
	Discuss results of preparations with colleagues					
	Find out about standing arrangement with the Beverly Hotel					
	Find out about the weather					
	Get information packs from York Tourist Information Office[3]					
	Help boss to decide on the best hotel					
	Inform boss about all the information received					
	Phone other hotels					
	Phone/e-mail hotel reception to make a booking					
	Prepare name tags[4] for visitors and local staff					
	Prepare a town map for visitors					
	Report back to boss about all the arrangements made					
	Send an e-mail to colleagues in the department					
	Wait for the hotel booking confirmation					
	Write out a rough "timetable[5]" for the various events of the visit					

[2] Fahrplan
[3] Fremdenverkehrsbüro
[4] Namensschildchen
[5] Zeitplan

2 Is there anything that should be added? – If so, amend the list.

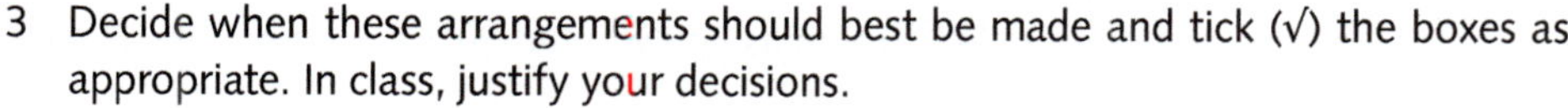

3 Decide when these arrangements should best be made and tick (√) the boxes as appropriate. In class, justify your decisions.

Write an e-mail.

Alan gets Jeremy, the office junior, to write an e-mail to Reception at the *Beverly Hotel* (reception@beverlyhotel.com) to make the booking. He confirms the details of Alan's telephone conversation with Juliet. *Sweets and the like* have no standing arrangement with any hotel in York. They leave it to the visitors to choose what type of breakfast they would like to have. And they will only pay for bed and breakfast. Any drinks from the minibar, etc. must be paid for by the visitors themselves.

Use the form and language of a business e-mail. And Alan has forgotten what the receptionist's first name was.

Do a role play.

Before you start on these tasks, work out what you want/need to say. Don't ask/ answer the questions all at once. Don't forget: Be polite and make a good impression.

Role A: (1) On behalf of *Sweets and the like* phone the *Beverly Hotel* again and ask Reception to book two additional rooms, as the Romanian party will be bigger than originally planned. Ask for the booking to be confirmed.

Role A: (2) You are Jeremy. You are phoning a taxi company in York to enquire about the prices for a minibus to pick up the Romanian visitors at Manchester Airport. The flight is due to arrive at 16.40 hrs on 25 October. There are eight persons altogether. You also want to know how much it will cost for three taxis to collect[1] the visitors at the Beverly Hotel and take them to the company premises on the outskirts of York (Brownhill Industrial Estate, Arondale Drive) on the mornings of 26 and 27 October. For the 28th you need transport back to Manchester Airport. Ask about special business rates and whether VAT is included. Also ask for a general list of taxi fares. You will be collecting offers from other taxi companies as well and then discuss the information received with your boss and ring back again later.

©araraadt-fotolia.com

[1] abholen

You will find the text for Role B on p. 204.

10.5 Passing on information

All the arrangements are in place now. Donald asks Jeremy to prepare a draft for an e-mail to his Romanian counterpart[1], Sorin Olaru. Just to be on the safe side[2], Donald checks Jeremy's draft. He finds 15 mistakes (language and facts!) which he asks Jeremy to correct. Can you make the necessary corrections?

[1] *hier:* Kollege/in

[2] auf „Numero sicher" gehen

Hi, everybody ①,

I am glad to tell ② you that all the arrangements for your visit have now been made. We found a nice guesthouse ③ for you in the centre of York and have booked six double ④ rooms and one single ⑤ room as you wanted ⑥. Of course, we will pay for bed and breakfast while you are here. We have also arranged for a minibus to collect you at Manchester Airport. The driver will greet ⑦ you in the departure ⑧ lounge and hold a sign with our name. The ride to your hotel should take about an hour and a half, depending on traffic, of course. We'll meet you there at 8 pm and then go out for lunch ⑨ at a nice restaurant. I hope that's OK with you.

For 26 and 27 October, we have arranged for taxis to drop you ⑩ at the hotel at 9 am. Our discussions and also the factory tour[1] (scheduled for the first day of your visit) will finish ⑪ at 9.30 am. We'll have lunch together in the staff canteen. There will also be no ⑫ opportunities to meet colleagues from other offices ⑬ during your visit. A reception is planned for the evening of the 26th. And our MD has refused ⑭ to join us for some of the events. In the afternoon of the 27th there will be some time for you to explore York and see York Minster[2].

I think that is all for the time being. If there are any questions or problems, do not hesitate to contact us.

Yours faithfully ⑮,

1 Fabrikbesichtigung
2 Münster, Dom

10.6 Saying "thank you"

After their return home to Craiova/Romania, Sorin Olaru of *Ciocolată Anghel* writes an e-mail to Donald Kemp of *Sweets and the like* to thank him and his team. His English is not very good. Replace the words in italics with appropriate terms from the box below. Note: there are more terms than you need.

• appreciate • efforts • enjoyable • factory • factory tour • great • grateful • • help • holiday • hospitality • improve • information • journey • • kind regards • morning/afternoon • opportunity • organised • programme • • safely • staff • stay • successful • valuable • welcome • would like •

donald.kemp@sweetandthelike.com

Visit to York

Good ① *day* Donald,

Our return ② *ride* to Craiova went according to plan and we landed ③ *securely* at Bucharest Airport.

I ④ *want* to thank you and your team for making our visit to your ⑤ *works* such an ⑥ *entertaining* event. Everything was well ⑦ *planned* and the ⑧ *schedule* gave us the ⑨ *chance* to learn a lot about your quality management system. We are ⑩ *thankful* for all the ⑪ *news* you gave us during the ⑫ *works visit* and in your presentations. All this is very ⑬ *precious* for our attempts to ⑭ *make* our quality control *better.*

Thank you also for the hard work of your ⑮ *workers* to make us feel ⑯ *loved* and also the ⑰ *friendliness* shown during our ⑱ *time* in York. We ⑲ *love* all this very much.

⑳ *Yours sincerely,*

Sorin

Head of Quality Control

©gustavofrazao-fotolia.com

Learn to express thanks on the phone.

Complete the telephone dialogue between Sorin and Donald. Write out Donald's role. Make sure Donald's answers fit in with what Sorin says. Here are some phrases to help you. The sentences are arranged in alphabetical order; and you don't need all of them.

thank you
much enjoyed
great
never forget
always remember
really good
superb
outstanding
spectacular
interesting
never seen

- And how was the journey?
- Bye, and all the best.
- Did you get home alright?
- Don't mention it.
- Fine. If you need any further help or have any questions, please do not hesitate to contact us.
- I'm glad you enjoyed your visit.
- I'm very pleased about that.
- If we can be of help, you know. – Anytime. Just give me a call or send an e-mail.
- Is there anything else we can do for you?
- No problem. That's the least we could do.
- Now, that sounds good.
- Oh, hello. It's good to hear from you. How are you?
- That's good to hear.
- That's very kind of you to say so.
- Yeah, alright.

©Sean K-fotolia.com

Donald: This is Donald from *Sweets and the like*. Good morning. What can I do for you?

Sorin: Oh, hello Donald. This is Sorin. I'm phoning about our visit to York.

Donald:

Sorin: Yes, no problem. The flights went very smoothly and we landed punctually and had a good car journey back home.

Donald:

Sorin: Yes. And what I wanted to say: The visit was super. Everything was so well organised.

Donald:

Sorin: We very much enjoyed the factory tour, and the discussions and presentations were immensely helpful for our work here in Craiova.

Donald:

Sorin: Yes, we learnt a lot about the way things work in your country. And we will now see how we can put that to good use here in Craiova.

Donald:

Sorin: We'll sure do that. And one more thing. We are very grateful for all the work of your staff and also the accommodation and transport arrangements. We couldn't have done all that from here.

Donald:

Sorin: Well, a big thank-you anyway. We very much appreciate everything you've done for us. Thank you very much indeed.

Donald:

Sorin: So, I wish you all the very best. Bye for now.

Donald:

Now act out this telephone conversation. 

As a German speaker, how would you express Sorin's statements in German? 

Revision

Talking about future events

1 *will* + infinitive is used to make predictions or express spontaneous decisions.
Examples: *It'll rain tomorrow. – I'll see you tomorrow then.*

2 *am/is/are going to* + infinitive is used to express a logical conclusion or a speaker's intention (non-spontaneous).
Examples: *It's very cold outside. I think it's going to be a frosty night. – I'm going to see my parents anyway.*

3 The *present continuous* is used to express a planned action that will take place in the future.
Example: *I'm meeting my boss at 9.00 am on Tuesday. – We're going to London tomorrow.*

4 *will + be* + present participle is used for events in progress in the future.
Example: *Tomorrow at this time, I'll be sitting on the train to the airport.*

5 The *simple present* is used for events in the future that occur regularly (timetable, programme).
Examples: *My train leaves at 7.45 hrs. – The show starts at 8 o'clock.*

Mediate. You want to say that … 

1 … das Flugzeug um 9.20 Uhr in Manchester landet.
2 … die Preise für Kaffee wegen der schlechten Ernte steigen werden.
3 … Sie Dienstag um diese Zeit in der Berufsschule sind.
4 … Sie heute den Bericht beenden werden.
5 … das neue Buch sicherlich sehr nützlich sein wird.
6 … Sie nächste Woche mit einem Kunden in Hannover sprechen.
7 … Sie die Angelegenheit heute Nachmittag mit Ihrer Chefin besprechen wollen.
8 … Sie morgen an der Sitzung teilnehmen wollen.

Use appropriate verb phrases to talk about future plans. The expressions in brackets are meant to help you. 

1 You plan to phone the taxi company tomorrow. (I …)
2 Your colleague has an appointment with the marketing manager next week. (He/she … - to see -)
3 Your company is thinking about trainings for the new software program. (In our company they … - to consider -)
4 Your job for next Tuesday is filing documents. (I … - to do -)
5 The conference room has to be got ready for the meeting on Thursday. (I …)
6 It's your boss's birthday next month. The office party is on Wednesday, 12 April. (My boss …; … to be due to …)
7 Time of meeting of Craiova party with Managing Director: Friday at 9.00 am. (The meeting … - to be …; full sentence , please)

10.7 How to act in formal situations

10.7.1 Greeting people

Info

In Britain and the USA, people are much less formal than in Germany. At work and also in their private lives, with neighbours for example, they use first names. However, using first names does not mean that there is a kind of friendship as often is the case in Germany. People usually introduce someone with their full name and they mostly use the family name when they meet someone as a customer.

Introducing a visitor to a colleague

(Speaker) *Good morning. David, I want you to meet Jeremy Finchley.*
(Visitor) *How do you do? Pleased to meet you. Oh, just call me Jeremy.*
(Colleague) *How do you do, Jeremy. I'm David. David Fairfax. But just call me David.*

Both speakers use the polite phrase *"How do you do?"* when they first meet. Then they invite each other to use their first name.

Note: The question *"How do you do?"* is just a form of greeting to which you reply with the same question. But people do not really want to know how you are. It is just a form of greeting someone when you meet for the first time. So, do NOT reply by saying *"Thank you. I'm fine"* or just *"(I'm) Fine."* If they really want to know, they'll probably ask: *"(And) How are you?"*

The polite forms *Mr, Mrs* or titles are only used when people find themselves in more formal situations. *Ms* is only used in letters. If you do not know the name of a person, use *Sir* or *Madam*, for example: *"Excuse me Madam/Sir."*

As a younger person, you should wait for the older or more senior person to take the first step; and that is asking you to call them by their first name.

Shaking hands

In Britain, until recently people did not shake hands when they met for the first time. So do not be offended[1] if this happens to you. But habits are changing. Again, wait for the more senior person to make the first move. In the U.S.A., it is fairly common to shake hands.

[1] beleidigen

Talk about greeting habits in other countries.

1 As young persons or good friends, how do you greet each other?

2 Find out from your classmates who have close contacts with other countries what habits they have observed in these countries (people meeting for the first time, people meeting regularly, greeting members of the family).

3 As a person not familiar with particular national or regional customs, how do you think you should/could behave in such situations?

10.7.2 Small-talk – Introduction

Info

In many business situations – and not only there – small-talk serves as an ice-breaker[1]. It brings people together who meet for the first time. It provides moments of relaxation[2] during coffee breaks or at lunch or even a cigarette break outside the building.

Leave business discussions to the conference room. And definitely[3], don't start talking about politics, religion, your financial affairs, your colleagues or your personal problems. So, what can you talk about? – The journey, the weather, the business premises, the kind of accommodation, the town/region to which you have come, important sports events, folklore (carnival, Christmas markets, local events). From there it's only a short step to finding out about common interests (sports, pastimes[4], travel etc.).

Feel confident[5] to take the initiative. A smile will go a long way[6] to establishing[7] contact. In breaks at meetings "May I join you?" can be a good start from where to move on. And the next move should be to ask the partner an open question (*How?, When?, What?, Where?, Why?* etc.). This gives your partner the chance to say a few words or sentences from which the next stages will develop more easily. Closed questions often lead to one-word answers. And then you need to think of another question.

1 „Eisbrecher"
2 Entspannung
3 ganz bestimmt
4 Freizeitbeschäftigung
5 sich zutrauen
6 ein großer Schritt sein
7 *hier*: anbahnen

Use open questions so that the conversation may continue.

1 Turn these questions into open questions. – You may have to use your imagination.
Example: *Did you have a good journey? – How was your journey?/What kind of journey did you have?*

1 Did you fly direct from Bucharest to Manchester?
2 Do you like the hotel?
3 Is your room nice?
4 Do you like our weather?
5 Have you been to this country before?
6 Did you enjoy the presentation/factory tour?
7 Will you go back immediately after the conference?
8 Have you had an opportunity to have a walk around town?

©Rawpixel-fotolia.com

2 What could the next sentence in these small-talk situations be?

A Where are you staying? – ______. – Yes, I know the hotel. And how do you like your room? – ______

B Have you been to this country before? – Yes, ______. – Is that so? And what did do you like about it? – ______

C What was the weather like in your country when you left this morning? – ______. – Interesting. And how do you find it here? – ______

D How long will you be staying this time? – ______. – That's not very long. And what will you do after your visit here? – ______

E You are saying you play football a lot. Which German team do you like best? – ______. – That's interesting to hear. And why do you say that? – ______

F And what is your town like? – ______. – I didn't know that./But that's very interesting to learn. – Is it very different from what you've seen here? – ______

Note the comments and question words in these short dialogues.

Practise making small-talk.

1 In class, discuss what you could say about the topics mentioned in situations A–F above.

2 What other topics would you suggest?

3 Form groups and work out the corresponding phrases in English. But first turn these ideas into idiomatic English.

1 Wie lange haben Sie (schon) Deutsch/Englisch etc. gelernt?
2 Mögen Sie Ihren Deutsch-/Englischkurs etc.?
3 Waren Sie schon einmal in Deutschland/England etc.?
4 Was hat ihnen gefallen?
5 Ist es bei Ihnen auch so heiß/kalt/nass?
6 Welche Sehenswürdigkeiten möchten Sie sich ansehen?
7 Wohnen Sie direkt in …?
8 Und wie kommen Sie zur Arbeit?
9 Gibt es in Ihrer Stadt einen guten Fußballverein?
10 Welchen Sport mögen Sie?/Treiben Sie selbst Sport?

Think about other phrases that you could/would use in small-talk in your companies/institutions.

Create small-talk situations.

1 In pairs, think up and act out a couple of small-talk situations. Make them longer than those in the task on pp. 135–136. (Those watching and listening should make suggestions for different developments of the conversations.)

2 Do the same in groups of three or four classmates. Before you start, agree on a topic, define your roles and prepare a few English phrases. Try to agree or disagree, share your experiences and/or opinions.

And remember to always be polite. – After all, you are talking to visitors to your company/institution.

Local/Regional customs[1]

Often, there are important traditional local or regional events that foreign visitors to Germany know nothing or very little about. In small-talk you can ask about special events in the visitor's country/region/home town.

[1] Bräuche, Brauchtum

Talk about special events.

Think of such events in your region/town and try to explain what is being celebrated[1] (Oktoberfest, St. Martin, Schützenfest (*marksmen's fair*), fun fairs, Weihnachtsmarkt etc.). Do research on the internet and look up relevant words in your (online) dictionary. Discuss your findings in class.

[1] feiern

10.7.3 Hospitality[1] and politeness

[1] *hier*: Gastfreundschaft

In business meetings with partners from other companies/institutions, you will find drinks (coffee, tea, cold drinks) and often some snacks on the table. Offering and asking for these politely is not always easy.

Decide which of these phrases are polite.

• Are there any soft drinks? • Could you pass the sugar, please? • Do you also have sandwiches? • Do you think I could have some green tea, please? • Give me the bottle opener. • Help yourselves to biscuits and cold drinks. We also have coffee or tea, whichever you prefer. • I'm afraid we only have mineral water. • I want some milk, please.	• I'll have coffee, if I may. • I'm a vegetarian and I don't eat cold meats. Could I have a cheese sandwich perhaps? • Is there anything missing? • If you require anything else, please let me know. • Hey, just pass the fruit bowl, will you? • There are more biscuits if you need them. • There is more of everything. Just shout. • Who wants tea or coffee?

Rephrase the less polite sentences. Use: Could I ...?, May I ...?, Would ... (perhaps)? Would it be possible ...?

Note

want means "ich will haben". – And don't forget to say *please* and *thank you*.

10.8 Business cards

Nobody in the business world can imagine a first face-to-face meeting without the "ceremony" of exchanging business cards.

What's your experience?

1 What are business cards good for? What do you think?
2 Does your company/institution have business cards? If so, who uses them?
3 Have you already seen people exchange business cards? Try and describe what they did and how they did it. How did they behave?
4 Can you describe the business cards that are used in your company/institution? Look at the design, the company logo, colours, information on the card, etc.
5 Look at the photos on p. 138 and describe the differences in the process of handing over the card. Which of the pictures comes closest to what you have seen yourself?

©Jenner-fotolia.com

©Andrey Popov-fotolia.com

©WavebreakMediaMicro-fotolia.com

Track 38

What's the use of business cards?

The business card is a form of self-introduction and also an advertising tool[1] for the company/institution that you, the cardholder[2], represent. First and foremost[3], business cards help the partners understand and remember each other's names. When you meet people for the first time, you state your name, of course. And so will your partner. But very often the partner does not fully understand, let alone[4] remember the name, especially when they meet several new people within only a few minutes, or when the name is pronounced very quickly or in a language or accent that they do not understand. So, when you get a business card from your partner, you can see the name in print and try to remember it. This is a great help if you want to call your partners by their names. Always a good thing to do, anyway.

It is also very useful for keeping in touch[5] later on, because the card shows the partner's job title[6], very often the department and sometimes other qualifications (university degree[7] or diploma). This information is usually not stated by the people introducing themselves for reasons of modesty[8]. And, obviously, the card carries the technical data for making contact[9] (company name and address, the partner's telephone and fax numbers as well as their e-mail address, sometimes their private address even). So, some people say, it is a kind of extension[10] of one's personality. Companies doing business abroad often take care to provide this information on the reverse[11] in the language of their foreign business partners.

Business cards are usually exchanged in a semi-formal environment, when you have said "Hello" shortly before a meeting (part of the greeting ceremony) and, depending on the customs of the country, shaken hands. Another situation is the coffee break, when people begin to learn more about each other. Mostly, cards are exchanged on a one-to-one basis and handed over and received with due respect[12] for the other person. It is expected that you look at it carefully and at least read the name and title. And the card is never put away in a wallet or a purse. In some countries a special etiquette[13] is observed[14]. The partners hand over and receive the card with both hands and bow[15] slightly while doing so.

[1] Werbemittel
[2] Karteninhaber/in
[3] zuallererst aber
[4] geschweige denn
[5] in Kontakt bleiben
[6] Stellenbezeichnung
[7] Hochschulabschluss
[8] Bescheidenheit
[9] Kontakt aufnehmen
[10] Ausweitung
[11] Rückseite
[12] gebührender Respekt
[13] Verhaltensregel
[14] *hier:* einhalten
[15] sich verbeugen

Work with the text.

1 Why is the business card helpful when you meet someone for the first time?
2 Why should you try and call your business partners by their names?
3 Apart from the name and job title, what "technical" information can you find on the business card?
4 Why, do you think, is it a good idea to also print the information in the partner's language?
5 Why, do you think, should the business card not be put away in a wallet or purse?

Unit 11 What it takes: Events and projects

©Rawpixel-fotolia.com

©pressmaster-fotolia.com

11.1 Let's get going!

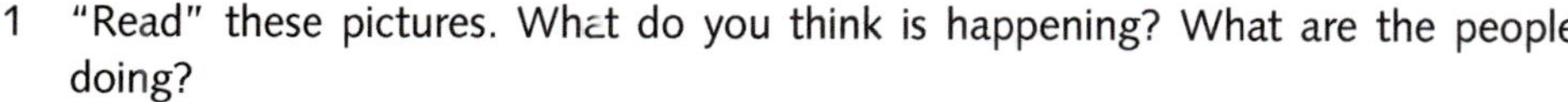

1 "Read" these pictures. What do you think is happening? What are the people doing?

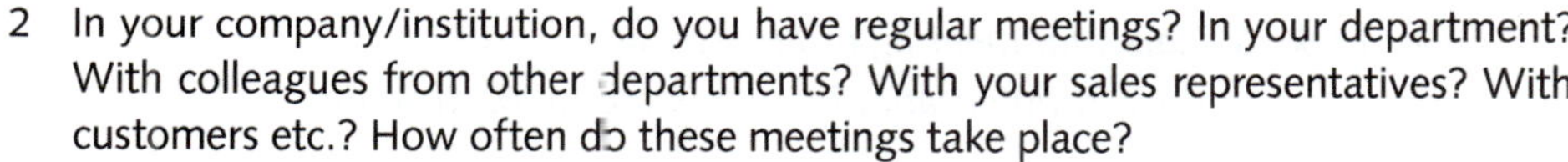

2 In your company/institution, do you have regular meetings? In your department? With colleagues from other departments? With your sales representatives? With customers etc.? How often do these meetings take place?

3 If you had the opportunity to take part, describe what happened in these meetings.

4 Who is responsible for arranging these meetings and who is involved in the preparation and the clearing up of the room after the event?

5 Have you been asked to help? Describe what you were asked to do.

6 How about seminars? – Does your company organise them? Or have you attended any? Describe your experiences.

©Rawpixel-fotolia.com

11.2 Getting ready for the event

Arranging an event requires a lot of thought, planning and organisation, and much of that well before the event itself. At different stages[1] there are several people taking care of[2] all the details.

Do you have any idea what needs to be done to prepare a meeting or a conference? Start drawing up a list – discuss your findings in class.

At Fawkes & Prim's Inc. in Detroit, the marketing manager for the toys product range, Pauline Greir, is preparing the annual conference for the field sales staff[3]. The plan is for a two-day event on the company premises. The participants will be staying in hotels. As this is the first time that she is doing this, she asks her office junior, David Grimes, to help her prepare a list of things they need to think of.

1 Stadium
2 sich kümmern um
3 Außendienstmitarbeiter *(pl)*

1 Ausbildungszentrum
2 Bereichsleiter/in
3 Mitarbeiter/innen der Abteilung
4 Zeitfenster
5 *hier*: Rücksendung
6 *hier*: Anmeldeformular
7 Erstattung
8 Reisekosten
9 Raumbedarf

Here is the result of their work.

- *reserve room in company training centre[1]*
- *inform staff canteen about need for extra meals & drinks*
- *book hotel accommodation*
- *contact guest speaker & agree on presentation topic*
- *contact division director's[2] office & invite her/him to formal dinner*
- *send out invitations to participants*
- *arrange formal dinner with hotel (conference participants & departmental staff[3])*
- *make technical arrangements for meeting room (get equipment)*
- *get sales people & headquarters staff to block time slot[4] for event ASAP*
- *draw up list of participants*
- *check return[5] of attendance forms[6]*
- *notify hotel about final number of guests for formal dinner*
- *draw up agenda/timetable*
- *organise presentation of new products; contact responsible product managers*
- *send out details about reimbursement[7] of travel expenses[8]*
- *order drinks & snacks for meeting room & breaks*
- *inform staff canteen & hotels about final number of participants & room requirements[9]*

It's time to get organised.

1 The list above represents the final result of Pauline's and David's brainstorming session. Turn these ideas into full sentences and use phrases such as the following: *we must (not forget to) …, someone should/needs to …, it will be necessary to …, we must see to it that ….*

2 Compare your ideas with the points mentioned above. Write down what needs to be added to that list.

3 Prepare a timeline[1] and pencil in[2] when, in your view, these activities and those you added to the list need to be taken care of. Use these stages:
- immediately,
- three to four months before the event,
- one to two months before the event,
- a week to a fortnight before the event,
- a couple of days before the event.

4 Use the criteria listed below to rearrange the "to do" list:
- need for internal communication,
- need for external communication,
- who can or should do the work: Pauline or David?

5 The "to do" list serves as a checklist for the person responsible for organising an event. List the kinds of persons or their jobs who should provide information on the work completed or give interim reports[3].

For points 3–5 above, discuss your results in class.

1 Zeitleiste
2 eintragen
3 Zwischenbericht

11.3 Problems with room bookings

Track 39

In the third year of his training, Tarik Yilmaz is doing a three-month work experience in the *Beaumaison Hotel* in Leeds, which is well known for its conference facilities[1]. Working in the back office, he gets a phone call from Susan, a colleague from Reception.

[1] *hier*: Konferenzräumlichkeiten

Susan: Hello. Tarik, is that you?

Tarik: Yes, it's me. What's up?

Susan: Well, I've got a client here who's enquiring about a two-day conference from 28 to 29 May. Have you got a conference room available for 25 to 30 people by any chance? Accommodation for the group is no problem.

Tarik: Well. Hold on a sec. Let me see. – I'm afraid it doesn't look too good. The Elmsgrove room is available on Friday, but only till 5 pm. We've got a family reception[2] there starting at six. It's fully booked[3] on Thursday.

Susan: That's too bad. They want to wrap up[4] their conference with a dinner party[5] which the management will also attend. I know they left it to the last minute really. But they're a very good customer. Is there nothing we can do??

Tarik: That really makes things rather complicated. Well, let me have a look again. – OK?!? Well, I think we could perhaps try and persuade the Bryson company to move to the Arndale. That's a bigger room. – Much better for their training anyway. Gives them more space. And if the Williams family reception gets moved to the Ennerdale?!? – It's a slightly smaller room, but should be much more comfortable for fifteen people anyway. – Yeah, I think that would do the trick[6].

Susan: Excellent. Sounds like a good idea.

Tarik: But, of course, we'd need to get the OK from both parties, the Brysons and the Williams. And there's one problem still.

Susan: And what's that?

Tarik: Well, there's the Lib Dem* meeting on Thursday night.

Susan: What about it?

Tarik: Well, they've booked the Arndale for that evening. So, we'd need to move them as well, so that the Bryson company can have the room for the whole day.

Susan: OK, I see. And what are the arrangements with the Brysons?

Tarik: Well, they're booked in for the whole of Wednesday 27th and for Thursday 28th. But their conference is only for two days. So I don't know when they'll be leaving on Thursday.

Susan: And the Lib Dem people? Do you happen to know when they'll be starting their function[7]?

[2] *hier*: Familienfeier
[3] ausgebucht
[4] *hier*: abschließen
[5] festl. Abendessen
[6] das ist die Lösung
[7] *hier*: Veranstaltung

©rilueda-fotolia.com

* Lib Dem is short for Liberal Democrats, a political party established in 1988 as a result of the merger of the Liberal Party and the Social Democratic Party.

Tarik: Sorry. No, I don't. Didn't take the booking.

Susan: Right then. I'll discuss the situation with the Brysons first. And if they finish their training session[8] at six or thereabouts[9], we should be in the clear[10]. If not, I'll talk to the Lib Dem people.

Tarik: Right. So, I'll make provisional[11] entries[12] then. And what's your client's name?

Susan: Willoughby & Sons.

Tarik: OK?!? And will I get the usual note[13] from you? You know, the confirmation[14] with names and dates and so on. And let me know what equipment they need for their conference.

Susan: Will do that. Thanks, Tarik.

[8] *hier*: Seminarsitzung
[9] so ungefähr
[10] *hier*: OK sein, in Ordnung gehen
[11] vorläufig
[12] Eintrag
[13] Notiz
[14] Bestätigung

Work with the text.

1 Explain what the problems are that Tarik and Susan are faced with.

2 What is the solution that Tarik and Susan agree on?

3 State what Susan has to do.

4 Look out for short verb forms and say what they stand for.

Familiarise yourself with the room plans.

Explain what Tarik has to change to enter the room reservations he agreed on with Susan.

Elmsgrove (seating[1] 30 persons)					
25 – 29 May	**Monday 25 May**	**Tuesday 26 May**	**Wednesday 27 May**	**Thursday 28 May**	**Friday 29 May**
9 – 10	*Wallingford Ltd*	*Turnbull plc*	*Bryson plc*	*Bryson plc*	
10 – 11	↓	↓	↓	↓	
11 – 12	↓	↓	↓	↓	
12 – 13	*Lunch*	↓	*Lunch*	*Lunch*	
13 – 14	*Saunders Ltd*	*Lunch*	*Bryson plc*	*Bryson plc*	
14 – 15	↓	*Turnbull plc*	↓	↓	
15 – 16	↓	↓	↓	↓	
16 – 17	↓	↓	↓	↓	
17 – 18	↓	↓	↓		*Williams family reception*
18 – 20	*Wortley FC*	↓			
20 – 22					

[1] mit einer Platzkapazität von

Arndale (seating 50 persons)					
25 – 29 May	Monday 25 May	Tuesday 26 May	Wednesday 27 May	Thursday 28 May	Friday 29 May
9 – 10	Clarks Ltd	Turnbull plc	Richley & Partners		
10 – 11	↓	↓	↓		
11 – 12	↓	↓	↓		
12 – 13	Lunch				
13 – 14		Lunch	Lunch		
14 – 15	ITC Ltd	Mullar & Partners	Richley & Partners		
15 – 16	↓	↓	↓		
16 – 17	↓	↓	↓		
17 – 18	↓	↓	↓		
18 – 20		↓	Leeds Drama Society	Horsley Lib Dems	
20 – 22					

The policy at the Beaumaison Hotel is to ask event organisers[1] to help stagger[2] the lunch breaks. This helps both the kitchen and the service staff[3]. And additionally, the waiting times at table can be reduced.

Which lunchtime slot[4] would you suggest for the conference that Willoughby & Sons are planning to hold on Thursday and Friday?

[1] *hier:* Veranstalter
[2] staffeln
[3] Bedienung(-spersonal)
[4] *hier:* Zeit

Do a role play.

Reception phones Tarik to pass on a telephone call from a client who has booked a conference for two and a half days. But the originally[1] agreed dates need to be changed. – Use the usual polite phrases at the beginning and the end.

Role A: You are a junior assistant acting for Madilena Baxter, the Personnel Manager at Swinton Ltd in Bradford. As the coach[2] who was to conduct[3] the training is seriously ill, you are forced to change the dates of the training. It is[4] now to[4] take place two weeks later. All the other arrangements remain unchanged. If there are any problems, you need to discuss things with your boss and will call back as quickly as possible.

You will find the text for Role B on p. 204.

[1] ursprünglich
[2] Ausbilder/in, Trainer/in
[3] leiten, durchführen
[4] sollen

11.4 Getting geared up for the training

A few days later, Tarik confirms the booking arrangements. Together with Sarah Quincy from Willoughby & Sons, he looks at a scanned illustration of possible seating arrangements for the group of 20 to 25 participants. These are the options available.

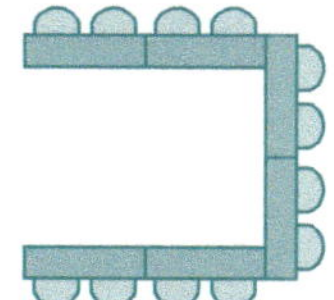

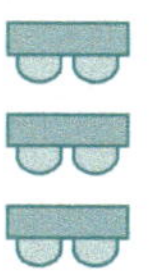

The staff training is planned to involve presentations by the trainer, group work and also group presentations. Apart from the trainer–trainee aspect, you may also want to consider one or two technical points: position of projector and screen, snacks and soft drinks (in the room – where?) or in the corridor.

1 Form groups of three or four and decide which of the options you would think is the most suitable for a training seminar[1]. Present your ideas in class and give reasons for your decision. Try to agree on one of the options shown on p. 143.

2 Tarik prepares a checklist for the Willoughby conference. Which equipment and utensils[2] should the hotel make available[3]? Which should be brought by the trainer or Willoughby? Tick the items in the list below and explain your choice.

[1] Schulung (-sveranstaltung)
[2] Gerätschaften
[3] zur Verfügung stellen

	Items for Elmsgrove	Beaumaison Hotel	Willoughby or trainer	To be discussed	Not required
1	Agenda/Timetable				
2	Ballpoint pens[1]				
3	Boardmarkers (erasable[2])				
4	Bottle openers				
5	Cloth				
6	Conference folder				
7	Crockery[3] and cutlery[4]				
8	Drinks coolers[5]				
9	Evaluation sheet[6]				
10	Laser pointer[7]				
11	Extension cable[8]				
12	Facilitator's toolbox[9]				
13	Flipchart				
14	Highlighters				
15	Hotel brochure				
16	Leeds tourist brochure				
17	List of participants				
18	Name tags[10]				
19	Pencils				
20	Pin boards[11]				
21	Programme				
22	Waste bins[12]				
23	Whiteboard				
24	Willoughby image brochures				
25	Wiper[13]				
26	Writing pads				

[1] Kugelschreiber
[2] löschbar
[3] Porzellan
[4] Besteck
[5] Kühler
[6] Bewertungsbogen
[7] Laserleuchtstift
[8] Verlängerungskabel
[9] Moderatorenkoffer
[10] Namensschildchen
[11] Pinwand
[12] Abfallbehälter
[13] Wischer

3 In an e-mail, Tarik confirms the arrangements made over the phone for the seating and the equipment of the Elmsgrove conference room.

Write an e-mail to Sarah Quincy (quincy@willoughby.com.uk) to which you attach the list on p. 144. Refer to the general booking confirmation sent by Susan on 2 March and yesterday's phone call. Mention the details of the room booking (name and times) and refer to the results of the discussion about the technical details. Thank Sarah for the decision of her company to choose *Beaumaison Hotel* as a venue for their conference.

Tarik writes a long e-mail in German to his friend, Selma Gökdal in Hanover, to explain the kind of work he has been asked to do at the *Beaumaison Hotel*.

11.5 Events as a marketing tool

Track 40

David Richards is an experienced coach who has been responsible for organising and doing many staff trainings. Here is what he has planned to say.

Ladies and Gentlemen,

[1] And finally a point that I think is very important. Events provide plenty of scope[1] for interaction[2]: participants with the presenters/coaches, customers with each other, salespeople with staff/colleagues from headquarters. Talking about business-related[3] and maybe also general issues allows for bonding[4] and networking[5] – effects which cannot be measured in money terms. And yet, they are very highly valued elements in the outcome of an event.

[2] Another point is that, apart from the content of the event, the participants get a feeling that the company they work for cares about their professional development[6]. One-day events in seminar hotels[7] or residential seminars[8] (involving an overnight stay[9]) go a long way to making staff "happy", simply by getting them away from the company premises into nice and comfortable surroundings. Here, training does not seem like work anymore. Such trainings are very costly, however. Therefore many businesses mostly use in-house trainings or even webinars[10] (these are trainings using an online seminar platform).

©Rawpixel-fotolia.com

[3] And with that I would conclude my little presentation. If you have any questions, do not hesitate to ask them. Thank you for your kind attention.

[4] On the one hand, companies need to create awareness[11] and goodwill outside. They organise roadshows[12] to make their products and services known to a wider public. They sponsor[13] events in the fields of sports and culture (festivals, concerts, exhibitions) which sometimes they attend in person, at the opening of events or at prize-giving[14] ceremonies for example. They also support traditional local or regional festivities[15].

[1] Spielraum
[2] soziale Interaktion
[3] geschäftlich
[4] Vertiefung von Kontakten
[5] Vernetzung
[6] berufliche Entwicklung
[7] Tagungshotel
[8] mehrtägiges Seminar
[9] Übernachtung
[10] Web-Seminar
[11] Bewusstsein
[12] *etwa:* mobile Verkaufsveranstaltung
[13] fördern, unterstützen
[14] Preisverleihung
[15] Fest

[17] Sitzung
[18] vernachlässigen
[19] oberste(r, s)
[20] Umgang mit Kunden
[21] Verhalten am Telefon
[22] nach Bedarf
[23] vertraut machen
[24] Fabrikbesichtigung
[25] zentriert
[26] (Ausstellungs-)Stand
[27] Firmenname
[28] *hier*: Firmenfarben

[5] Good morning to all of you and welcome to this seminar on event management. Before we start with our work, I would like to very briefly introduce myself. My name is David Richards, and I will be your coach for the two sessions[17] this morning.

[6] Goodwill is also an objective that is not to be neglected[18] when businesses organise seminars and trainings for their staff. Of course, the primary[19] objective is to bring employees up-to-date with new developments in many job- or business-related areas, to train them to use new software or technical equipment, to acquire skills in customer handling[20] or dealing with complaints, telephone manners[21], etc.

[7] I think you will agree that there are few businesses in which events do not have a role to play in the annual calendar. Some of them occur regularly, and organising them has almost turned into a routine activity. Other events are arranged as the need arises[22].

[8] On the other hand, events are often organised within the business. They address existing customers to familiarise[23] them with new products, train them in how to use them and inform them about new product developments. Factory tours[24] (for customers and/or the general public) are part of the customer-/user-focused[25] form of event-marketing. In addition to the transfer of information, the hospitality that a business offers its visitors (the welcome they receive, the food and drink they can enjoy "for free", maybe give-aways, etc.) plays an important role in creating goodwill.

[9] Throughout my professional career, I have been working in event management. I think that to begin with, it's a good idea to learn what event management is about. And after that I propose that we do some practical work. I hope that's OK with you?!?

[10] On many of these occasions they set up stands[26] to market their products and services. The corporate name[27], its logo and colour coding[28] become visible to a wider public. And the people at the stands or giving prizes etc. lend a human face to the business.

Work with the text.

1 This time David's notes have got a bit muddled. Try and piece them together in the proper sequence. Look for the structuring phrases at the beginning of the sections.

2 Give each paragraph a short title.

3 What strategies do companies use to become "visible" to the public?

4 What do companies use in-house[1] events for when they address existing customers?

5 Mention possible topics of in-house seminars.

6 What do companies do to create goodwill among their staff?

7 How can the costs of trainings be kept low?

8 Mention forms of interaction that can occur during training sessions.

[1] firmenintern

From the list below, find definitions for the terms in the box. There are more terms than you need.

• bonding • coach • customer handling • evaluation • feedback • • goodwill • interaction • networking • promotion • residential conference • • seminar • sponsoring • training • venue • webinar •

1 communication (oral and written) with one or more people
2 dealing with the people who buy a company's goods or services
3 developing and maintaining a good relationship with many people for business reasons
4 forming a close relationship with so.
5 giving money or goods to support an event (sports, music, arts etc.)
6 meeting in a small group to discuss a particular topic, may take half a day or longer
7 meeting to learn new skills or update existing skills
8 meeting using online facilities to discuss a topic
9 meeting with overnight accommodation to discuss a topic or acquire knowledge or skills
10 positive attitude towards a company

Think of definitions for the terms not needed in the preceding activity.

Revision

The passive

The passive is used to put emphasis on the action rather than on the agent.
Example: *The participants were invited by mail. – The department head/They invited the participants by mail.*

Forming the passive is not really difficult. The forms of *to be* in the appropriate tenses are combined with the past participle of the main verb. Here is a schedule of the key tenses:

Tense	Active	Passive
Simple present	*I call*	*I am called*
Simple past	*I called*	*I was called*
Future I	*I will call*	*I will be called*
Present perfect	*I have called*	*I have been called*
Past perfect	*I had called*	*I had been called*
Future II	*I will have called*	*I will have been called*
Present progressive	*I am calling*	*I am being called*
Past progressive	*I was calling*	*I was being called*

The passive is often used in situations where the agent is not really known or not relevant.
Example: *All of us were asked this question. – Our head office was built more than 50 years ago.*

If necessary, the agent can be mentioned at the end of the phrase using the preposition *by*.
Example: *My boss will send you an e-mail. – An e-mail will be sent to you by my boss.*

Revision (cont'd)

The passive is found in fixed expressions such as: *It is thought/said/reported/believed that …* (Man meint/glaubt/sagt, Leute meinen/sagen; Es wird gesagt/berichtet, dass …; … soll … haben, angeblich) to quote from a source that is not mentioned.

The verbs *have* and *get* are often used to express a passive meaning.

Examples: *The car got damaged in the accident.* – Das Auto wurde bei dem Unfall beschädigt.
I had my hair cut yesterday morning. – Ich habe mir gestern die Haare schneiden lassen.

Some verbs are active in form but passive in meaning.

Examples: *This product sells well.* – Dies Produkt verkauft sich gut/lässt sich gut verkaufen.
The lock opens easily. – Das Schloss ist leicht zu öffnen/lässt sich leicht öffnen.
My new car drives smoothly. – Das neue Auto fährt sich angenehm/lässt sich gut fahren.

Learn to use the passive.

©Rawpixel-fotolia.com

1 Turn these phrases into the passive.

1. We must not neglect the idea of goodwill.
2. In our business we organise seminars whenever necessary.
3. The coach trained us in the use of the new software.
4. Our company does a lot to sponsor cultural events.
5. But we also support local sports clubs.
6. You can ask questions at the end of my presentation.
7. This year our MD will present the prizes for the best team performance.
8. As of[1] next year we will organise regular coaching sessions[2] for our staff.
9. It is impossible to measure the effects of networking in money terms.

[1] von/vom … an
[2] Training, Schulung

2 Render these ideas in idiomatic sentences. Do not translate them word for word. Use the passive or structures with a passive meaning.

1. Sie hat sich den Bericht ausdrucken lassen.
2. Das neue Software-Paket verkauft sich gut.
3. Der Antrag wurde mit großer Mehrheit angenommen.
4. Man hat mir den Auftrag gegeben, heute die Ablage zu machen.
5. Angeblich gibt es nächstes Jahr zwei Seminare für Auszubildende.
6. Sie soll gesagt haben, dass die Abteilung neu organisiert wird.
7. Es heißt, dieses Produkt wird nicht mehr beworben.
8. Die Seminarvorbereitung wird von der Personalabteilung gemacht.
9. Man hat uns gewarnt, dass unsere Firma von der Konkurrenz (*the competition*) gekauft werden würde.

11.6 Project work

There are people out there who argue[1] that a lot of project work is a waste of time. From your experience in your company/institution so far, would you agree or disagree? Give reasons for your views. Exchange your experience with your classmates.

[1] behaupten

Read these statements about project work and put your first thoughts into words.

Project management is easy. You have an idea. You fix a deadline. You set a budget. You choose the right people. And then you just leave it to the team.

If you don't have the right mix of planning, monitoring and controlling, you won't be able to complete a project on time, on budget and with good results.

Good project management has to do with skills in strategic thinking, measuring, organising, analysing, developing, executing.

Project management is about initiating[1] a task, planning the stages, executing the work, controlling the results and completing the work so that the implementation[2] stage can begin.

Project work involves five stages: conceptualisation[3], teambuilding, strategy definition, execution, conclusion[4].

[1] einleiten, beginnen
[2] Umsetzung
[3] Konzepterstellung
[4] Abschluss

1 From your experience with project work in your company/institution, which points would you add?

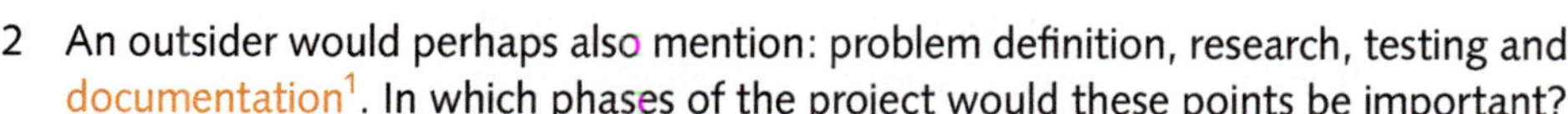

2 An outsider would perhaps also mention: problem definition, research, testing and documentation[1]. In which phases of the project would these points be important?

3 Draw up a list of tasks in the field of project work that would involve the help of office workers. Consider these areas:

- Building a team
- Communicating[2]
- Documentation
- Finance & control
- Holding meetings
- Idea and application
- Milestone reports[3]
- Planning

If in your training you have had any experience with the organisation of projects, state what kind of work would be required for each of these points.

[1] Erstellung von Unterlagen
[2] Informations-, Gedankenaustausch
[3] Meilenstein-, Zwischenbericht

Improve your language competence.

1 Below you will find some verbs and noun phrases. However, they have got into a muddle[1]. Try and put together meaningful idiomatic combinations. Use your (online) dictionary if necessary.

[1] durcheinander geraten
[2] ehrgeizig

Verbs	Noun phrases
• to coordinate • to draw up • to file • to invite so. • to keep • to meet • to prepare • to set • to solve • to write •	• a deadline • a problem • a record of spendings • a report • a timetable • ambitious[2] targets • the documents • the minutes • the project work • to a meeting •

2 Technical English can be very simple. Find the right English terms for the German nouns. Note: There are more English terms than you need.

German terms	English terms
Abschlussbericht	(time) schedule
Arbeitspaket	buffer time
Fortschrittsbericht	cost estimate
Kostenschätzung, -voranschlag	final report
Lenkungs-, Steuerungsausschuss	interim report
Netzplantechnik	network/critical path analysis
Projektabnahme	progress report
Projektphase	project acceptance/approval
Pufferzeit	project manager
Terminkontrolle	project phase/stage
Terminplan	project schedule
Vorgangsnummer	schedule/progress control
Zwischenbericht	steering committee
	transaction number
	work package

Do a role play.

Der/die Leiter/in der Entwicklungsabteilung *(engineering dept.)* von Müllering Transportsysteme AG ist für ein internationales Projekt zur Entwicklung von Software für den Betrieb von Transportbändern *(conveyor belt)* zuständig. In zehn Tagen soll eine Sitzung stattfinden, auf der verschiedene Fortschrittsberichte vorgelegt und diskutiert werden sollen. Sie warten noch auf die Ergebnisse aus Italien und Großbritannien.

Role A: Sie arbeiten in der Entwicklungsabteilung Ihres Unternehmens. Ihr/e Chef/in hat Sie gebeten, den italienischen Partner anzurufen und zu veranlassen, den Bericht schnellstmöglich einzureichen. Geben Sie ihm fünf Arbeitstage Zeit, das zu erledigen. Versuchen Sie höflich aber bestimmt zu sein.

You will find the text for Role B on p. 205.

Unit 12 Presenting

12.1 Let's get going!

Remember the presentations you have listened to and answer the questions below.

- What were the topics?
- Was there a presentation that blew you away[1]? Why?
- Which parts or elements of that particular presentation do you remember? State your reasons.

©Rawpixel-fotolia.com

[1] vom Hocker hauen/reißen, begeistern

And how about **your** last presentation???

- How did you feel while preparing and delivering your presentation?
- Was there anything that did not go as planned?
- Were there any difficulties you came across?

THINK! PAIR! SHARE!

12.2 Preparing a presentation

How to avoid[1] common mistakes when preparing a presentation in a foreign language

When it comes to presentations in a foreign language, many people tend to desperately[2] seek help in order to get it absolutely right. However, a mistake that is frequently made is asking a friend or family member for help. They will then write the complete text for the presenter, who just has to "rehearse[3]" that text once it is time for their presentation.

This is the point where things can go wrong. You may well be able to read out the text. However, tricky words which you might not have used yourself if you had written the text on your own could cause some problems. Often the pronunciation will be wrong. And since the text was written by someone else, you might not have a clue[4] what you are actually talking about. This will make answering questions a very hairy[5] matter.

Furthermore, since the vocabulary used is often far too complex for your target audience[6], the listeners will not be able to follow your presentation. If someone has even made the mistake of learning[7] the whole text by heart[7], listening to their presentation will be utterly agonising[8].

Track 41

[1] vermeiden
[2] verzweifelt
[3] einüben
[4] keine Ahnung haben
[5] heikel
[6] Zielpublikum
[7] auswendig lernen
[8] eine Qual sein

©ra 2 studio-fotolia.com

9 scheinbar
10 makellos
11 Chaos
12 unverständlich

The once seemingly[9] flawless[10] presentation may end up in a mess[11] of mispronounced words and unintelligible[12] information and, in the end, may miss the whole point of the task in the first place.

Experts therefore recommend that you write the text yourself, without copying whole sentences from Google Translator, and also that you keep it simple in order to make the presentation understandable.

Note

If you use online dictionaries, you may find a 'PLAY' or speaker button next to the English word. Just click on it and listen to the pronunciation.

In the past, your boss was not entirely satisfied when you and your colleagues had to deliver presentations for foreign customers. He found the text above on the internet and asks you to prepare a well-structured guideline for your German colleagues with tips on how to avoid common mistakes.

How can you avoid other problems you have had in the past and also future problems? Collect your ideas in class to create a checklist full of useful tips for your next presentation.

Learn to use the language of presentations.

Copy the table below and fill in the **Useful phrases** in the appropriate[1] sections. Find idiomatic German equivalents.

1 angemessen, passend

English	German
Introduction	
…	…
Main part	
…	…
Conclusion	
…	…

Useful phrases

Thanks for listening.
Let me go back to …
Please/You may recall what I said earlier about …
Do you have any questions before we continue to my next point?
This leads/brings me/us to my next point.
And now I'll come to the end/the final part of my presentation.

My presentation is divided into ... parts: ...
Today's presentation covers the following points: ...
Thank you all for being here today.
In conclusion/to sum up/to summarise, I'd like to ...
I'd like to begin/start by ...
Today's topic is ...
Turning to ... / Alright, let's move on to ...
Let's continue by ... / Next, I'd like to ...
I'd like to fill you in on (some of) the details of ...
We'll come back to that later.
First(ly), second(ly), ... , and finally ...
To give you an example, ... / An example will show you how/why ...
Please take/have a brief look at ...
I'd like to introduce myself: I am ... /My name is ... and I am in charge of ...
As you can clearly see here, ... / This chart/graph shows you ...
If you have any questions, please wait until the end of the presentation. There will be ample[1] time to answer them then.
I'd like to take this opportunity to show you .../outline[2] ... for you/give you an overview of ...

[1] reichlich, genügend
[2] umreißen, skizzieren

1-minute talk

Use the phrases above and on p. 152 and prepare a 1-minute talk.

Talk about a product or a service that your company offers or something (= an object) you use in your company/institution every day.

- Try to create a sort of hype[1] around your product, service or object.
- Use adjectives and expressions from the boxes below and on p. 154.
- Look at the things that are wrong with your product, service or object and change them into positive aspects, if possible. (Example: an old, huge and heavy smartphone → it is robust and durable[2]!)

[1] Rummel, Wirbel
[2] strapazier-, widerstandsfähig

Adjectives		
amazing	efficient[3]	stunning[6]
powerful	awesome[4]	magical
productive[1]	great	remarkable[7]
incredible	wonderful	easy
unbelievable	fast	premium[8]
exciting	outstanding[5]	beautiful
phenomenal[2]	fantastic	top-notch[9]

Say these adjectives with a lot of enthusiasm: fantastic!!!

[1] leistungsfähig, ertragreich
[2] phänomenal
[3] wirkungsvoll, wirksam
[4] großartig, toll
[5] hervorragend, ausgezeichnet
[6] verblüffend, umwerfend
[7] bemerkenswert, erstaunlich
[8] hochwertig
[9] erstklassig

1 Vergnügen
2 hervorragend, erstklassig
3 Durchbruch
hier: bahnbrechend
4 fortschrittlich, fortgeschritten
5 *hier*: Ingenieurskunst, -leistung

Catchy sentences	
the best way to (do x) it's really easy to (do x) it's such a pleasure[1] (to do x) it's a revolution it just feels right it's a world class product it's a superbly[2] designed (product)	an incredible breakthrough[3] product it's just fun it's going to change the way we do x it's the most advanced[4] piece of (technology/clothing/stationery/engineering[5]) I don't have to change myself to fit the product, it fits me.

12.3 Project: Presenting your company

As your company is about to attend a trade fair in England, you have been given the task of delivering a presentation about your company for interested visitors. Use presentation software to prepare it. Please refer to Unit 3 of this book. On pp. 30–31 you will find an example of a company presentation, some useful phrases and also an idea of how to structure it. Of course, the structure there is not final. You may add whatever information about your company that you think is important or interesting for your audience, for example:

- the legal form[1]
- the industry your company operates in
- the department you are currently working in and your current tasks
- the name of the current CEO[2] (chief executive officer[2]) or MD (managing director) of your company
- important events like mergers[3], takeovers[4]/acquisitions[5], etc.

1 Rechtsform
2 Vorstandsvorsitzende/r
3 Fusion, Zusammenschluss
4 Übernahme
5 Aufkauf

Note

In English, the term ***industry*** is more widely used and also refers to sectors outside manufacturing/production, e.g. insurance, banking. The German equivalents are: Branche, Sektor, Zweig. Be careful: the English word ***branch*** means Filiale, Zweigstelle.

Info

Legal forms

German legal forms do not always have direct counterparts in other countries. Below you can see legal forms which are roughly equivalent to those in Germany.

Germany	UK	USA	Europe
Aktiengesellschaft (AG)	Public limited company (plc/PLC)	Corporation (Inc./Corp.)	Societas Europaea (SE)
Gesellschaft mit beschränkter Haftung (GmbH)	(Private) Limited company (Ltd/LTD)	Limited liability company (LLC)	–
Kommanditgesellschaft (KG)	Limited partnership (LP/L.P.)		–
Offene Handelsgesellschaft (OHG)	General partnership		–
Einzelunternehmen, eingetragener Kaufmann (e. K.)	Sole proprietor/trader/owner		–

Note

Remember to make use of the features of your presentation software:
- Show your company logo.
- Show pictures of your company, e.g. buildings, machinery, people.
- Use a template[1] in your company's corporate design[2], if available.
- Remember to make use of the things you have learnt about preparing presentations such as how to design slides[3] (e.g. not too much text per slide, contrasting[4] font[5] and background colour).

[1] Vorlage
[2] einheitliches Firmendesign
[3] Folie
[4] sich abhebend, kontrastierend
[5] Schrift(art)

Give feedback.

To evaluate your classmates' presentations, you can use the sheet on page 205.

Mediate.

In order to deal with questions that might arise during or after your presentation, you have prepared the list below. Read it and find English equivalents. Be as polite as possible.

1 Könnten Sie die Folie zur Firmengeschichte noch einmal zeigen?
2 Warum sind die Verkaufszahlen im letzten Jahr gesunken?
3 Könnten Sie den letzten Punkt noch einmal erläutern?
4 Warum haben Sie die Niederlassung in England geschlossen?
5 Welche Pläne für die Zukunft haben Sie?
6 Wie viele Azubis beschäftigen Sie?
7 Welche Produktneuheiten wollen Sie demnächst auf den Markt bringen?
8 Welche sind Ihre wichtigsten Märkte?
9 Wollen Sie noch mehr Geld in die Weiterbildung *(professional development)* Ihrer Beschäftigten investieren?
10 Was können Sie zur Rolle von Frauen in Ihrem Betrieb sagen?

Revision

"Some" and "any"

Be aware of the difference between *some* and *any*.

Some is used in positive statements and polite questions (offers and requests).
Examples: *Chris found some money in the pocket of his jacket.* (etwas Geld)
Can you give me some of these folders? (ein paar von diesen Ordnern)

Any is used in negative statements and questions that might prompt positive or negative answers.
Examples: *I don't have any friends.* ((gar) keine Freunde.)
Do you have/Are there any questions? (irgendwelche/noch Fragen)
Is there any milk left? ((noch) etwas Milch)

Any is used in statements which contain a negative word other than *not*, such as *hardly*, *never*, *barely*, or *without*, or when there is a suggestion of doubt, e.g. with *if* or *whether*.
Examples: *There can hardly be any doubt about it.* (eigentlich keinerlei Zweifel)
I wonder whether any of you have done their homework. (überhaupt jemand)

These rules also apply to the compounds of *some* or *any*:
somebody/anybody, something/anything, somewhere/anywhere, etc.

Fill in *some* or *any* or one of their compounds.

1 Yes, I've got _____ time this afternoon to discuss the marketing project.
2 I'm afraid we don't have _____ printer paper anymore.
3 What I'd really like now is _____ fresh air.
4 Are you hungry? I'll get you _____ to eat from the cafeteria.
5 Do you know _____ about the meeting that took place yesterday?
6 Yesterday, _____ broke the photocopier.
7 It's so noisy in here! I can't hear _____!
8 The folder has to be _____ in this office.
9 Where's Rick? I can't find him _____.
10 I hope you learnt _____ from your mistake.
11 I've invited _____ of our customers to our next fair.
12 I don't need _____ help with the filing. I can do it myself.

Translate the sentences below.

1 Manche unserer Kunden möchten unseren Newsletter nicht mehr bekommen.
2 Gibt es irgendwelche Informationen darüber, wer der neue Abteilungsleiter wird?
3 Kann ich noch irgendetwas für Sie tun?
4 Irgendjemand hat gestern Abend das Licht im Büro angelassen.
5 Bis jetzt habe ich keine Angebote für unsere neuen Büromöbel erhalten.
6 Ich benötige jemanden, der die Gäste aus Wales am Flughafen abholt.
7 Ich habe noch nichts von unserem Lieferanten gehört.
8 Unser 24-Stunden-Service ist etwas, das andere Unternehmen nicht bieten.

12.4 Describing graphs & diagrams

Tamara Klein is a German trainee doing a practical in the Irish company Innes LTD, which operates in the real estate[1] industry. Their activities involve property development[2] and management, services relating to the purchase and sale of commercial[3] and private properties[3], etc. Tamara has been given some data highlighting various points in the history and performance of the company. Her task is to prepare slides for a presentation at a conference of the management team at their headquarters.

Later, this information is to be made available to potential investors that Innes LTD are trying to attract, partly due to their currently somewhat difficult financial situation. In order to show how profitable an investment in this company could be. Tamara has drawn up several charts comparing the performance of their biggest competitors[4] in the Irish market. She shows the results to her boss to get his approval before finalising the charts.

1 Immobilie(n)
2 Grundstückserschließung, Immobilienentwicklung
3 Gewerbeimmobilie
4 Wettbewerber, Konkurrent

12.4.1 Pie chart

Tamara realises that percentages[1] are best shown as a piece of a circle to give you a quick idea of the share of each category. Therefore she decides to show the contributions of Innes's operations in different locations in Ireland to the total revenue of the group in a pie chart.

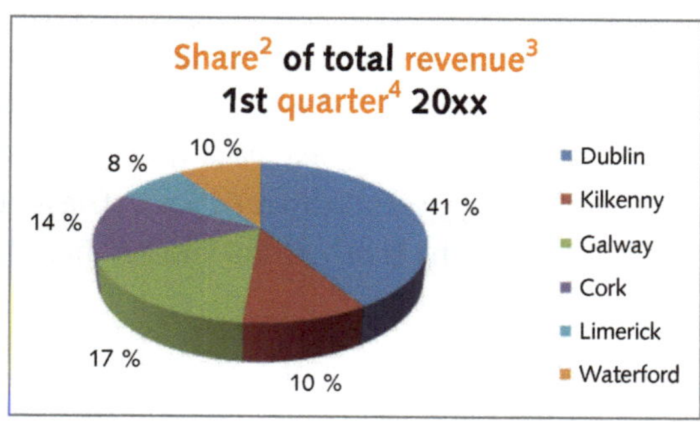

[1] *hier*: prozentualer Anteil
[2] Anteil
[3] Erlöse, Umsatz(-volumen)
[4] Quartal

Useful phrases

X makes up approximately[1]/nearly/almost half of our sales.

Y accounts for[2] just over/just under a third of the total amount.

X has a percentage of 20 per cent, compared to/with Y which has/whereas/ Y has (only) 18.5 per cent.

The red/green/yellow/... slice[3] represents a share of 45 per cent.

As you can see, X constitutes[4] a significant[5]/negligible[6] proportion[7] of the total amount.

[1] ungefähr, circa
[2] ausmachen, entfallen auf, betragen
[3] Anteil, (Kuchen-)Stück
[4] ausmachen, darstellen
[5] wesentlich, bedeutend
[6] vernachlässigbar, unbedeutend
[7] Anteil

Note

to account for is a useful verb phrase when dealing with figures/statistics. The best translations are "entfallen auf", "betragen" and "ausmachen". But in German the structure is different: „Auf Deutschland entfallen .../Der Anteil Deutschlands an ... beträgt ..."

Describe the pie chart above. Use the phrases in the box.

12.4.2 Bar chart

From her theoretical training in a German vocational school, Tamara knows very well that bar charts are used to visualise comparisons of different data for a given time period, e.g. comparing sales of different companies, staffing levels[1], investments or monthly/quarterly results[2] of a business unit[3].

[1] Personal(be)stand
[2] Quartalsergebnis
[3] Geschäftsbereich, -einheit

Useful phrases

Comparisons: X is higher/lower/bigger/smaller/more successful/less productive **than** Y.
X is (not quite/twice/three times) **as** big/functional/secure **as** Y.
X has grown more/less//faster/more slowly **than** Y.
X has acquired **more** customers **than** Y.
X has made **less** money **than** Y. *(uncountable)*
X has sold **fewer** items **than** Y. *(countable)*

Rankings: X is the highest/lowest//most/least valuable (of …)
X is followed by Y (with …), and finally we have Z with …
X comes first with … , Y comes second with …
X comes in first place with … , Y comes in last with …
First/second/third/next/last/last but one is X.
At the top/bottom, you can find X.

[1] Rentabilität, Gewinnsituation

In preparation for the visit of a potential investor at the end of the week, Tamara has prepared the bar chart below showing the profitability[1] of key competitors in comparison with that of Innes LTD.

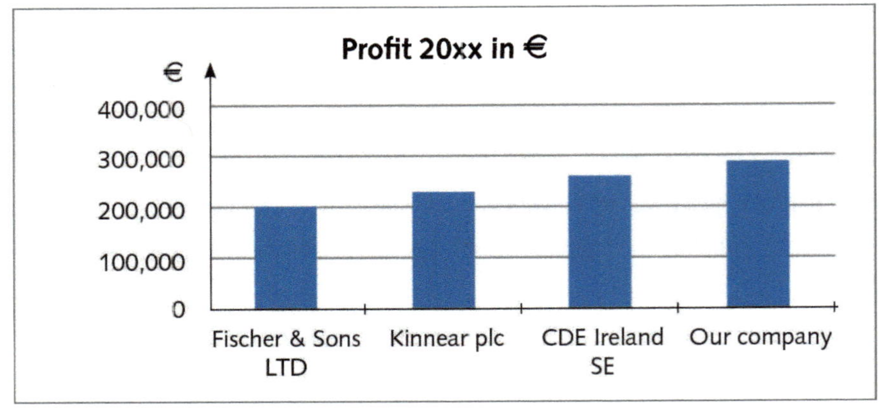

Describe the bar chart and turn to the Useful phrases for help.

Mediate. Note: Do not translate word for word.

In preparation for a company presentation to foreign visitors to be given by her head of department, Tamara has written down the information below. Now she only has to render[1] this information in English.

[1] wiedergeben, übertragen

Unser Absatzergebnis im letzten Jahr war positiv. Insgesamt erreichte der Absatz ein Allzeithoch *(all-time high)* von €2.772.500. Der Anstieg für das gesamte Jahr betrug *(to amount to)* 2,7 Prozent im Vergleich zum Vorjahr. Im ersten Quartal stiegen unsere Absätze nur leicht auf €695.630 an. Dabei zeigten insbesondere unsere Verkäufe im Raum Dublin einen Anstieg um mehr als 10 Prozent *(by … per cent)*. Unsere Verkäufe in Galway gingen allerdings um mehr als 7,5 Prozent zurück. Diese positive Entwicklung hielt *(to continue)* auch im zweiten Quartal an. Der Umsatz erreichte *(to reach)* €727.350 und war somit *(thus)* um 3 Prozent höher als im zweiten Quartal des Vorjahres. Das dritte Quartal war sehr enttäuschend, denn der Umsatz ging im Vergleich zum *(compared with/to)* Vorjahr *(year before/earlier)* um mehr als 7,5 Prozent auf €464.980 zurück. Dies ist das schlechteste Quartalsergebnis in den letzten fünf Jahren. Im letzten Quartal waren wir in allen unseren Filialen sehr erfolgreich und erreichten mit €886.540 einen Zuwachs von mehr als 10 Prozent. Das ist der höchste Quartalsumsatz in unserer Geschichte. Eine ähnliche Entwicklung konnten wir auch in den früheren Jahren beobachten.

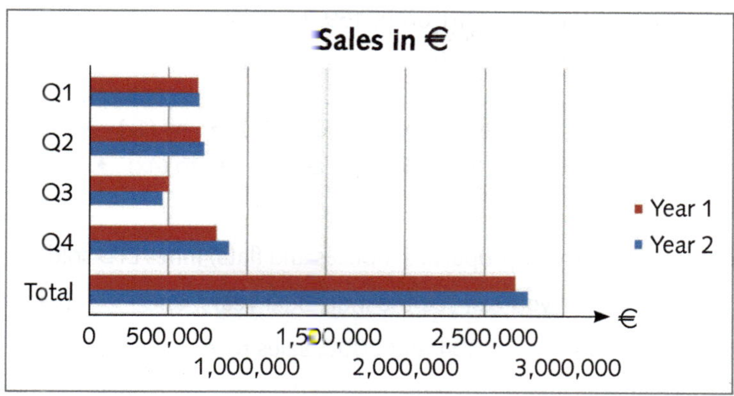

Convert this bar chart into a line graph.

Draw a line in a different colour for each year and add a third line for the year just ended. Use the figures in brackets (Q1 €724,805; Q2 €750,125; Q3 €445,427; Q4 €980,350 = €2,900,707).

Compare the quarterly results for each of the two years and work out the changes per quarter and for the years in percentage terms.

Think of a new set of figures and ask your partner to draw the graph.

12.4.3 Line chart

Tamara is also thinking about line charts (also called line graphs) to visualise the developments at Innes LTD (e.g. for turnover[1], marketing spending[2] or staffing levels, etc.) over a period of time and decides to show the number of properties sold in the graph below.

1 Umsatz
2 Marketingausgaben

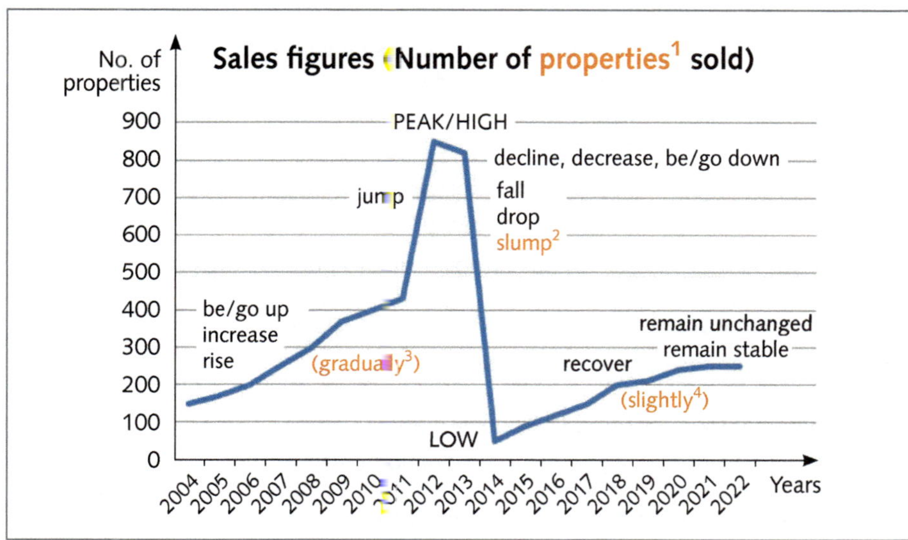

1 Immobilie
2 *hier*: abstürzen
3 stetig, kontinuierlich
4 geringfügig, leicht

Translate the terms used in the chart.

Have a close look at the terms and where they are positioned. Put them into three categories: upwards, downwards, no change.

Here is a description of the line chart on p. 159. Use the prepositions from the box below. Some are needed more than once.

• at (1x) • before (1x) • between (2x) • by (1x) •
• from … to (1x) • of (2x) • on (3x) • to (4x) •

[1] Achse
[2] sich erholen
[3] Wohnungsmarkt
[4] Hochkonjunktur

This line chart shows how many properties (houses and flats) Innes LTD sold _____ 2004 and 2022. _____ the x-axis[1] you can see the individual years, and _____ the y-axis the number of properties sold. _____ 2004 and 2008, sales rose gradually _____ 150 units _____ 420 units. Then they jumped sharply _____ 430 units _____ a peak _____ 850 units. Following this peak, sales declined slightly _____ 820 units. After that they dropped sharply _____ the all-time low _____ 50 units. Then sales recovered[2] slightly and remained stable _____ 250 units sold. You can clearly see when the crisis _____ the housing market[3] hit the company. Fortunately, we have now managed to return _____ the level of sales we had reached _____ the boom[4].

Note

When describing a line chart, bear in mind that you are talking about developments in the past!

*From 2020 to 2023 the price **went** up.*

Make sure you use the correct forms of the past tense of your verbs!

Learn about word formation.

Change the underlined words. If there is a noun, use a verb instead. If there is a verb, use a noun. Pay attention to adjectives and adverbs.

Example: There has been a slight recovery of sales figures in the last two months.
→ Sales figures have recovered slightly in the last two months.

1 Our turnover dropped dramatically due to poor advertising.
→ There was a _____ _____ in our turnover due to poor advertising.

2 There has been a steady rise of the customer base of our competition[1].
→ The customer base of our competition _____ _____ .

3 Our production costs increased steeply last year.
→ We experienced a _____ _____ in production costs last year.

4 A sharp decline in orders forced our company to lay off[2] a few workers.
→ Our company had to lay off a few workers because orders _____ _____ .

5 After the software update, complaints suddenly jumped to an all-time high.
→ The software update led to a _____ _____ of complaints to an all-time high.

[1] Konkurrenz, Wettbewerber
[2] freisetzen, entlassen

Info

How to describe a (line) chart

STEP 1: Overview

✓ Study the chart: First, read the title and subtitle of the graph. Then look at the source, if available.

✓ Check which values[1] are shown horizontally (x-axis) and vertically (y-axis).

STEP 2: Description

✓ Before you start, make sure you understand what you have been asked to do.

✓ Use the information obtained from Step 1 for a short introduction. Begin your presentation by stating the title and the source. Then describe the units on the x-axis (time periods) and the y-axis (quantities/units). Don't forget that your audience will see this chart for the first time and needs some time to understand what it is about.

✓ Depending on your task, describe the development for each time period or show a general trend over several periods.

✓ Mention striking[2] developments, e.g. all-time[3] highs[4] or lows[5]. If possible, give reasons for changes.

✓ Try and state why this chart is relevant[6].

[1] Wert
[2] auffällig
[3] Allzeit-
[4] Hoch, Höchststand
[5] Tief, Tiefststand
[6] bedeutsam, wichtig

When the boom began to lose momentum[1] and there were the first signs of an emerging[2] crisis, Innes LTD decided to reduce its spending on its advertising/marketing efforts[3]. A cost-cutting programme[4] was introduced in all departments. Tamara uses the data available to show the development of spending in the marketing department. This table is to be put into an information pack for the potential investors as well, but needs to be checked by the department heads[5] first.

[1] an Fahrt verlieren
[2] auftreten, sich herausbilden
[3] Aufwand
[4] Sparprogramm
[5] Abteilungsleiter/in

Describe the line chart below using the steps from the Info box.

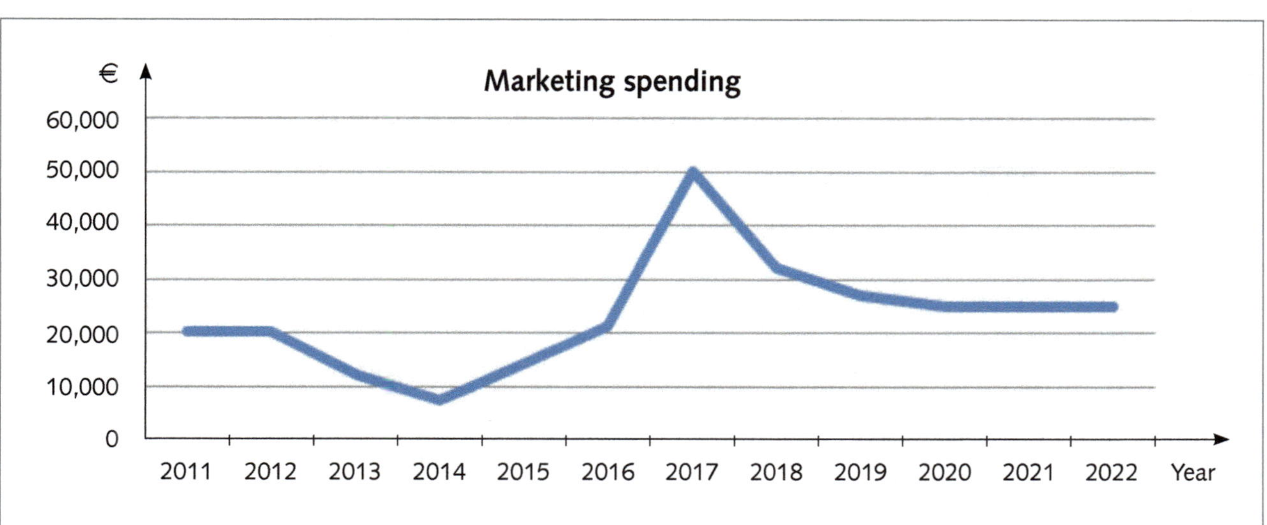

12.4.4 Preparing and presenting data

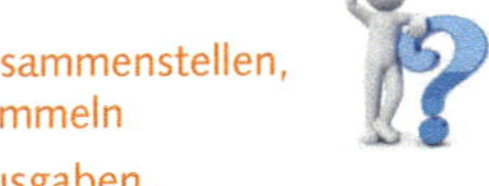

The data of staffing levels and staffing structure for the various locations of Innes LTD have already been compiled[1] in a table. The table also shows the total expenditure[2] for all types of staff in these locations.

[1] zusammenstellen, sammeln
[2] Ausgaben, Aufwendungen

Innes LTD: Staffing levels								
Year	**Branch**	**Dublin (HQ)**	**Kilkenny**	**Galway**	**Cork**	**Limerick**	**Water-ford**	**Total**
2020	Full-time	15	6	8	5	2	3	39
	Part-time	8	1	2	1	1	3	16
	Temporary[1]	5	2	1	1	1	0	10
	Total	28	9	1	7	4	6	65
	Staff costs	819,600	285,600	363,600	229,200	114,000	172,800	1,984,800
2021	Full-time	12	5	6	3	2	2	30
	Part-time	7	1	1	0	1	3	13
	Temporary	8	3	2	3	1	1	18
	Total	27	9	9	6	4	6	61
	Staff costs	739,200	265,200	285,600	169,200	114,000	152,400	1,725,600
2022	Full-time	10	4	3	1	2	1	21
	Part-time	2	1	0	0	0	3	6
	Temporary	13	3	4	5	2	2	29
	Total	25	8	7	6	4	6	56
	Staff costs	656,400	226,800	187,200	128,400	112,800	132,000	1,443,600

[1] zeitlich befristet, Zeit-, vorübergehend

Tamara has been asked to use this table as the starting point for a number of Power-Point slides that are also to be shown to the potential investors to visualise the changes in the composition[1] of staff and the development of staff costs for each location and for Innes LTD as a whole.

[1] Zusammensetzung

Present the data.
Study the chart carefully before dealing with the tasks below.

1 Decide on how to visualise the data and use the appropriate types of graphs.

2 With the information in the table above, prepare the corresponding graphs using spreadsheet software[1].

3 Present the data with the help of your graphs.

[1] Tabellenkalkulationsprogramm

Unit 13 Going to a trade fair

©davis-fotolia.com

©Sorbis-shutterstock-fotolia.com

13.1 Let's get going!

Let's talk about your experience with fairs.

- Have you ever been to a trade fair[1]? What was your experience?
- Have you seen advertisements for fairs? Which?
- Some cities call themselves "Messestadt". Can you mention any names?
- Which German trade fairs do you know about? Mention names and locations, if possible.
- Does your company/institution take part in fairs? – What can you say about this?

[1] Messe, Ausstellung

13.2 Getting information

Track 42

The engineering company[1] MarKestTech GmbH in Schwetzingen is a specialist manufacturer of measuring and testing equipment[2]. The management have decided to make a push[3] to further develop their business activities in the UK. They have been able to establish a good customer base already, but feel that the market offers many more opportunities. Anka Winters, who works there as a trainee office junior, has been asked to find out from their British representative[4] Tim Myers, based in Leeds, which fairs could be particularly suitable. And this is what Anka wrote.

> Dear Tim,
>
> I'm writing to you today on behalf of our management team[5].
>
> It's been decided to try and expand our UK operations by taking part in a specialist trade fair[6] for the industrial sector[7] in which we operate. And we would kindly ask you to find out about fair events for the engineering industries[8] in Britain.
>
> For the time being, it's only a question of getting as much information as possible about relevant[9] fairs. Please also let us know about the locations and the facilities[10] there, the dates and possibly also the costs involved[11].
>
> Could you please do that ASAP and let us have the results of your enquiries?
>
> Kind regards,
>
> Anka

[1] Maschinenbauunternehmen
[2] Mess- und Prüfgeräte
[3] energisch daran gehen
[4] (Außendienst-)Vertreter/in
[5] Führungsmannschaft
[6] Fachmesse
[7] Branche
[8] Maschinenbau
[9] einschlägig
[10] *hier*: Angebot für Aussteller
[11] *hier*: anfallende Kosten

Work with the text.

1 In a few words, say what Anka asks Tim to do.

2 Do you remember what ASAP stands for?

3 Decide which of the words and phrases in the e-mail (Box A) can be replaced by a synonym (Box B). Note: there are more synonyms than you need.

A Words and phrases in the e-mail (chronological order)	B Synonyms (alphabetical order)
for	at this stage
taking part	business activities
operations	check out
industrial sector	develop
find out	facilities
just now	industry
getting	obtaining
acceptable	on behalf of
locations	organisation
equipment	participating
	suitable
	venues

A couple of days later Tim replies.

Track 43

Dear Anka,

Thank you for your e-mail. I've checked out various websites and also phoned a number of exhibition centres[1]. The results are very disappointing indeed. Apart from Birmingham, London and Manchester, the exhibition centres do not host[2] any major[3] international trade fairs for the manufacturing[4] and engineering industries[4]. The events shown in the fair calendars very often are one-day events only aimed at[5] a general business public[6], tradespeople[7] and DIY enthusiasts[8]. To me, this does not seem worth taking into consideration, especially in view of[9] our product range and the kind of customers that we are trying to win.

For your information, I have attached details of three trade shows that could possibly be of interest.

It might be an idea to consider a participation[10] in the Aero Engineering Event; whether as a visitor or an exhibitor[11] is for the management to decide. I cannot really make any recommendation.

I'm sorry I can't be more positive.

Kind regards,

Tim

[1] Messezentrum
[2] veranstalten, ausrichten
[3] groß
[4] verarbeitende Industrie
[5] sich richten an
[6] *hier*: Fachpublikum
[7] Handwerker *(pl)*
[8] interessierte Heimwerker
[9] *hier*: wenn man … bedenkt, im Hinblick auf
[10] Teilnahme
[11] Aussteller

Note

There is a slight difference in meaning: ***fair*** refers to an event where goods are shown that can be purchased; ***exhibition*** is used above all for events where goods are shown (in the fine arts). But there is no clear dividing line, as you can see in the texts in this Unit. In the end it comes down to language usage. Just learn the words as shown here.

Work with the text.

1 In the text, find expressions showing that Tim is not very happy.

2 Prepare a list of terms and phrases that refer to trade shows.

Anka phones the managing director to give her/him a brief summary of the content of Tim's reply to her mail. Summarise the content of the e-mail on p. 164 in German.

Attachment to Tim's e-mail

In the attachment Anka finds this information:

28–29 Sep	Northern Manufacturing & Electronics This event in Manchester (EventCity Exhibition Space[1]) showcases[2] products from the electronics and electrical goods, manufacturing, repairs and maintenance industries.
25 Oct	Engineering Testing Show The 1-day show held in Derby (Roundhouse) showcases products related to technological developments in the engineering testing[3] industry and in the business services[4], education & training industries.
2–3 Nov	Aero Engineering Show The outstanding UK-based event held in Birmingham (National Exhibition Centre – NEC) for the aero-engineering industry offers excellent B2B dealings[5] and business development and networking opportunities. The focus is on R&D, design, testing, supply chain, production, assembly, components and MRO engineering. With 7,000+ UK companies working in aeronautics engineering, the event is of interest for companies operating in related fields[6] such as manufacturers or component suppliers.

[1] Ausstellungsfläche
[2] zeigen, ausstellen
[3] technische Erprobung
[4] Dienstleistungen für Unternehmen
[5] *hier*: Geschäfte, Geschäftsmöglichkeiten
[6] *hier*: verwandtes Gebiet

Note

B2B (business to business) = activities/communication between companies (marketing term), cf. also ***B2C (business to consumer)*** = activities/communication between companies and customers/consumers

R&D (research & development) = F & E (Forschung & Entwicklung)

MRO (maintenance, repair and operations) = Instandhaltung, Reparatur & Betrieb

"+" after a numeral is a short form meaning ***more than***.

Work with the text.

Anka finds the technical vocabulary confusing. Here is a list of the German terms to help her understand. Try and find the English equivalents in the attachment on p. 165. If need be, use your (online) dictionary.

Bildung & Ausbildung	Liefer-, Wertschöpfungskette
Dienstleistungen für Unternehmen	Luftfahrt(-technik)
Flugzeugbau	Montage, Zusammenbau
Gestaltung	Technische Erprobung
Instandhaltung, Reparatur & Betriebstechnik	Vernetzung, Netzwerkaktivitäten
Komponentenbau	Wartung, Instandhaltung
	Zulieferer für Bauteile

Anka shortens the information in the attachment and prepares a table with just the key points for the management team. Draft a list in German.

Anka, on her own initiative, phones Tim to find out whether he has any strong views[1] with regard to participating in[2] or just visiting any of these events. In groups, think about suggestions.

In small groups, work out and then act out the telephone dialogue between Anka and Tim.

1 klare/eindeutige Meinung
2 teilnehmen an

13.3 Fair business in Germany

Anka has never been to a trade fair before and wants to know more about these events. Read what she found on the internet:

Fairs worldwide – some facts
31,000 fairs staged[1] worldwide every year
1,200 fair venues[2] worldwide
4.4 million exhibitors
260 million fair visitors[3] p.a.[4]
German exhibitors spend an average of €170,000 p.a.

1 veranstalten, ausrichten
2 Messestandort
3 Messebesucher
4 p.a. = per annum – jährlich

DIGITAL+ Track 44

©D. Wessels

Germany accounts for about 10 per cent of the worldwide trade fair business[1]. This may partly be due to the history of fairs in Germany. In the Middle Ages, the fairs in Frankfurt and Leipzig enjoyed[2] an excellent reputation far beyond[3] their regions, something which they have been able to maintain and build on. And then there is Germany's geographical position in the very centre[4] of Europe – a huge market of more than 500 million consumers almost on the doorstep[5].

Originally, fairs were a kind of shop window for the whole range of regional trades and industries[6]. This is still true for many local or regional fairs. But generally speaking[7], the trend has been to more specialisation[8] and internationalisation[9].

1 Messegeschäft
2 *hier*: haben
3 weit über … hinaus
4 mitten in
5 vor der Haustür
6 Handwerk u. Gewerbe
7 allgemein gesehen
8 Spezialisierung
9 Internationalisierung

Today fairs are organised for a large number of industries such as vehicle production, logistics, printing, food, hotel & catering, electronics, aviation, leather goods, jewellery, tourism, caravanning, outdoor sports, equestrianism, to mention but a few. At the same time, many fairs have become truly international. Some events in Germany attract up to 50 per cent of exhibitors and 30 per cent of visitors from abroad.

Attending fairs[11] is a must for manufacturers and service providers[12], for buyers in industry and commerce[13], the distributors[14] (in the wholesale[15] and retail trades[16]) and also for those specialists who need to keep up to date[17] so that they can run their businesses[18] efficiently. New products, recent developments and the range of services can be shown and explained to the public at large[19]. Exhibitors can see what their competitors are offering. Such events are also ideally suited[20] for maintaining and developing contacts with existing foreign customers. In many cases visiting them in their respective[21] countries would be too costly in terms of[22] expenses and time required. And in addition, the general public can get a comprehensive overview of what is available or new in the market.

Communication and information are key activities at fairs. Conversations in fair booths[23] provide an opportunity to talk to prospective buyers, to strengthen existing customer relations, to find out about market trends and to get an idea of the general situation in the market. And of course, a fair is a market in its own right[24]. Fairgoers[25] get (detailed) product information orally[26] or in written form. They can sample[27] products, can look at competing products[28] displayed at other stands, can compare prices and terms and then decide what to do when they get home. Obviously, the exhibitors expect their business to develop further, especially because of the contacts with new customers.

Therefore, a trade fair is an ideal marketing tool[29] in B2B and B2C communication. More general fairs are organised for both the interested parties in the field and the general public. But whatever the kind of fair, fairs mean big business for the hotel & catering trade, fair stand designers[30], hostesses, language experts, taxis and many others.

[11] Messebesuch
[12] Dienstleister
[13] Handel
[14] Vertriebsgesellschaft
[15] Großhandel
[16] Einzelhandel
[17] sich auf dem Laufenden halten
[18] Unternehmen leiten
[19] breite Öffentlichkeit
[20] gut geeignet
[21] jeweilig
[22] hinsichtlich
[23] Messestand
[24] für sich genommen
[25] Messebesucher/in
[26] mündlich
[27] probieren
[28] Konkurrenzprodukt
[29] Marketinginstrument
[30] Messestandgestalter

Specialist terms

1 Use your (online) dictionary to check out the German for the industries listed in the third paragraph (ll. 14 - 18).

2 Which of them are you interested in? State your reasons and discuss them in class.

Please answer these questions.

1 Why is Germany an important location for trade fairs?
2 How did the fair activities develop?
3 Mention some specialisations of trade fairs.
4 Give examples showing the degree of international appeal of the fairs held in Germany.
5 Why is attending fairs a must for manufacturers and service providers?
6 Why do specialists and the general public go to fairs?
7 Describe the role that communication plays for both the exhibitors and the fairgoers.
8 List some of the sectors that benefit from trade fairs.

13.4 Preparing for the fair

[1] Strategietreffen
[2] sich dranmachen

In a strategy meeting[1] and based on the information provided by Anka, it is decided that two engineers will visit the Northern Manufacturing & Electronics in Manchester and also that the company will participate in the Aero Engineering Show in Birmingham. There is still plenty of time (eight months) to get organised. So they set about[2] planning.

What needs to be done to get prepared for the fair participation? In groups, collect ideas.

13.4.1 Things to do

Together with her boss, Christian Hinterseer of the Marketing and Distribution Department, Anka comes up with these ideas.

[1] Zugang
[2] Messegelände
[3] Auftragnehmer
[4] Standfläche
[5] Flussdiagramm
[6] Messegesellschaft
[7] *hier*: Transport organisieren
[8] Ausstellungsstück
[9] Reisevorbereitungen
[10] *hier*: bekannt machen, vermarkten
[11] Messeteilnahme
[12] Fachzeitschrift
[13] Verkaufsprospekte
[14] anwerben, einstellen
[15] Freikarte

No.	Task	Christian's job	Anka's job	Time-frame
1	Arrange access[1] to exhibition grounds[2] for staff and contractors[3]			
2	Book stand space[4]			
3	Draw up and circularise a flowchart[5] of activities before the fair starts			
4	Find out about charges for stand space and facilities (water, electricity, cleaning, etc.)			
5	Find out about hotel accommodation and make bookings			
6	Get information from the National Exhibition Centre			
7	Have texts translated and brochures printed			
8	Invite selected customers to reception on fair stand			
9	Make booking with fair organisers[6]			
10	Make transport arrangements[7] for exhibits[8]			
11	Make travel arrangements[9] for Schwetzingen staff			
12	Market[10] fair participation[11] in trade magazines[12] (British & Irish)			
13	Order food and drink for visitors & staff			
14	Organise English courses for staff attending the fair			
15	Plan for the design and construction of fair stand			
16	Prepare suitable texts for fair catalogue			
17	Prepare sales literature[13] (general and product-related)			
18	Recruit[14] local staff to welcome fair visitors to the stand			
19	Select products to be shown			
20	Send circular to customers with complimentary tickets[15]			

1 Did Christian & Anka forget anything? Compare their list with your ideas.

2 A lot of work needs to be done. So Christian & Anka share it out. Decide who is going to do what. Tick the appropriate boxes in the table on p. 168.

13.4.2 Action plan

Christian and Anka have worked out a fairly detailed action plan[1] for everything that should be done before the fair.

[1] Aktionsplan

Timeframe	Before the event		
6 months to go	Set business objectives[1]	Define business policy for UK market, agree budgets, book space	Make fair participation known through e-mail and social media contacts
4 months to go	Stand design	Finalise plan for the stand; contact stand designers[2], get quotes[3] and decide	
2 months to go	Finalise all activities	Confirm floor space[4] with fair organisers, order furniture, electrics[5], Wi-Fi, audio-visual equipment etc.	
3 weeks to go	Organise stand activities	Customer relations: plan meetings at the stand, send out invitations	
2 weeks to go	Better be safe than sorry	Contact all suppliers & service providers[6]: double-check[7] all arrangements	
1 week to go	Staff briefing[8]	Rehearse[9] with staff, explain duties & rotas[10], give useful tips; sort out remaining problems	
Show time			

[1] Geschäftsziel
[2] Standdesigner, Messebauer
[3] Angebot einholen
[4] *hier*: Standfläche
[5] Elektrik
[6] Dienstleister
[7] nochmals prüfen
[8] Anweisungen ans Personal
[9] proben
[10] Dienstplan

1 Decide when approximately[1] the things listed above have to be done. Use the categories in the timeframe[2] column on p. 168.
Also consider:
   1 What has to be done immediately?
   2 What has to be done immediately before the fair starts?
Add your ideas that are not covered in the list above.

2 Anka has been asked by Christian to explain the chart in a meeting of the management team and some colleagues of the sales department. Use the information in the table to make an oral presentation.

[1] ungefähr
[2] Zeitfenster, -raum

Share in the follow-up work[1] after the fair.

What happens after the fair (assessing the success, following up[2] the fair contacts, etc.) is very much up to the management, the sales and the marketing people. But not only. Form groups for each of the points 1 to 3 below.

1 Do you have any ideas what should be done to follow up new business contacts?

2 In what way could an office trainee support any of these activities?

3 And do not forget the costs. Think of what exactly has to be paid for (staff, goods and services, etc.). – And technically, what are the steps involved?

Draw up lists for all these points.

[1] Nachbereitung
[2] nachverfolgen

13.5 Contacting customers

Track 45

The management have decided to invite all existing British customers to a reception on the fair stand on the evening of the first day of the fair. Anka has been asked to put the German version of the invitation circular into English. This is what it looks like after Tim's corrections have been made.

[1] Fachzeitschrift
[2] eintragen
[3] Kalender
[4] Messeveranstalter
[5] Konstruktion im Flugzeugbau
[6] *hier*: zur Verfügung stehen
[7] Höhepunkt
[8] erkunden, ausloten
[9] Zusammenarbeit
[10] Gang
[11] einlösen, eintauschen
[12] (sehr) herzlich
[13] Zettel, Abschnitt
[14] Produktneuheit

©Tanongrattana-shutterstock.com

Dear Customer,

You may have noticed from trade magazines[1] that the **AERO ENGINEERING SHOW** in Birmingham will be held in a few weeks' time. The event will take place at the National Exhibition Centre (NEC) from 2 to 3 November. Be sure to pencil in[2] this date in your diary[3].

As we have learnt from the fair organisers[4], several hundred companies in aeronautics engineering and related fields will be presenting their products. So, the fair promises to be an excellent opportunity for exhibitors and visitors alike to get an overview of the current trends in aeronautics design[5] and manufacturing. And in addition, many firms from the maintenance and repair industries will be attending the fair as well. An entire hall has been set aside[6] for exhibitors of measuring and testing equipment.

MarKestTech GmbH have decided to take part in this highlight[7] in the British fair calendar. We feel we want to be closer to our customers, have an opportunity to talk to you about our very exciting recent developments and, of course, to explore[8] possibilities for even closer cooperation[9].

We would like to invite you to meet us at our stand in Hall 4, Aisle[10] B14. Enclosed please find two vouchers which can be redeemed[11] online for complimentary tickets. Just go to the NEC website, click "Tickets", enter the voucher code and then print out your tickets.

On Thursday, 2 November, at 5 pm, there will be a reception on our stand to which we cordially[12] invite you. Kindly use the attached slip[13] to let us know whether you will be attending this event.

For your information we have also enclosed our latest brochure and hope you will find some new products there that may be of interest for your business. We will exhibit some of these product innovations[14] on our stand.

We very much look forward to meeting you at the fair in a few weeks' time.

Yours sincerely,

Christian Hinterseer

Marketing and Distribution

Work with the text.

1 Give each paragraph a short title.

2 Please answer these questions.

1 Where is the fair to be held?

2 How many companies will be exhibiting at the fair?

3 Which industries will be represented at the fair?
4 Why have MarKestTech GmbH decided to participate in this event?
5 How can MarKestTech GmbH customers get their tickets?
6 Why should MarKestTech GmbH customers return the slip?
7 What can the customers find in the brochure?

3 Find words and phrases that are meant to arouse the interest of the reader.

4 Decide which of the terms and phrases in the letter on p. 170 could be replaced by one of the following:

• are also sending you • developments • discover • discuss with you • enterprises • exchanged	• exhibition • fairgoers • furthermore • may have read in • new products • outstanding occasion	• participating in • please detach and return the slip • showcasing • we have enclosed • would be delighted to see you

13.6 Changing a reservation

A couple of weeks before the start of the fair, the management of MarKestTech GmbH have decided to ask Anka to join them on the trip to Birmingham, because the English-language skills[1] of the other staff, the Managing Director, her boss and two of the product managers are not very good. But she has continued to improve her English in evening classes[2] and spent a couple of holidays with her exchange partner in Coventry, not far from Birmingham. She now needs to phone the hotel in Birmingham to change the reservation.

[1] Sprachkompetenz
[2] Abendkurs

Do a role play.

Before you start on this task, work out what you want/need to say. Don't ask/answer the questions all at once. And don't forget: you want to be polite and make a good impression.

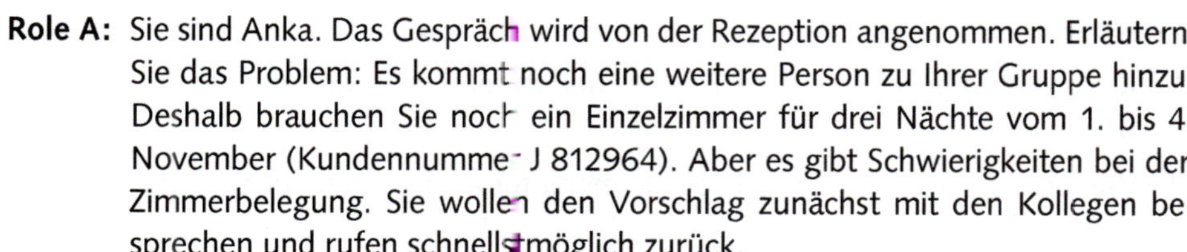

Role A: Sie sind Anka. Das Gespräch wird von der Rezeption angenommen. Erläutern Sie das Problem: Es kommt noch eine weitere Person zu Ihrer Gruppe hinzu. Deshalb brauchen Sie noch ein Einzelzimmer für drei Nächte vom 1. bis 4. November (Kundennummer J 812964). Aber es gibt Schwierigkeiten bei der Zimmerbelegung. Sie wollen den Vorschlag zunächst mit den Kollegen besprechen und rufen schnellstmöglich zurück.

You will find the text for Role B on p. 206.

Revision

Progressive forms

The progressive forms, also called continuous forms, are used to talk about activities that take some time before the action is completed. These forms can be used in most tenses. Very often the statements are accompanied by expressions that say that the action lasted or will last for some time.

Examples:

Present progressive – something is happening at the moment of speaking

(Right now) I'm looking at the graphs showing the development of our staff numbers.

But: *I watch the news every night.* (repeated action) – *I live in Berlin.* (general statement)

Past progressive – ongoing event in the past

Yesterday at this time I was writing a letter to my friend.

Past progressive – an ongoing event is interrupted

I was writing an e-mail when my boss came in.

But: *I went to a concert last week.* (event/action completed in the past)

Future progressive – action in progress at some time in the future

Tomorrow at 8 o'clock I will be seeing a client.

But: *I'll talk to you later today.* (intention) – *It'll be a busy week.* (prediction)

Present perfect progressive – used for events that started in the past and are still continuing or whose effect is still being felt

We've been discussing this problem for weeks now.

But: *I haven't been to this exhibition yet.* (relation to the present time)

Past perfect progressive – ongoing event until a point in the past

I had been looking forward to going to this fair. But in the end I couldn't.

But: *I hadn't seen the car coming when I hit it.* (an event in the past comes before another)

Future II progressive – action in progress in the future seen from a point after this event

I'm sure that by the time you get there she will have been trying to reach you on the phone.

But: *By this time tomorrow I will have been to the bank to get some money.* (an event in the future is completed before a certain time)

The simple forms refer to events that occur frequently, to habits or to facts.

Learn to use the progressive forms.

Which verb form is correct?

1 My boss had been living/had lived in London for 5 years and then took up a job in Glasgow.

2 We looked/have been looking at the menu for a long time, but can't make up our minds what to eat.

3 I was just keying/just keyed data into the computer when my boss interrupted me.

4 I drink/am drinking fruit juice every morning, but I didn't this morning.

5 She was warning/warned me about the dangers of drinking too much coffee.

6 I like/am liking my new job in the logistics department.

7 My colleague is telling/tells me that I should check my e-mails first thing every morning.

8 Tomorrow at this time I will sit/will be sitting on the plane to Birmingham.

Use the simple or the progressive form. Express these ideas in English.

D – E

Sagen Sie, dass

1 Sie in Darmstadt wohnen.
2 er gerade einen Bericht schreibt.
3 Sie gerade nach Hotelunterkünften in Birmingham gesucht haben.
4 Sie bis jetzt noch nie auf einer Messe waren.
5 er sich gerade einen Bericht angesehen hatte, als das Telefon schellte.
6 Sie gleich mit Ihrer Chefin sprechen wollen.
7 er seit mehr als 3 Jahren Französisch lernt.
8 Sie morgen um diese Zeit schon Ihre E-Mails beantwortet haben.

13.7 How to get there

When you travel to a place that you don't know, it's always good to get some advice[1] beforehand[2] from someone who knows their way around[3]. This also goes for[4] drivers who can use their sat nav[5] or for smartphone users.

[1] Rat(schlag)
[2] vorab
[3] sich auskennen
[4] zutreffen auf
[5] Navigationsgerät

13.7.1 Learn to read a site map[1]

1 Are you a good at giving directions[2]? Why do you think so?
2 Are there any differences between males and females when it comes to giving and receiving directions?

Maps of any kind use colour coding[3] and signs (a lot of them used internationally) to make it easier for users to find their way around[4].

[1] Lage-, Übersichtsplan
[2] Weg erklären
[3] Farbmarkierung
[4] sich zurechtfinden

Note

British motorways are numbered M1, M4, M45, etc. Major roads carry numbers such as A1, A11, A925. Similar to the numbering in Germany, the single-digit numbers refer to long-distance motorways or roads.

On the site map of the National Exhibition Centre on p. 174 find the following:

1 the railway station,
2 the motorway junction[1] J6,
3 the West Midlands bus stop D,
4 the shuttle bus stops and the toilets on the Car Parks North complex,
5 the gates G1 to G5,
6 the Atrium and Piazza entrances.

Describe exactly where on the site map you found these places.

[1] (Autobahn-)Anschlussstelle

The NEC and The NEC Arena site plan

www.necgroup.co.uk

To Birmingham New Street Station
Bickenhill Lane
Premier Travel Inn
Express by Holiday Inn
N10a
N10b
N10
N9b
N12
N11
N9a
N8b
N8a
M6 Junction 4
M6/M1
G5
G4
Birmingham International Airport
Terminal 1 (Main Terminal)
Terminal 2 (Eurohub)
Air-Rail Link
Piazza entrance 2
NEC House
Warehouses
N4
N6
N3
N7
N2
N5
Hall 19
Hall 18
Hall 17
Hall 20
Hall 6
Hall 7
Hall 8
Hall 16
Atrium
Atrium entrances
B'ham Int. Rail Station
Hall 3
Hall 3a
Hall 2
Piazza
Hall 4
Pedestrian Skywalk
Hall 1
Hall 5
Hall 9
Hall 10
Hall 11
Hall 12
N1
North Way
G3
G1
West Car Park
Pavilion
Piazza entrance 1
Hilton Birmingham Metropole Hotel
The NEC Arena
Pendigo Lake
Forum
East Way
E1
M42
E3
E2
Birmingham
Crowne Plaza Hotel
G2
South Lorry Park
South Way
S6
E4
S3
S5
S7
E5
A45
6
To London Euston Station
M40/M5
M42
A45
Coventry
N
W
E
S

Key

Hall 9 Exhibition hall
Information Point - telephone 0121 767 3888
Medical Centre
Car parks
South: S3, S4, S5, S6, S7
East: E1, E2, E3, E4, E5
North: N1 - N12
West: West Car Park
The NEC plantation

(A) Car park for people with disabilities
(B) Outdoor Exhibition Area
(C) Taxis
(D) West Midlands bus stop
(E) Shuttle bus to halls
(F) Footbridge to rail station
(G1) to (G5) Gates 1 to 5
Toilets (car park)

P169(5072) 244889/05 10/05

the nec arena
birmingham

13.7.2 Learn to give directions

Using the site map of the National Exhibition Centre, Anka works out which routes customers of MarKestTech GmbH should take to get to Hall 4 of the exhibition site.

Useful phrases

Turn left/right at the (first/second/... set of) traffic lights/(first/second/...) crossing.

Go/walk/drive straight on for about ... yards/metres.

Take the first/second ... road/street on the left/right.

Then you come to/reach ...

Follow the signs for ...

Leave the motorway at junction ...

You will see a (tall building, little park, ...) on your left/right.

On your left/right there is ...

Walk/drive/go past the ...

When you come to ... it's only a few ... steps/yards/metres till you reach the ...

Our office is in the ... building on the ... floor.

Be careful. There is a speed restriction[1] on this section of the road/motorway.

Take the filter[2] to the left/right.

Stay in the left/right/centre lane.

You will join a dual carriageway[3]/three-lane road.

[1] Geschwindigkeitsbeschränkung
[2] *hier*: (Abbiege-)Spur
[3] vierspurige Straße

Prepare short written directions for the fair visitors. Explain your directions to your classmates.

1 From the railway station to Hall 4.
2 From the M42 to the East and South Car Parks.
3 From the centre of Birmingham on the A45 to West Car Park.
4 The route from Birmingham Airport (Terminal 1) to Hall 4.
5 The shortest routes from the car parks E1 to E5 to Hall 4.
6 The shortest routes from the car parks S1 to S7 to Hall 4.
7 The shortest routes from West car park to Hall 4.

13.8 Share your experience of fairs.

Talk about your own experience of local/regional events.

1 When did these fairs take place? Are they regular events?
2 Where did they take place? Indoors or in the open air?
3 How and where were they advertised?
4 What were the goods displayed or sold?
5 Who do you think the visitors were?

©D. Wessels

1 What kind of role do outdoor craft fairs play in the activities of your local community?

2 Can you make out a difference between indoor and open-air fair events? Describe some of the characteristic features.

13.9 Revise your vocabulary

In the puzzle below, find words that fit these definitions:

1 anything one can eat	11 someone who goes to see and buy goods displayed
2 area that can be used	12 something that is made to be sold
3 closed-in place where goods are shown	13 space in exhibition hall where people walk
4 company showing goods	14 space where a play is performed
5 event where goods are shown	15 time in which something can be done
6 event where goods are shown and sold	16 to display goods to the public
7 going to an event to show one's goods	17 to give special attention to something
8 large area where goods are displayed	18 to receive and entertain guests
9 list showing who is to do certain jobs	19 to work out what something should look like
10 person/company who is given a job to do something	20 train or bus regularly going back and forth between A and B

E	U	T	R	A	D	E	■	F	A	I	R	A	I
U	P	I	B	M	A	E	G	A	E	H	L	P	O
G	D	M	S	H	S	L	F	S	A	I	S	L	E
I	R	E	H	D	H	P	O	I	B	G	R	E	X
L	O	■	U	E	O	B	O	O	T	H	U	W	H
S	T	F	T	S	W	Y	D	G	O	L	V	S	I
P	A	R	T	I	C	I	P	A	T	I	O	N	B
A	P	A	L	G	A	W	A	E	T	G	C	A	I
C	K	M	E	N	S	T	A	G	E	H	O	F	T
E	M	E	■	Z	E	P	E	A	Y	T	N	G	I
W	R	A	S	I	P	R	O	D	U	C	T	I	O
R	E	V	E	H	B	N	D	A	M	C	R	K	N
F	A	I	R	G	R	O	U	N	D	D	A	W	A
A	N	D	V	S	T	U	P	E	A	L	C	G	Z
K	F	A	I	R	G	O	E	R	A	M	T	P	O
Z	O	N	C	G	P	C	N	B	W	H	O	S	T
F	T	P	E	X	H	I	B	I	T	O	R	T	H

Note

Some terms have two parts which are separated by a black square. The letters in the highlighted squares tell you that a "room" must be "built" to show the goods at a fair.

					■												

Unit 14 Working in human resources (HR)

14.1 Let's get going!

1 In class, find out and compare what contacts and experiences you have had with the people from the HR department[1] when you applied for a trainee post as office junior.

2 Describe in what form HR work is visible in your business/institution.

3 How many people work in HR in your business/institution? What are their functions?

©DOC RABE Media-fotolia.com

4 On the basis of your experience with HR up to now, would you consider working there when you have completed[2] your training? Say why or why not.

1 Personalabteilung
2 *hier*: beenden, abschließen

Info

The term "human resources management" or simply HR has replaced the more old-fashioned concept of "personnel management". As far as language is concerned, people (and the skills, knowledge and experience they have) are now treated as one of the three factors of production[1] which in traditional economic theory were: land (soil[2] and raw materials), labour[3] (availability of workers) and capital (goods used for the production of other goods). For most people, activities in human resources are linked to employing and paying workers. But HR is much more than that.

1 Produktionsfaktor
2 Boden
3 Arbeit

In groups of three or four, find at least five words (nouns, verbs, adjectives) that can be linked to human resources. Compare your lists and throw out those words that occur more than once. Replace them by others. Try and put together word families (e.g. job interview, to interview, interviewee)

14.2 Interview with an HR manager[1]

DIGITAL+
Track 46

As part of her project work for her school, Lizzy Hamilton is doing some research into the work done in an HR department. She has arranged an interview with the HR manager of a major food processing company[2] in her hometown of Dundee. In addition to fruit and vegetables purchased from other sources, the company also uses locally produced vegetables and soft fruits (strawberries, raspberries, red and black currants[3], etc.) to make frozen fruit and vegetables, fruit preserves[4], jams etc. for the sale in supermarkets as well as to the hotel and catering trade[5]. Lizzy wants to find out what exactly HR work involves and has prepared a list of questions she wants to ask the HR manager, Geoff Bryant.

1 Personalleiter/in
2 Lebensmittel verarbeitendes Unternehmen
3 rote u. schwarze Johannisbeeren
4 Fruchtkonserven
5 Hotel- und Gaststättengewerbe

Study Lizzy's list and then find out which of the answers a) to j) below given by the HR manager relate to which question.

1 *What do you do to get new employees?*
2 *How do you select a new employee from a long list of candidates?*
3 *What is the final stage in the recruitment[1] process?*
4 *How about the chances of getting on in your job?*
5 *How do you assess[2] people's work?*
6 *How about training?*
7 *What do you do about harassment[3] at work?*
8 *Did you ever have to reduce staff?*
9 *Did you ever have to dismiss[4] people?*
10 *How often do you have to deal with disputes[5] and matters of discipline?*

1 *hier*: Personalbeschaffung
2 bemessen, bewerten
3 Belästigung
4 entlassen
5 Streit(igkeit), Auseinandersetzung

The answers of Geoff Bryant, the HR manager

Track 47

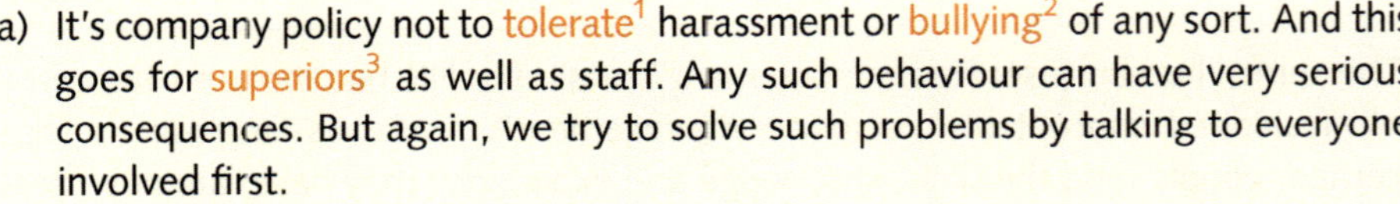

a) It's company policy not to tolerate[1] harassment or bullying[2] of any sort. And this goes for superiors[3] as well as staff. Any such behaviour can have very serious consequences. But again, we try to solve such problems by talking to everyone involved first.

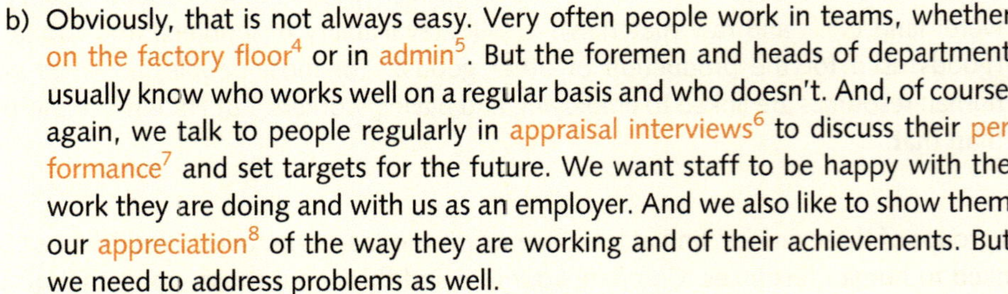

b) Obviously, that is not always easy. Very often people work in teams, whether on the factory floor[4] or in admin[5]. But the foremen and heads of department usually know who works well on a regular basis and who doesn't. And, of course, again, we talk to people regularly in appraisal interviews[6] to discuss their performance[7] and set targets for the future. We want staff to be happy with the work they are doing and with us as an employer. And we also like to show them our appreciation[8] of the way they are working and of their achievements. But we need to address problems as well.

c) Of course, we need to draw up a contract of employment[9] in which we lay down[10] all the important details of employment, that's to say the job title[11], salary or wage, employee benefits, working hours, holiday entitlement[12], etc. This has to be signed by both parties.

©Stock Photo Pro-fotolia.com

d) Promotion[13] is very important to motivate staff and to show that we appreciate the quality of their work. Empowerment[14], that means giving people more responsibility, more scope for deciding things on their own, is very important as well. The transfer[15] to another post within the company is another tool[16] that we like to use – recruitment from within[17] as we call it. In some exceptional[18] cases, we grant people a bonus or maybe a pay rise[19].

1 dulden
2 Belästigung, Mobbing
3 Vorgesetzte/r
4 *hier*: in der Produktion
5 *(coll.)* Verwaltung
6 Mitarbeitergespräch
7 Leistung
8 Wertschätzung
9 Arbeitsvertrag
10 niederlegen
11 Stellenbezeichnung
12 Urlaubsanspruch
13 Beförderung
14 Ermächtigung
15 Versetzung
16 Werkzeug, Instrument
17 interne Personalbeschaffung
18 außergewöhnlich
19 Gehaltserhöhung

e) It's never easy to cut jobs[20] and make people redundant[21], because we're aware of the huge problems for the people concerned and their families. And everybody involved here feels the emotional strain[22]. But as a company we need to re-invent[23] ourselves from time to time to follow developments in the market or give up product lines that are not really profitable anymore.

f) That often depends on what kind of post we need to fill. We normally advertise[24] vacancies[25] on the company website, on the websites of job agencies[26] and in local newspapers. And we also look for trainees in schools and colleges.

g) That doesn't happen very often. That's the very last step we would take if there are really big problems, and I mean big, with a particular person regarding the quality of their work or their unacceptable[27] or offensive behaviour[28] in the workplace. But again, we like to solve such problems by talking to those concerned.

h) Well, it goes without saying[29] that for a big employer such as our company, training our staff is very important. We do a lot of initial training[30] for school leavers both in admin and on the shop floor[31]. We organise regular trainings for our existing staff to upgrade[32] their skills and to familiarise them with new developments, for example in health and safety, to enable them to use new equipment and machinery or new software. Some of these trainings are in-house[33]; and we outsource[34] others.

i) Well, this doesn't happen very often. Most of the disputes among staff are settled[35] within the team or in discussions between those concerned and their superiors. Only when things get really out of hand[36] do we as HR people get involved as mediators[37].

j) Well, recruiting[38] is a very complex process. Of course, we look at the applicants' CVs, their cover letters, skills, etc. very carefully. Occasionally, we organise assessment centres. Finally, it's the person we're interested in. Will they fit into our teams? Are their qualifications and experience as well as their personal qualities suitable for the job? Are they willing to contribute[39] to the success of our business? These are the really important points.

[20] Stellen streichen
[21] (Personal) entlassen
[22] seelische Belastung
[23] neu erfinden
[24] *hier*: ausschreiben
[25] freie Stelle
[26] Personalvermittler
[27] nicht hinnehmbar
[28] beleidigendes Verhalten
[29] selbstverständlich
[30] Erstausbildung
[31] in der Fertigung/Produktion
[32] aktualisieren, ausbauen
[33] (firmen)intern
[34] fremdvergeben, auslagern
[35] beilegen
[36] außer Kontrolle geraten
[37] Vermittler/in
[38] Personalbeschaffung
[39] Beitrag leisten

Work with the text.

1 Use one sentence each to express the activities mentioned in points a) to j).

2 Find suitable headings for the statements a) to j).

Now act out the interview. Try to rephrase the questions to make them sound more natural.

Expand your vocabulary and learn about types of word formation.

Very often nouns or adjectives are formed by adding a syllable to the verb.

Example: *to inform – information – informative*

Use *-al, -ment, -ance, -tion, -ing, -er/-or* to form nouns from the verbs in the box below. You will find quite a few words in Geoff Bryant's answers. Warning: In some cases there is a change in spelling.

to appraise to assess to describe	to dismiss to educate to employ	to fire to harass to pay	to post to supervise to terminate

In groups of three or four, find words (verbs or nouns) where similar patterns can be used. Create a list similar to the following example:

Verb	Noun(s)	Adjective
to program(me)	program(me) programmer	
to inform	information informer	informative

1 In each of the nine boxes below, words and phrases are grouped together which are similar in meaning. In some cases you may not know the exact meaning. But you can guess what the key idea of the terms in each of the boxes is. In groups, work it out and explain it to your classmates.

1	continuing education in-house training initial training upgrading skills	2	dismissal firing lay-off redundancy	3	benefits job title monthly pay regular working hours
4	CV personal data sheet reference résumé	5	assessment centre job advertisement job description job posting on the internet	6	at the workplace in the office on the factory floor on the shop floor
7	pay rise performance bonus promotion recruitment from within	8	achievement measurement appraisal interview performance assessment performance review	9	foreman head of department supervisor team leader

2 Use your (online) dictionary to find out about the meaning of the terms and phrases in the boxes above. Then try to describe the differences in the items in each of the boxes. Do this in groups.

3 Decide which of the headings a) to l) below are the most suitable for the terms and phrases in boxes 1 to 9 above. There are more headings than you need.

a) developing employee skills b) ending a contract of employment c) getting a job d) leading positions in a business e) measuring the quality of work f) place of work	g) points covered in a contract of employment h) rewarding[1] good work i) staff mobility j) tools used to recruit[2] new staff k) wages and salaries[3] l) workplace organisation

[1] belohnen
[2] (Personal) einstellen, beschaffen
[3] Löhne & Gehälter

Note

The difference in meaning between "wages" and "salaries" is not quite clear anymore. The term *salary* was *mainly* used for those working in admin-related jobs paid on a monthly basis, whereas *wage* was used for those working in production (originally paid on a daily or weekly basis). This distinction is disappearing.

4 Use the ideas expressed in points a) to l) on p. 180 to prepare a list of the work that in your view has to be done by staff in an HR department.

14.3 Activities in the HR department

1 Decide which of the administrative activities[1] listed below you might be asked to do or have done already during your training in the HR department. Also say under which of the headings ① – ⑦ they could be classified. Tick off (√) the boxes as appropriate.

[1] Verwaltungs-, Bürotätigkeiten

① Recruitment ② Promotion ③ Training ④ Dismissals and redundancies[1] ⑤ Wages and salaries ⑥ Performance interviews[2] ⑦ General staff administration

[1] Kündigung & Entlassung
[2] Mitarbeitergespräch

	Task	My job	Heading
1	Assisting wages clerk with data input[1]		
2	Checking the return[2] of assessment interview reports[3]		
3	Collecting data concerning staffing levels in company departments		
4	Collecting data from questionnaires[4] after a training session		
5	Coordinating a time schedule for job interviews		
6	Filing new job descriptions in employees' records[5]		
7	Helping prepare notices[6] to staff members of annual pay rises		
8	Posting a notice of staff training in company magazine		
9	Preparing a bar chart of total staff costs for the past ten-year period		
10	Preparing statistics for staff redundancy plan[7]		
11	Preparing seminar rooms for in-house training sessions		
12	Putting up vacancy notices[8] on the company notice board		
13	Putting letters of dismissal[9] into envelopes		
14	Sending promotion notices[10] to payroll clerk[11]		
15	Sorting staff appraisal documents[12] alphabetically		

[1] Dateneingabe
[2] Rückgabe
[3] Bericht über Mitarbeitergespräch
[4] Fragebogen
[5] *hier*: (Personal-)Akte
[6] Mitteilung, Ankündigung
[7] Sozialplan
[8] Stellenausschreibung
[9] Kündigungsschreiben
[10] Beförderungsmitteilung
[11] Lohnbuchhalter/in
[12] Beurteilungsbogen

2 To the fellow students in your group, describe and discuss your work that you may have been asked to do in your training period in HR. Compare what you may have experienced.

3 Having done a four-week work placement in an HR department in her final year, Lizzy explains to her German friend, Leonie, in an e-mail what kind of work she has been sharing in. Write the e-mail in German and use some of the information in the list on p. 181.

Revision

Asking questions (1)

In questions, the normal SPO (subject – verb – object) word order changes and the subject moves into second place after the first part of the verb.

Yes/No questions

There is no question word (interrogative). The question starts with a part of the verb.

Examples: *Can I offer you a cup of tea?*
V_1 S V_2 indir. obj. dir. obj.
Did you read the mail I sent you yesterday?
V_1 S V_2 dir. obj.

Note: Do **not** answer yes/no questions by simply saying ***yes*** or ***no***. That is considered impolite. You need a shortened sentence that takes up the verb in the question.

Examples: ***Are*** *you ready to start? – Yes, I* ***am****.* Or: *No,* ***I'm*** *not.*
Did *you read the e-mail I sent last night? – No, I* ***didn't****. So sorry.* Or: *Yes, I* ***did****.*
Will *you be seeing Ms Anderson today? – No, I* ***won't*** *(= will not). / No, I don't think I* ***will****.* Or: *Yes,* I (think I) ***will***

Learn to deal with yes/no questions.

1 Answer the questions below.

1 Did you ask your boss whether you can have the day off next Tuesday? – Yes/No, ______

2 Have you been to Turkey already? – Yes/No, ______

3 Will you be seeing Eileen at evening class tonight? – Yes/No, ______

4 Has he had his lunch break yet? – Yes/No, ______

5 Are you sure this is the right way of dealing with this problem? – Yes/No, ______

6 Would you rather finish the job now? – Yes/No, ______

7 Did she get some help from Thomas? – Yes/No, ______

8 Will you be there tomorrow at 8 o'clock? – Yes/No, ______

2 Ask your partner yes/no questions that relate to their work (in the HR department). The partner should answer these questions. Use the pattern in sentences 1–8 above.

Revision

Asking questions (2)

Questions beginning with an interrogative start with question words such as *who, whom, whose, which, what, why, how, where, when,* etc.

If the information you ask about is the subject of the sentence, there is no change in the word order. In this case, the interrogative **is** the subject or part of the subject.

Examples: ***Which catalogues*** *are in these parcels? – All those to our customers abroad.*
interrogative S V prepositional obj.

Which customer *placed an order for 250 office chairs? – That was our customer from Baltimore.*
Interrogative S V dir. obj. prepositional obj.

The word order changes if the element you are asking about is some other part of the sentence. In this case, the interrogative is used in first place and followed by the first part of the verb (V_1). This is then followed by the subject (S) and the second part of the verb (V_2) and then the other parts of the sentence.

Examples: *When can we expect the consignment of printers?*
interrogative V_1 S V_2 dir. obj.

How did you prepare for this test?
interrogative V_1 S V2 prepositional obj.

Whose address are you looking for?
interrogative + prep. obj.1 V_1 S V_2 prep. obj.2

Sometimes the interrogative consists of two parts *(e.g. to whom, with whom, for whom, about what, for what, from where)*. In these cases, the *wh*-part is the first word in the question and the other part is moved to a position after the verb. The interrogative *whom* then changes to *who.*

Examples: ***Who*** *did you talk* ***to*** *just now?*

What *did you talk* ***about*** *at dinner?*

Where *does she come* ***from****?*

Apply what you learnt.

1 Ask questions about the part of the sentence printed in italics. Use the interrogatives in brackets.

1 She sent off the letter *yesterday morning.* (When?)
2 He discussed *the matter* with her on the phone. (What?)
3 *We haven't heard from our customer in Liverpool yet.* (Why?)
4 She's been away on business *for a week.* (For how long?)
5 We've just got a big order *for printer toner*[1]. (For what?)
6 She talked to the department head *about the complaint* yesterday afternoon. (About what?)
7 He went *to the stationer's*[2] to get some printing paper. (Where?)
8 John came *all the way from Manchester* this morning. (From where?)

[1] Druckertoner
[2] Schreibwarengeschäft

2 It's your turn now. Ask your partner questions. Choose a topic (work in your department, getting your trainee post, latest purchase of a large item, holiday, etc.) and then take turns. Ask and answer at least five questions using question words from the box above.

14.4 An interesting job advertisement

Having passed her school leaving exams, Lizzy decides she wants to get some work experience before going on to college to do a full-time one-year course in secretarial, administration and office skills. After some extensive[1] internet research she finds this job advert from a Dundee-based property development company[2] quite attractive.

1 umfangreich
2 Immobilienentwicklungsgesellschaft
3 Praktikum
4 Immobiliengesellschaft
5 Unternehmen
6 umsetzen
7 *hier*: sanieren
8 Immobilienverwaltung
9 gestalterisch
10 hochmodern
11 erzeugen, schaffen
12 Nutzer, Bewohner
13 angemessener Ertrag
14 städtisch
15 interessiert
16 ausführen, erledigen
17 Dateneingabe
18 auffüllen
19 Büromaterial
20 fließend
21 kompetent
22 soziale Kompetenz
23 Initiative ergreifen
24 Auftreten
25 begierig, bemüht
26 (= curriculum vitae) Lebenslauf
27 An-, Begleitschreiben
28 Probezeit

Junior Office Assistant
(paid work experience[3])

Dundee, centre
Posted — 20 days ago
Contract type — temporary (12 months maximum)

Description

Fantastic opportunity to join an exciting and busy property company[4] as a junior office assistant.

PCN UK Ltd is a young and fast-growing enterprise[5]. We develop and implement[6] concepts to regenerate[7] properties and turn them into attractive places for people to work and live.

We attach great importance to intensive property management[8]. We offer creative[9] solutions and state-of-the-art[10] designs. We generate[11] value for our occupiers[12]. We promise our investors fair and stable returns[13].

Currently we are working on projects in many big urban[14] centres in England and Scotland. We are based in London.

For our busy Dundee office we are looking for an enthusiastic and keen[15] young person to join and support our hard-working team.

Your duties

- You will perform[16] general office and admin duties.
- You will answer phone calls and take messages.
- You will perform reception duties (greeting clients and advising staff of their arrival).
- You will organise incoming mail and prepare outgoing mail.
- You will assist with IT issues and data entry[17].
- You will top up[18] printers and photocopiers with paper.
- You will order toners and cartridges for printers and photocopiers.
- You will check and order stationery[19].
- You will manage meeting room bookings.
- You will arrange tea and coffee for meetings.
- You will keep meeting rooms tidy.

Your skills

- You are fluent[20] in English, both spoken and written.
- You are well-organised.
- You have good telephone manners.
- You are proficient[21] in the use of Microsoft Office programs.
- You have excellent interpersonal skills[22].
- You are proactive[23].
- You are a quick learner.
- You have a pleasant demeanour[24].

This is a good opportunity for someone seeking to start their career and gain some experience of working in an office. If you are hard-working and eager[25] to learn, send us your CV[26] with your cover letter[27].

The post is for an immediate start with a probationary period[28] of three months.

Salary: £15k

Please send your online application to recruitment@pcn.com quoting Ref.-No. 762398.

Work with the text.

1 Answer these questions on the text.

1 How does PCN UK Ltd describe itself?
2 What do they do for their customers and their investors?
3 Where does the company have its headquarters?
4 Why does the company need an office junior?
5 List the tasks relating to dealing with people.
6 What are the tasks with regard to meeting rooms?
7 Which of the skills listed in the advert can be acquired at school or college?
8 How can an interested person apply?
9 What does £15k stand for? (Find out how much this is in euros.)

Apply now!
job vacancies
job openings
We want you!
Your career with us!
Now hiring
Job fair
Vacant positions
Join our team!
Applications invited

2 It is generally said that a job advert has four or five sections:

- description of the job,
- expected candidate profile,
- information about how to apply,
- name and location of the employer and the place of work,
- profile of the employer.

Where do you find this information in the advert? What is the order of the information provided by the employer?

3 Find words or terms in the text that correspond to the definitions or synonyms below.

1 for a limited period of time 2 land and buildings 3 lively 4 industrious 5 refilling	6 getting things done before being told 7 well-developed ability to communicate 8 good behaviour 9 time span to find out about the abilities of a new employee 10 modernise older properties

14.5 Applying for a job

Track 48

A job application, whether sent via the internet or in the traditional form by post, is a kind of visiting card of a person trying to get a job. It is meant to attract the reader's attention. And therefore it must stand out from the rest in terms of[1] appearance[2], structure and content. Bear in mind that the recruiter[3] has to read through dozens of applications or even more. On average[4], so experts say, staff in HR do not spend more than two or three minutes on going through an application whether written or sent online. Therefore, keep it short and concise[5]. Don't be a time-waster[6]. The cover letter[7] and the CV are the candidate's most powerful "selling tools". So, obviously you want to get it right.

1 was … anbelangt
2 Erscheinungsbild, *hier*: Form und Gestaltung
3 Personalbeschaffer
4 durchschnittlich
5 knapp
6 Zeitverschwender
7 An-, Begleitschreiben

14.5.1 How to present yourself in a CV

Track 49

1 Lebenslauf
2 außerschulisch
3 Teilzeit-
4 Zusammenhang

In a CV, or résumé[1] in American usage, a candidate provides a clearly organised overview of her/his achievements and skills. Very early in your career, your performance in school (subjects and grades, extra-curricular[2] activities) is an important element in the decision of whether to invite you for an interview or not. But your experience in part-time[3] work outside school, your skills, your interests/hobbies, your team-related or social activities also play a major role. And don't forget that the way you present the information about yourself requires some attention, although in principle, content is more important than form. Make sure there is some coherence[4] between the requirements of the job advert and your application.

From the internet and a handbook, Lizzy got some ideas on how to present the information about herself. And this is what she has come up with: a traditional chronological approach.

1 Schulabgänger/in
2 Organisations-
3 wirksam, effektiv
4 Computer- und Informationstechnologie
5 Auffüllen der Regale
6 Lager
7 Pflegeheim
8 Verlag
9 Hospitation
10 Texterfassungskompetenz
11 Zwischenstufe
12 Empfehlungsschreiben

Lizzy Hamilton

3c Brook Street, Broughty Ferry, Dundee DD5 1LX
Tel. 07342 1234567 (mobile) E-mail lizhamil011@bt.com

Objective: Office junior

Personal statement

Ambitious school leaver[1] with strong organisational[2] and administrative skills, able to work effectively[3] as a team member or independently, good IT skills, committed and eager to learn

Education

2011–2017	Eastern Primary School		
2017–2022	Monifieth High School		
	National 5 exams in:	English (B)	Maths (C)
		Geography (B)	History (C)
		French (D)	ICT*[4] (B)
		Music (D)	Art (A)

Work experience

2020–2022	Broughty Ferry Supermarket	Assisting with shelf-filling[5], Working in the stockroom[6] (at weekends and during school holidays)
	Monifieth Nursing Home[7]	General duties (early evenings)
2022	4-week work placement with DCT Publishing[8] Work shadowing[9] in the HR department, assisting with office routines (July)	

Activities & interests

Badminton in Tayside 14–18 team (Broughty Ferry Sports Club)
Cycling
Aerobics
Reading

Information & communication technology

Familiar with standard Microsoft Office applications
Good keyboarding skills[10]
Basic skills in programming

Languages

English (native speaker)
French (intermediate[11])
Gaelic (beginner)

References[12] will be supplied on request

* ICT = information and computer technology

Note

In the Scottish school system, students take National 5 exams (similar to the GCSE O-level exams in England and Wales) after five years in secondary school. They can then take up work or they may continue their school education for another year before going on to university or college.

You know how to write a CV?!?

1 State what you like or dislike about this CV.

2 How does Lizzy refer to the skills required in the job advert?

©Photo-graphee.eu-fotolia.com

3 Would you consider Lizzy's application for the post of Junior Office Assistant as described in the advertisement on p. 184 as good enough to invite her for an interview? State your reasons.

4 In the modern type of CV, the chronological order is changed, and the most recent activities are put first. This may not be such a good idea for a school leaver. Discuss the advantages and disadvantages.

5 Some information that you find in a standard German CV is missing here. – Which? Can you think of any reasons for leaving out such information? Discuss your findings in class.

6 Imagine you are applying for a post in an English-speaking country after the completion[1] of your current training. Write your own CV in English. Go back to Unit 1 for the education and training terminology.

7 Compare Lizzy's CV with your own. Describe the differences.

1 Abschluss, Beendigung

14.5.2 The cover letter

Track 50

The cover letter usually is the first page of a candidate's profile[1]. For online applications, its format/layout as well as the text can be the same as in the traditional printed version. Normally this letter should not be longer than about half an A4 sheet (about 15 to 18 lines of text at the very most). It is meant to attract the recruiter's attention. Don't repeat details from your PDS (personal data sheet)[2]. What you say should be relevant[3] for the position you are applying for. Therefore make clear that you think you have the qualifications and experience for the job. And of course, your motivation for joining a particular company should become obvious. Most cover letters use this structure:

- Reference to the source of information and application for the advertised post,
- Reason for applying and job-specific qualifications,
- Motivation and suitability[4] for the job,
- Availability[5] for an interview and contact,
- Polite close.

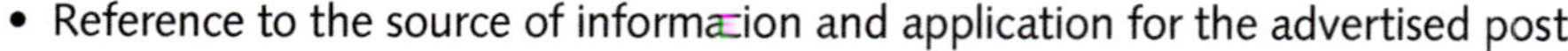

1 Kurzbiographie
2 Personalbogen, Lebenslauf
3 einschlägig, wichtig
4 Eignung
5 Verfügbarkeit

Lizzy writes an e-mail to recruitment@pcn.com to send her personal profile. Use the bits of text below to put together a short e-mail. The sentence beginnings are capitalised and put in bold. And the sentence ends are marked with a full stop. There are seven sentences altogether.

Good morning,

getting some experience of office work

a career in office work.

I hope you will

consider my application.

I am interested in such a position.

at any time.

If you have any queries

I saw your posting[1] of the

can be a sound base for the college course

And I think

Having just finished school

you can contact me

my personal profile.

that I am planning to begin

Please find attached

My aim is to start

with National 5 exams in eight subjects

temporary vacancy for a Junior Office Assistant

on the internet.

in autumn next year.

Kind regards,

Lizzy Hamilton

Attachments: Cover letter
Personal profile

[1] Anzeige, Inserat

©Tupungato-fotolia.com

Now read Lizzy's cover letter.

Lizzy Hamilton
3c Brook Street, Broughty Ferry, Dundee DD5 1LX
Tel. 07342 1234567 (mobile)   E-mail lizhamil011@bt.com

18 August 20..

Junior Office Assistant (Ref.-No. 762398)

Dear Madam or Sir,

On the internet I noticed your posting of a vacancy for a junior office assistant. I would like to apply for this temporary post.

As you will see from my personal profile I am a school leaver with National 5 exams in a broad range of subjects. Before going on to a college of further education to do a one-year full-time course in secretarial, administration and office skills, I would very much like to get some practical experience in a role such as the one you are advertising. I think that this hands-on[1] approach[2] will enable me to make the best possible use of the education I will be getting at college.

The job description in your posting indicates that there will be many opportunities to familiarise myself with general office routines. And at the same time, I think I can apply the skills and knowledge I acquired[3] in some of the courses I took in school. I feel that the ICT course has given me a good understanding of both the technical and practical aspects of communication. The art course has helped me to develop my creative talents further and provided me with some understanding of the various art forms, colour coding and shapes. My teachers and my classmates consider me to be a well-organised person with good manners who can act of her own accord when there is a job to be done.

You will find my personal profile attached. I am willing to start working with you straightaway and am available for an interview at any time. Please contact me by phone or e-mail to arrange an appointment.

Thank you very much for considering my application and I look forward to hearing from you in the near future.

Yours faithfully,

Lizzy Hamilton

Lizzy Hamilton

[1] praxisbezogen
[2] Ansatz
[3] sich aneignen, erwerben

efficient
experienced
qualified
hard-working
highly motivated
skilled
keen
gifted
eager to learn
super-organised

Work with the cover letter.
Please identify the parts of the cover letter.

Find expressions in the letter that mean the same as those listed below. Work in groups, each taking one set of terms and phrases.

• advertisement • college education • CV • graduate • insight into[1] • one year of work experience • personal data sheet	• real-life • soon • sound grounding[2] • tasks • to be proactive whenever necessary • to enrol for a course • to get in touch	• to get to know • to wish to be considered a candidate for • to look at • to post a job opening • to really want • to use • wide

1 Einblick
2 solides Fundament

Find out how and with what kind of language Lizzy refers to the job advert.

Write a cover letter.

You want to apply for the post of Junior Office Assistant in an English-speaking country. Use the notes below:

- Stellenausschreibung im Internet gefunden
- Interesse an Tätigkeit im Ausland wegen der Sprache und Erfahrung
- Ausbildung als Bürokauffrau/-kaufmann abgeschlossen (Dauer, Abschlussnote)
- ein Jahr Berufserfahrung in ihrer Ausbildungsfirma
- jetzigen Aufgabenbereich nennen/beschreiben
- Interesse an Erfahrung in neuem Arbeitsgebiet <u>oder</u> an Erweiterung der Kompetenzen im jetzigen
- Verbesserung der Englischkenntnisse in Abendkursen (Prüfungen: Cambridge Business English [Vantage], KMK-Prüfung [Stufe II])
- Beginn der Tätigkeit verhandelbar *(negotiable)*, aber 4 Wochen Kündigungsfrist *(period of notice)*.

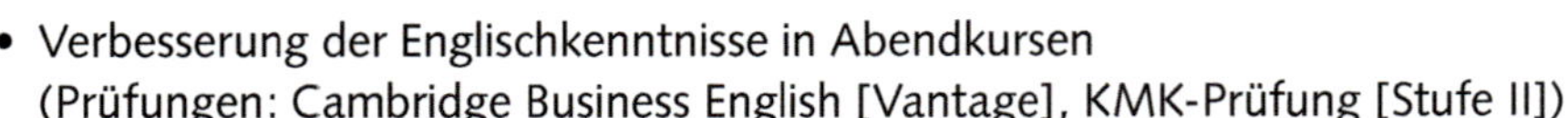

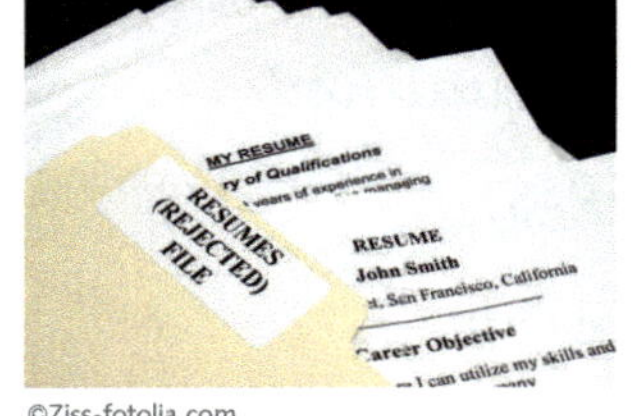

©Ziss-fotolia.com

Type out your letter and any extras on your computer and produce a nicely presented A4 cover letter. Use the proper terms to give information about your (German) school education and qualifications. (Go back to Section 1,4 in Unit 1)

Note

"kündigen" is best translated by *to give notice*.

Phrases: mit einer Frist von 4 Wochen kündigen = *to give four weeks' notice.*
Die Kündigungsfrist beträgt … Wochen. = *The period of notice is … weeks.*

Die KMK-Zertifizierung

Berufliche Schulen können auf freiwilliger Basis eine Prüfung anbieten, so dass sich Schülerinnen und Schüler ihre Fremdsprachenkenntnisse zertifizieren lassen können. Die Prüfung besteht aus einem schriftlichen und einem mündlichen Teil und kann auf verschiedenen Niveaustufen abgelegt werden, die sich am Gemeinsamen Europäischen Referenzrahmen für Sprachen (GER) orientieren. Die Prüfungen sind bestanden, wenn jeweils mindestens die Hälfte der ausgewiesenen Punktzahl erreicht wird; ein Ausgleich ist nicht möglich.

Die Dauer der Prüfung richtet sich nach der von Ihnen gewählten Niveaustufe:

Niveaustufe	entspricht GER	Dauer der schriftlichen Prüfung	Dauer der mündlichen Gruppenprüfung
I	A2	60 Minuten	15 Minuten
II	B1	90 Minuten	20 Minuten
III	B2	120 Minuten	25 Minuten

Auf dem Zertifikat sind die geprüfte Sprache, das Niveau, Ihre Teilergebnisse in den einzelnen Bereichen und Ihr Gesamtergebnis ausgewiesen. Die Zertifikatsprüfung steht in keinerlei Zusammenhang mit der Benotung im Zeugnis.

1. Schriftliche Prüfung (maximal erreichbar: 100 Punkte)

Diese besteht in der Regel aus vier Aufgaben. Sie dürfen ein allgemeines zweisprachiges Wörterbuch verwenden. Beim Hörverstehen hören Sie die Texte zweimal und mit angemessenen Pausen.

Aufgabe	Punkte	Inhalt der Aufgabe
1. Hörverstehen	20	Teil 1: Sie hören eine Nachricht und tragen Informationen in ein vorgefertigtes Formular ein. Teil 2: Sie hören einen berufsbezogenen Text (z.B. ein Interview oder einen Vortrag) und beantworten offene Fragen zum Inhalt.
2. Leseverstehen	20	Sie lesen einen berufsbezogenen Text und beantworten offene Fragen zum Inhalt.
3. Produktion	30	Sie erstellen einen Geschäftsbrief auf Englisch.
4. Mediation	30	Sie bekommen einen deutschen oder englischen Text und übertragen diesen in die andere Sprache.

2. Mündliche Prüfung (maximal erreichbar: 30 Punkte)

Die mündliche Prüfung wird in der Regel als Gruppenprüfung mit zwei Prüflingen durchgeführt. Normalerweise bekommen Sie eine angemessene Vorbereitungszeit, um eine an Ihrer Schule oder von Ihrem/r Lehrer/in erstellte Aufgabe zu bearbeiten. Dies ist meist ein Dialog, den Sie zusammen mit Ihrem/r Partner/in vortragen, z. B. zwischen einem/r Anrufer/in mit einer Beschwerde und einem/r Mitarbeiter/in im Service. Außer dem gemeinsamen Teil führen Sie auch noch ein Einzelgespräch mit Ihrem/r Lehrer/in, z. B. über Ihre Ausbildung, Ihren Betrieb, Ihre Pläne nach bestandener Ausbildung usw.

Quelle: http://www.kmk.org/fileadmin/Dateien/veroeffentlichungen_beschluesse/1998/1998_11_20-RV-Fremdsprachen-berufliche-Bildung_02.pdf

Musterprüfung 1 – KMK Niveau II

Aufgabe 1 – Hörverstehen **20 VP**

Teil 1 (Anrufbeantworter) 8 VP

Ihre Firma erwartet einen Gast aus Indien, der gegen Mittag ankommen sollte. Als Sie morgens ins Büro kommen, hören Sie folgende Nachricht, die er nachts auf den Anrufbeantworter gesprochen hat. Verfassen Sie eine Telefonnotiz **(Anlage 1)** für Ihre/n Vorgesetzte/n. Sie hören die Nachricht zweimal.

Anlage 1 (Hörverstehen Teil 1)

Track 52

GESPRÄCHSNOTIZ

Datum:		
Anrufer:		[1]
Telefonnummer:		[1]
Betreff:		[1]
Nachricht:		[4]
E-Mail:		[1]

Teil 2 (Podcast) 12 VP

Track 53

Sie hören einen Podcast über häufige Fehler, die von Auszubildenden gemacht werden.

Beantworten Sie die Fragen stichwortartig auf Deutsch. Sie hören den Podcast zweimal.

1 Worüber möchte Alan Beaudrie sprechen? (1)
2 Was sollten Auszubildende tun, um in der Firma gut auszusehen? (2)
3 Warum ist es laut des Experten wichtig, den ersten Fehler zu vermeiden? (1)
4 Wie zeigen Auszubildende ihr geringes Interesse? (1)
5 Erklären Sie, warum es wichtig ist, in einem Betrieb zu arbeiten, in den man gerne geht. (2)
6 Nennen Sie den dritten Fehler. (1)
7 Welche Gefahr läuft man, wenn man versucht, den dritten Fehler unbedingt zu vermeiden? (2)
8 Welchen Stellenwert hat unabhängiges Arbeiten laut Herrn Beaudrie? (2)

Aufgabe 2 – Leseverstehen **20 VP**

Lesen Sie den nachfolgenden Text durch und beantworten Sie die Fragen in ganzen Sätzen auf Deutsch.

Ensuring a long-lasting business relation with your supplier

Jonathan Myers and Dan Langdon are owners of a company dealing in laptop components. They have been having discussions with a potential new supplier in Korea, Kim Tae-yong, as well with their long-standing supplier in Indonesia, Sehat Sutardja. They would like to continue working with Sutardja. But they also see opportunities and advantages in doing business with a new source of supplies, as Myers and Langdon are sure that the Korean components would be a useful addition to their current range because they are apparently good value for money. Furthermore, Myers and Langdon assume that the parts will be well received by their customers.

What is holding the two men back from working with the new supplier are environmental issues. Having done some research, they found out that Kim Tae-yong does not care much about working conditions and ensuring that his raw materials are obtained from sustainable production. This might cause problems, as Myers and Langdon have to meet certain EU requirements. On the other hand, Sutardja's prices have been rising quite significantly over the past 18 months. Therefore, ensuring the continuing production of supplies at competitive prices could be a new challenge for them.

Myers' and Langdon's main goal this year is to comply with the new ISO standards; this is why they have called their Indonesian supplier, because meeting the new ISO standards not only means relying on a supplier with an excellent environmental policy but also providing information on any raw materials or products (source, production, processing) that have been delivered to Sutardja.

In order to see whether the new potential Korean supplier can fulfil the necessary requirements, Myers plans to visit the production site to get a first-hand idea of the production process and to discuss the environmental issues that are holding them back from working with Tae-yong at the moment. He has made a questionable offer that might turn out to be a trick to lure them into a long-standing business arrangement where, at a later point in time, an 'unavoidable' increase in prices might follow.

Apart from the environmental issues, Langdon and Myers also need to watch their costs. Sutardja has already agreed to meeting environmentally friendly production standards. This has involved rising costs over the past one and a half years. While Myers is visiting the Korean supplier, Langdon, together with two of his engineers, will visit Sutardja's facilities to find ways of reducing production costs. In an e-mail, Sutardja had mentioned an unusually high rate of defective parts over the past six months – both Sutardja and Langdon are hoping to address this issue.

The two visits will hopefully help Myers and Langdon with their decision that will greatly influence the future of their company. Both suppliers have their advantages and disadvantages, and in the end the two men have to see whether complying with the new ISO standards and lowering production costs would be feasible.

(464 words)

1 Nennen sie den Grund, warum die beiden Firmeninhaber an einem neuen Lieferanten interessiert sind. (2)

2 Erläutern Sie, warum Myers und Langdon zögern, Geschäfte mit dem neuen Lieferanten aufzunehmen. (3)

3 Erläutern Sie, was Myers und Langdon dazu bewegt hat, mit ihrem Stammlieferanten neu zu verhandeln. (3)

4 Erklären Sie, wieso es zur Erfüllung gewisser ISO Standards notwendig ist, auch den Lieferanten mit ins Boot zu nehmen. (4)

5 Nennen Sie die Gründe für den Besuch des koreanischen Lieferanten. (2)

6 Welche Taktik wendet der koreanische Lieferant angeblich an, um eine Zusage der beiden Firmeninhaber zu bekommen? (2)

7 Erklären Sie, durch welche Ursachen die Kosten des Stammlieferanten gestiegen sind und wie versucht werden soll, die Kosten wieder zu senken. (4)

Aufgabe 3 – Schriftstücke erstellen (Produktion) **30 VP**

Sie arbeiten für Liquimetall GmbH, die europaweit zu den führenden Herstellern in der Metall verarbeitenden Industrie gehört, und wurden von Ihrer/m Vorgesetzten beauftragt, für die Einrichtung der neuen Konferenzräume in ihrer Außenstelle in München potenzielle Lieferanten ausfindig zu machen. Der bisherige Lieferant kommt nicht in Frage, da die Qualität der Ware mangelhaft war und die Lieferungen mehrmals verspätet eintrafen.

Wie es der Zufall will, haben Sie einen Werbeprospekt in der Post gefunden und fragen bei den Lieferanten an; vor allem ein englischer Büromöbelhersteller hat es Ihnen angetan.

Verfassen Sie eine Anfrage in englischer Sprache und berücksichtigen Sie die folgenden Punkte:

- Datum, Anrede, Betreff
- Kurze Vorstellung der eigenen Firma
- Erläuterung, warum ein neuer Lieferant gesucht wird
- Benötigt werden hochwertige Stühle, Konferenztische, Regale, Schreibtische.
- Wichtig sind Ihnen gute Qualität, Ware muss auf Lager sein, kurze Lieferfristen.
- Bitten Sie um Zusendung des Katalogs sowie der gültigen Preisliste.
- Fragen Sie nach etwaigen Rabatten bei Abnahme größerer Mengen, Skonti.
- Formulieren Sie einen geeigneten Schlusssatz.

Verwenden Sie **Anlage 2.** Formulieren Sie ganze Sätze.

Anlage 2 (Produktion)

Liquimetall GmbH
Marschstraße 356
81929 München
Tel. 089/290136100
info@liquimetall.de

©Jan Engel-fotolia.com

Mr Jeff Buchanan
Furniture & More
1 Thorpe Rd.
Norwich
NR1 1WZ
United Kingdom

____

....

....

....

....

....

....

....

....

Aufgabe 4 – Übertragen eines Textes (Mediation) **30 VP**

Im Rahmen des Erasmus+ Mobilitätsprogramms wird eine Gruppe ausländischer Auszubildender Ihren Betrieb besuchen. Gemeinsam mit einem anderen deutschen Auszubildenden wurden Sie beauftragt, eine kurze Einführung auf Englisch für die Gäste vorzubereiten.

Entnehmen Sie hierzu die nötigen Informationen aus dem deutschen Infotext Ihrer Firma und formulieren Sie ganze Sätze.

Beschränken Sie sich auf folgende Punkte:

- Standorte des Unternehmens
- Rolle des Unternehmens in Europa und der Welt

Firmenhistorie & Rolle des PERCEVAL KONZERNS

Fast alle unsere Produkte bieten Qualität „Made in Germany" – und das seit 1881. Das beweisen zum Beispiel unsere beiden Standorte in Stuttgart: Im Osten der Stadt sitzen unsere Verwaltung und die Produktion; unser Logistikzentrum im Gewerbegebiet „Vogelsang" bietet genügend Platz für viele tausend Artikel.

Neben der Produktion am Firmensitz in Stuttgart werden Teile unserer Produktpalette auch im bayrischen Erdingen hergestellt. Einen weiteren Produktionsstandort gibt es in St. Gallen in der Schweiz. Rund 630 Mitarbeiter arbeiten an den Standorten in Stuttgart, weitere 450 an den Standorten in Bayern und der Schweiz.

Die gesamte Perceval Group – mit ihrer Kernmarke PAPEL – zählt mit einem Produktionsvolumen von mehr als 15.000 Tonnen pro Jahr zu den größten Papier verwertenden Unternehmen Europas. Die Unternehmensgruppe ist mit ihren Marken in sieben europäischen Ländern vertreten.

Der Perceval Konzern stellt an den drei deutschen und dem Schweizer Standort jedes Jahr Millionen Schulhefte, Kalender, Blöcke, Geschäfts- und Notizbücher her und erwirtschaftet damit einen Umsatz von mehr als 130 Millionen Euro pro Jahr.

Der Perceval Konzern als Global Player

Die Welt wird zum Dorf – das Internet hat in vielen Haushalten Einzug gehalten und sorgt dafür, dass Menschen überall auf der Welt miteinander kommunizieren können. Die Globalisierung mit ihrem Wunsch nach immer schnell verfügbaren Produkten stellt auch unsere Logistik vor neue Herausforderungen. Vom Logistikzentrum „Vogelsang" beliefern wir Kunden in ganz Deutschland und im benachbarten Ausland.

Immer neue Märkte kommen für uns hinzu. So wird der Perceval Konzern unter anderem durch Kooperationen mit schwedischen und norwegischen Kalender- und Papierherstellern immer internationaler.

Inzwischen exportieren wir Schulhefte, Kalender, Blöcke, Geschäfts- und Notizbücher sowie Geschenkpapier in mehr als 50 Länder in aller Welt. Zu unseren wichtigen Auslandsmärkten gehören die Schweiz und Österreich; wir beliefern zahlreiche Kunden in Ost- und Nordeuropa. Darüber hinaus haben wir sogar Verbindungen, die bis nach Namibia oder Japan reichen.

(302 words)

(Quelle: brunnen.de (stark verändert))

Musterprüfung 2 – KMK Niveau II

Aufgabe 1 – Hörverstehen **20 VP**

Teil 1 (Anrufbeantworter) 8 VP

Sie hören eine Nachricht auf Ihrem Anrufbeantworter ab. Füllen Sie die Gesprächsnotiz **(Anlage 1)** stichwortartig auf Deutsch aus. Sie hören die Nachricht zweimal.

Anlage 1 (Hörverstehen Teil 1)

Track 54

GESPRÄCHSNOTIZ		
Datum:		
Anrufer:		[1]
Telefonnummer:		[1]
Betreff:		[1]
Nachricht:		[4]
E-Mail:		[1]

©3dmavr-fotolia.com

Teil 2 (Dialog) 12 VP

Sie hören ein Interview zwischen dem Moderator einer Radiosendung und einem Unternehmer zum Thema „Franchising". Sie hören das Interview zweimal.

DIGITAL+ Track 55

Beantworten Sie die Fragen stichwortartig auf Deutsch.

1 Welche Franchisen betreibt Danny Jones und seit wann tut er dies? (2)

2 Weshalb hat sich Danny Jones für diese beiden Franchisen entschieden? (4)

3 Welchen Rat hat Danny Jones für Leute, die daran interessiert sind, Franchisenehmer zu werden? (3)

4 Wie beurteilt Danny Jones seine Zeit als Franchisenehmer? (2)

5 Was sind die Zukunftspläne von Danny Jones? (1)

Aufgabe 2 – Leseverstehen **20 VP**

Lesen Sie den nachfolgenden Text durch. Beantworten Sie die Fragen stichwortartig auf Deutsch.

Working in multi-national teams

In recent years, globalisation has led to an increase in the degree of international cooperation at work. Nowadays, it is quite common to work together with people from different cultural backgrounds – not only in the actual office, but also online in virtual spaces. Thanks to this, new ideas or solutions might be found, and this again can lead to an increase of productivity. However, diversity can also cause severe problems. Besides the obvious problems of language, cultural differences pose a risk to the progress of a project. There might be misunderstandings or your behaviour might be offensive to someone else. Normally, it is the job of management to ensure that multi-national members of a team work together smoothly. However, reading our brief guidelines will also help you when you have to deal with such situations should you ever be involved in such teamwork.

Names

Some of your international colleagues might have names you have never heard. You might not even know which part of the name is the first name and which is the last name. So, make sure that you understand the names and can also pronounce them. Furthermore, don't forget to find out how to properly address your colleagues, for example whether titles are important.

The language barrier

Even if someone is rather fluent in a second language, he/she might not be able to accurately express what he/she is thinking in sufficient detail. And someone who is less fluent might not say much or nothing at all because he/she feels ill at ease. However, some input from these people might be very important for your team or project; and you don't want it to be lost. So, try to address everyone in your team and get them to talk by using polite and not forceful questions. This leads us to our next point.

Politeness

Bear in mind that in some cultures it is considered impolite to say "no" or to openly disagree with what your boss or the majority think. So, a "yes" might easily mean "yes, but ..." or even "no." In order to be certain, make sure that "yes" means "yes" or ask different questions which can't be answered with a simple "yes" or "no."

Doing things in different ways

Different mentalities are the biggest obstacle when it comes to working efficiently. Germans who tend to plan everything down to the last detail might consider Americans to be rushing head over heels into a project when they get started with nothing but a basic idea and a good intuitive feeling. Americans on the other hand, who are used to bosses who allow them to have a lot of freedom, might think that German bosses, who like giving orders, don't trust their staff. In order to avoid such situations, you have to find out which cultural problems could arise before they actually do and discuss them within the team.

(491 words)

1 Auf welche Arten arbeiten internationale Teams zusammen? (2)
2 Welche Vorteile kann die Arbeit eines internationalen Teams mit sich bringen? (2)
3 Welche Probleme können sich in einem internationalen Team ergeben? (3)
4 Inwiefern verursachen die Namen der internationalen Arbeitskollegen Probleme? (2)
5 Wie sollte man mit den Namen der internationalen Kollegen umgehen? (2)
6 Worin liegt die Problematik der Sprachbarriere? (3)
7 Warum bedeutet ein „ja“ nicht immer „ja“? (2)
8 Welche zwei Probleme können sich bei der Zusammenarbeit von Deutschen und US-Amerikanern ergeben? (3)
9 Wie lassen sich kulturelle Probleme vermeiden? (1)

Aufgabe 3 – Schriftstücke erstellen (Produktion)

30 VP

Sie arbeiten für die Weiss AG, einen Hersteller von Süßigkeiten. Ihr Unternehmen wird im nächsten Jahr an der IFE (International Food and Drink Exhibition) teilnehmen, einer Lebensmittelmesse im Exhibition Centre London (ExCeL). Ihr/e Vorgesetzte/r plant, zu diesem Anlass Ihre britischen Kunden zur Messe einzuladen und hat Sie deshalb mit dem Verfassen einer Rundmail beauftragt.

Verfassen Sie eine geschäftliche Mail in englischer Sprache und berücksichtigen Sie die folgenden Punkte:

- Betreff, Anrede
- Kundeninformation: Teilnahme an oben genannter Messe, Zeitraum: 19. bis 22. März.
- Einladung zum Empfang in der „re:mix lounge" im Hotel „Aloft London ExCeL" direkt vor dem Messegebäude. Datum: 20. März, 10:00 Uhr. Anschließend Messebesuch möglich, pro Kunde 2 Freikarten.
- Bitte um Rückmeldung bis zum 31. Januar.
- Kunden, die nicht am Empfang teilnehmen können, sind trotzdem herzlich eingeladen, während der Messe unseren Stand zu besuchen (Standort: Halle Nord, direkt beim Eingang N9).
- Formulieren Sie einen angemessenen Schlusssatz.

Verwenden Sie **Anlage 2**. Formulieren Sie ganze Sätze.

Anlage 2 (Produktion)

An:	mailinglist_UK
Betreff:	

....

....

....

....

....

....

Aufgabe 4 – Übertragen eines Textes (Mediation) **30 VP**

Situation: Ihr/e Vorgesetzte/r überlegt, Mitarbeitern/Innen die Möglichkeit zu geben, von zu Hause aus zu arbeiten. Er/Sie hat dazu einen Artikel auf Englisch gefunden, den er/sie für gut befindet. Um die Mitarbeiter/Innen zu informieren, hat er/sie Sie gebeten, auf Basis dieses Artikels ein Infoblatt zu entwerfen, auf dem

- die Vorteile und die Nachteile von Telearbeit genannt werden und
- das die Tipps aufführt, die Arbeit von zu Hause erfolgreich macht.

Verwenden Sie **Anlage 3**.

Turn working from home into a success story

There are many advantages to working from home: You don't have to commute to work, thus avoiding traffic and crowded public transport. Additionally, you can enjoy the comfort of your own home and don't have to deal with noisy co-workers. However, there are also some drawbacks: Staying focused might be difficult with your children around or chores like dirty dishes or a pile of laundry waiting to be done. Giving in to these distractions will cause your productivity and efficiency to suffer.

In order to help you, we have put together a list with six tips that will make working from home easier.

Have a designated workspace

Don't set up your home office in your living room – a couch and a coffee table cannot really serve as substitutes for office furniture. You definitely need a special corner, a basement or an entire room so that you feel like you have gone to work.

Focus on your work

Dealing with distractions will not be that easy, especially at first. During your working hours, force yourself to ignore the laundry, gardening, dish washing or cleaning. A proper work mindset is important and yet another reason for having a designated workspace.

Set designated working hours

If you don't pay attention, working from home might easily become a 24-hour job. Needless to say, this will do you no good. You will have to find out what your right work-life balance should be. So set home office hours and follow them. And when it is time to call it a day, close the door to your home office and enjoy the evening.

Have the right equipment

A fast and reliable internet connection is a must if you decide to work from home. Furthermore, you will require suitable programs that will let you work efficiently – especially programs that allow you to share content with your co-workers.

Keep in touch with your co-workers

After a while, most teleworkers miss the opportunity for social interaction with their co-workers. However, with the right tools it is easy to stay connected. Instant messaging services, video conference software or even good old-fashioned telephone calls give you the means to check in, share ideas and communicate. Another benefit of this: you will not be forgotten or even passed over for promotion.

Stretch your legs or enjoy a change of scenery

Sitting at your desk all day is neither good for your concentration nor your health. Make sure you get up regularly for some form of light exercise, e.g. walking around or stretching.

You can also work "off-site", leaving your home. It is quite easy to find coffee shops which offer free Wi-Fi and even some space for people to work.

(453 words)

Anlage 3 (Mediation)

INFOBLATT TELEARBEIT

Vorteile:

....

....

Nachteile:

....

....

Tipps für die erfolgreiche Arbeit von zuhause aus:

....

....

....

....

Unit 3 Finding my way in the company

3.4.4 Practise using telephone numbers.

Buch S. 38

Listen to these messages and write down the numbers and also the names of the towns that you hear.

1 Our number is 01244 for Chester and then 86 55 023. I'll repeat: 01244 for Chester and then 86 55 023.
2 You can reach us at 0141 for Glasgow and after that 975 43 43. I'll say it again: 0141 for Glasgow and after that 975 43 43.
3 Call us under 857 for Boston and dial 96 781 718. I'll repeat: our number is 857 for Boston and dial 96 781 718.
4 Please ring the following number: 0131 for Edinburgh and then 605 02 06. I'll repeat the number: 0131 for Edinburgh and then 605 02 06.
5 You can reach us as follows: 313 for Detroit. And the number is 12 45 847. So it's 313 for Detroit and the number is 12 45 847.
6 Would you please ring 01253 for Blackpool. And the number is 138 78 54. Here is the number again: 01253 for Blackpool and after that 138 78 54.
7 For further information, ring 440 for Cleveland. And then dial 47 74 781. I'll repeat, ring 440 for Cleveland and then dial 47 74 781.
8 My daytime number is 01482 for Hull. And then dial 88 65 718. Here is the number again: 01482 for Hull and my number is 88 65 718.

3.4.5 Listen to this telephone call. Make notes of the details.

Buch S. 41

Lena Westermann is taking the call. But the caller, Patricia Soames, wants to talk to Mr Sven Braukmüller.

Lena: Guten Morgen. Westermann von der Firma Odenthal GmbH. Was kann ich für Sie tun?

Patricia: Good morning. Sorry, I don't speak much German. Could we speak English, please?

Lena: OK. But my English is not very good. I'll try.

Patricia: Excellent. Thank you. I would like to talk to Herr Br..., Brauk... Excuse me. The name is so complicated.

Lena: Do you mean Herr Braukmüller?

Patricia: Exactly. That's him. Could I speak to him, please?

Lena: I'm very sorry, but he is not in the office this morning.

Patricia: Oh, that's a shame. I need to talk to him very urgently.

Lena: Hmn. Would you like to leave a message then?

Patricia: Yes, I think I would. Very good of you.

Lena: And what is the message?

Patricia: Please tell him that Pat phoned, Patricia Soames from Sykes Ltd in Birmingham. It's about the meeting the day after tomorrow[1]. We're having some problems with some of the participants[2] who can't travel. It's really very urgent.

Lena: OK. So the message is: could Mr Braukmüller please call you back immediately, because you are having some problems with the meeting the day after tomorrow. Some people can't travel. Is that right?

Patricia: Very good. That's it, exactly.

Lena: OK. – Just a moment please. I've got that then. And could you please tell me your name again?

Patricia: No problem. My name is Pat, Patricia Soames.

Lena: And could you spell your name, please?

Patricia: Yes, of course. S O A M E S from Sykes Ltd in Birmingham.

Lena: OK. And, just in case, could I have your telephone number, please?

Patricia: My number is 0044 for Britain, and then the area code is 121 for Birmingham. And our number is 660 34 58.

Lena: OK. I think I've got that. I repeat. Your number is 0044 121 660 34 58. And your name is Patricia Soames.

Patricia: That's perfect. Your English is really very good. Well done.

Lena: Thank you. And I'll make sure Herr Braukmüller gets the message when he comes in.

Patricia: That's very kind of you. Thank you and goodbye.

Lena: Goodbye.

[1] übermorgen
[2] Teilnehmer/in

Role play Buch S. 42

Role B You are Wendy, the receptionist of Sampson Engineering Ltd. The company normally does not do organised visits. But you'll try to reach the public relations officer, Ann Johnston. You find out that she is not in the office and won't be back until the day after tomorrow. You take down the name and number of the caller. You promise that Ann will call back as soon as she's back in the office.

Unit 5 Getting supplies

5.2.3 Make a telephone enquiry.

Buch S. 62

Role play

Role B You work at the reception desk of Burns Sports Equipment Ltd. You receive an enquiry about sports equipment for children. And you promise to get it sent off[1] immediately. You don't understand the address at first and ask for it to be repeated and for parts of it to be spelt. You promise that the literature will be sent off straightaway[2].

[1] Versand veranlassen
[2] sofort

Unit 6 Handling orders

6.5 Chasing up a fax order

Buch S. 77

Listen to this telephone conversation.

Brian		Julia
Leicester Office Supplies. Brian speaking. How can I help you?	→	
	←	This is Julia Strasser. I'm working at McCallum Engineering. And I sent you a fax a few days ago. Have you got it?
Sorry, a fax you said? And who did you send it to?	→	
	←	Yes, a fax. To your company.
No particular name or anything?	→	
	←	Nooh, to your company.
OK. And what was it about?	→	
	←	We need some office materials very quickly.
OK. Office materials, you say? Just a sec. – I think I've got the fax now. Is it for envelopes[1], printer paper, cartridges[2] and a lot of other stuff[3]?	→	
	←	Yes, I think you are right. That must be our order.
And what's the problem?	→	
	←	We need everything at once.
And what do you mean by "at once"?	→	
	←	We must have everything tomorrow morning.
Tomorrow morning, eh?? - Now, that's really very short notice. And why don't you check your stocks earlier, may I ask? – We're closing in half an hour. You realise that?? And I'm not sure that we've got everything in stock[4], anyway.	→	
	←	But we did. And we sent our order three days ago. And nothing has happened. Now we need the things very fast. Please!?!
OK. OK. – I don't know what went wrong there. But I'll see what I can do. I'll just put together what we've got in stock. And then, I'll have to send a van[5] round first thing[6] tomorrow. And what we can't supply now we'll just have to send later. Is that alright with you then?	→	
	←	That is very good of you. Thank you very much. And I hope you HAVE got everything in stock.
I'll do what I can. Alright?!	→	
		Good. I like that. Thank you and goodbye.

[1] Briefumschlag
[2] (Tinten-/Drucker-)Patrone
[3] Zeug
[4] auf Lager, vorrätig
[5] Lieferwagen
[6] als allererstes

Unit 8 How to deal with complaints

8.6 Role play

Buch S. 109

[1] während

Role B You are Ms Sylvia Hayes of Translog Logistics LTD. Find out what your partner is phoning about. Try to be very understanding and helpful. Ask for the details of the addressee and the consignment number. But you cannot find the documents immediately. You will ask your colleagues and promise to phone back later. Stay calm throughout[1] this phone call.

Unit 10 Dealing with visitors

10.4 Getting things organised

Buch S. 130

Role play 1

Role B You are working at the reception desk of Beverly Hotel. *Sweets and the like* want to make a booking for two additional single rooms. Check the dates again and confirm the booking (one double room and six single rooms). All other terms remain unchanged.

Role play 2

[1] Taxifahrt

Role B You are the secretary/receptionist of *York Taxis*. You will be asked to give information on the fares for taxi rides[1] in York itself and between Manchester and York. The rates for the rides in York are fixed (basic rate of £2.50, mileage rate £2.10, waiting time £30.00 per hour, flat rate for the minibus to Manchester £75.00). There are no business rates, and VAT is included in the price.

Unit 11 What it takes: events and projects

11.3 Problems with room bookings

Buch S. 143

Role B You are Tarik. Swinton Ltd wants to change the dates of their conference originally arranged for two and a half days from Wednesday, 1 June to Friday, 3 June, midday. The group needs a room seating 25 people. The conference is to be held exactly two weeks later. All your rooms are fully booked for that period. You can only offer a much larger room seating a hundred people. The other possibility to have the meeting is three weeks later. Your partner cannot make a decision now. You promise to make a provisional booking for Wednesday, 22 June to Friday, 24 June. But the offer is firm for three days only. You repeat the dates.

11.6 Project work Buch S. 150

Role B Sie arbeiten für den italienischen Partner in diesem Projekt und wissen, dass ihr Bericht nicht termingerecht fertiggestellt worden ist. Das Team ist augenblicklich mit vielen anderen wichtigen Dingen beschäftigt. Aufgrund von Informationen aus der Teamleitung gehen Sie aber davon aus, dass der Bericht innerhalb von einer Woche fertig sein wird. Sie versprechen, dass Sie alles tun werden, das früher zu erledigen.

Unit 12 Presenting

12.3 Project: Presenting your company Buch S. 155

A	Content		++	+	O	–	– –	
1	Handling of the content	interesting, engaging[1], well-informed speaker						not interesting, not very engaging, poorly[2] informed speaker
2	Structure	introduction – main part – conclusion, comprehensible[3]						no introduction, no or unclear structure
3	Visualisation[4]	meaningful[5] graphs and tables, clear and understandable, appealing[6] design (colours, pictures)						no (meaningful) graphs/tables, too much text/detail; unclear
4	Length	appropriate						too long/short
B	**Language**		**++**	**+**	**O**	**–**	**– –**	
5	Delivery	free or with little help (prompt cards[7]), good flow						read out from a sheet of paper, learned by heart, blackouts, too fast/no breaks
6	Voice	not too loud/low, dynamic, clear articulation[8], with emphasis[9]						too loud/low, monotonous, difficult to understand
7	Style	appropriate vocabulary, suitable[10] for the audience, provides necessary help for understanding unknown terms, good use of presentation phrases						slang, long and/or complicated sentences, use of unclear terms
C	**Body language**		**++**	**+**	**O**	**–**	**– –**	
8	Eye contact	often, everyone feels addressed						only looks at one person or her/his sheet/prompts or at the computer screen
9	Facial expressions[11], gestures[15] and posture[16]	confident[12], open, appropriate and punctuating[18]						exaggerated[13], stiff[14], artificial, fidgeting around[17]
D	**Overall impression and any other pieces of advice you want to give your classmate**							

1 *hier*: einnehmend, fesselnd
2 dürftig, schlecht
3 nachvollziehbar, verständlich
4 Visualisierung, Veranschaulichung
5 aussagekräftig
6 ansprechend
7 Stichwortkarte
8 Aussprache
9 Betonung
10 passend
11 Mimik
12 selbstbewusst, souverän
13 übertrieben
14 steif
15 Gestik
16 Körperhaltung
17 herumzappeln
18 *hier*: unterstreichend, mit Hervorhebung wichtiger Punkte

Unit 13 Going to a trade fair

13.6 Changing a reservation

Buch S. 171

Role B You are the receptionist at Hotel Belvedere. A client has made a trade fair booking for three nights for early November. Ask for the reference number. The booking is for five single rooms at the early booking rate of £250 per night including cooked breakfast. At this late stage you don't have any single rooms anymore. But because of a cancellation[1] only a few minutes ago, a double room has become available at the price of £450. So two of the party will have to share. But you need an answer ASAP.

[1] Stornierung

Vocabulary

Chronologische Wortschatzliste

Diese Liste enthält alle Wörter und Phrasen der Einheiten 1–14 in chronologischer Reihenfolge. Die Übersetzungen geben die im Textzusammenhang sinnvolle Bedeutung der Einträge wieder. Die Nennung der Abschnitte (Nummern und Titel) in den Einheiten erleichtert das Auffinden.

Unit 1 My first day at work

1.1 How to introduce yourself

training	Ausbildung
office management assistant	Kaufmann/-frau für Büromanagement
company	Unternehmen
to introduce os.	sich vorstellen
colleague	Kollege, Kollegin
workplace	Arbeitsplatz
teamleader	Teamleiter/in, Leiter/in des Teams
(to do an) internship	Praktikum (machen)
to apply	sich bewerben
to train	eine Ausbildung machen
to become	(beruflich) werden
office junior	jüngere(r) Mitarbeiter/in im Büro
secondary school	Real-, Haupt-, Sekundarschule
snorkelling	Schnorcheln
final exam	Abschlussprüfung
to pass (an exam)	(eine Prüfung) bestehen
A-levels	*etwa:* Abitur
to decide	entscheiden
economics	Wirtschaftswissenschaften

Introducing oneself

to mention	erwähnen
achievements	Erfolge, Leistungen
depending on	abhängend/abhängig von
amount	Menge
(the/a) kind of	(die/eine) Art von
to vary	variieren, sich verändern
to consider	in Betracht ziehen
audience	Zuhörer *(pl.)*; Zuschauer
it just takes	man braucht nur
to attend school	Schule besuchen
to graduate	Schule abschließen
finals	Abschlussprüfung
scheduled	geplant

Simon's first day at work

department	Abteilung
trainee	Auszubildende/r
to start out as	beginnen als
opposite	gegenüber
to look after so.	sich um jdn. kümmern
a couple of weeks	ein paar Wochen
applicant	Bewerber/in

Writing skills

informal	formlos
internal	innerbetrieblich
addressee	Empfänger/in
flush left	linksbündig
in capital letters (caps)	in Großbuchstaben
immediate(ly)	unmittelbar, direkt; sofort

1.2 How to equip one's workplace

equipment	Ausstattung, Ausrüstung, Geräte
tools	Werkzeuge, (Hilfs-)Mittel
employer	Arbeitgeber
to want so. to do sth.	wollen/mögen, dass jd. etw. tut
to arrange	einrichten, anordnen
to feel comfortable	sich wohl/zuhause fühlen
keen	begierig, sehr interessiert
paper clip	Büroklammer
punch	Locher
computer keyboard	Rechnertastatur
screen	Bildschirm
writing pad	Schreibblock
staples	Heftklammern
file folder	Aktenordner
printer	Drucker
memory stick	Speicherstick, Memory-Stick
ring binder	Ringhefter, Ringbuch
printer paper	Druckerpapier
window envelope	Fensterbriefumschlag
biro	Kugelschreiber
board marker	Boardmarker
container	Behälter
ink	Tinte
sticky tape	Klebeband
highlighter	Textmarker
pen tray	Stiftablage
index cards	Karteikarten
printer cartridge	Druckerpatrone
post-it note	Post-it Notiz(-zettel)
device	Gerät
hanging file	Hängeordner
meeting	Sitzung, Konferenz

1.3 How to become an office junior

career	Karriere, Berufslaufbahn
particularly	besonders; insbesondere
overtime	Überstunden
office-based	Büro-
impression	Eindruck
career path	Berufslaufbahn, beruflicher Werdegang
responsibility	Verantwortung
office manager	Büroleiter/in
to obtain further qualifications	sich weiter qualifizieren
junior role	Stelle von untergeordneter Bedeutung
at least	zumindest, mindestens
GCSE (General Certificate of Secondary Education) O-levels (= ordinary level) *[GB]*	Hauptschul-, Realschulabschluss, Abschluss Sekundarstufe I
job description	Stellenbeschreibung
A-level (advanced level) *[GB]*	*hier*: Fachprüfung im engl. Abitur (fortgeschrittenes Niveau)
experience	Erfahrung
training on the job	Ausbildung im Betrieb
office routines	Büroroutinen
experienced	erfahren
to work towards	hinarbeiten auf
vocational qualification	berufliche Qualifikation
business administration	Betriebswirtschaft

1.4 Talking about school

primary school	Grundschule
secondary education	Schulbildung in der Sekundarstufe I, Sekundarschulbildung
subject	(Schul-/Studien-)Fach
to include	einschließen, umfassen
apprenticeship	Ausbildung (*meist gewerblich*)
NVQ (national vocational qualification) *[GB]*	staatlicher Berufsbildungsabschluss
extracting	*(Rohstoffe)* Abbau
engineering	Ingenieurwesen
manufacturing	Herstellung, Produktion
to provide	zur Verfügung stellen, bereitstellen
communicating	Kommunikation(-swesen)
to continue	fortsetzen
school-leaving age	Ende des schulpflichtigen Alters
pre-school education	Vorschulerziehung
primary education	Grundschulausbildung
elementary school	Grundschule
junior high school	Mittelschule
secondary education	Sekundarschulausbildung
(senior) high school	Oberschule, Gymnasium
tertiary education	Hochschulausbildung
at the age of	im Alter von
average grade	Durchschnittsnote
comprehensive school	Gesamtschule
form teacher	Klassenlehrer/in
grade	Note
pupil	Schüler/in
school report	(Schul-)Zeugnis
school year	Schuljahr
student	Schüler/in; (Student/in)
summer holidays/ vacation *[AE]*	Sommerferien
to attend school/classes	zur Schule/zum Unterricht gehen
to decide to go to … (school)	sich entscheiden, zur … Schule zu gehen
to do a work experience	ein Praktikum machen
to fail an exam	eine Prüfung nicht bestehen, in einer Prüfung durchfallen
to leave school	von der Schule abgehen
to repeat a year	ein Jahr wiederholen
to resit an exam	eine Prüfung wiederholen
to spend (time) abroad	(eine Zeit) im Ausland verbringen
to start kindergarten/ school	in den Kindergarten/die Schule gehen
grammar school	Gymnasium
secondary school	Haupt-, Realschule, Sekundarstufe I
vocational school	Berufsschule, berufsbildende Schule
graduation from high school *[US]*	(*etwa*) Abitur
to do one's A-levels *[GB]*	Abitur machen
to graduate from high school *[US]*	seinen Schulabschluss machen
high school diploma *[AE]*, O-level exams *[GB]*; secondary school-leaving certificate	Hauptschul-, Realschulabschluss, Abschluss der Sekundarstufe I
secondary school leaver; high school graduate	Realschulabgänger/in
PE (physical education)	Sport
Home Economics	Hauswirtschaft(-slehre)
Fine Arts	Kunst
Combined Sciences	Naturwissenschaften
Design & Technology	Gestaltung & Technologie
Business Studies	Betriebswirtschaftslehre
Computer Studies	Informatik
Food & Nutrition	Nahrung & Ernährung
Environmental Management	Umweltmanagement
Commercial Studies	Handelskunde
to capitalise	großschreiben

Unit 2 Working in an office

2.1 Office work: What's it like?

pros and cons	Vorteile und Nachteile
customer	Kunde, Kundin
challenging	schwierig, anspruchsvoll
to have sth. explained	etw. erklärt bekommen
to look over so.'s shoulder	jdm. über die Schulter sehen, jdn. kontrollieren
to get on	vorankommen, klar kommen
dress code	Kleiderordnung
to come down to	darauf hinauslaufen
cubicle	Bürozelle, Kabine
open office	Großraumbüro
to make small-talk	Smalltalk machen, sich unterhalten
a waste of time	Zeitverschwendung
to chat	plaudern, klönen

2.2 The ideal office junior

to interview	Vorstellungsgespräch führen
prospective	zukünftig
activity	Tätigkeit
outside	außerhalb von
super organised	blendend organisiert, mit super Organisationstalent
detail-oriented	detailbewusst, -genau
accurate	genau, präzise, sorgfältig
trustworthy	vertrauenswürdig, verlässlich
reliable	zuverlässig
self-motivated	(selbst)motiviert
good communicator	wort-, sprachgewandt, mit verbindlichen Umgangsformen
verbal and written	mündlich und schriftlich
tidy	sauber, ordentlich
neat appearance	gepflegte Erscheinung, gepflegtes Äußeres
job advert	Stellenanzeige
to rearrange	neu anordnen

2.3 The time spent at work

working hours	Arbeitszeit
working day	Arbeitstag
standard working week	normale Arbeitswoche
regular working hours	normale Arbeitszeit
(to work) flexitime	Gleitzeit (arbeiten)
flexitime account	Gleitzeitkonto
core hours/time	Kernarbeitszeit
to start/leave early	früh anfangen/Schluss machen
(to take) a day off	freier Tag; einen Tag frei nehmen
(to take) time off	frei; sich frei nehmen
(to work) overtime	Überstunden (machen)
lunch break	Mittagspause
coffee break	Kaffeepause
annual holiday/leave/ vacation *[AE]*	Jahresurlaub

2.4 The job

administrative assistant	Verwaltungsassistent/in
team assistant	Teamassistent/in
office assistant	Büroassistent/in
to pick up	mitnehmen, abholen
mail room	Postzimmer
outgoing mail	Postausgang, ausgehende Post
administrative work	Verwaltungsarbeit
clerical work	Schreib-, Büroarbeit
to file (away)	Ablage machen
to sort	sortieren
enquiry	Anfrage
to layout	gestalten
report	Bericht
spreadsheet	Tabelle, Diagramm
to create a spreadsheet	Tabelle anlegen
project documents	Projektunterlagen
to take and pass on messages	Nachrichten annehmen & weiterleiten
to check (out)	überwachen, prüfen
supplies	Vorräte
to place an order	Auftrag erteilen
under the direction of	unter der Anleitung von
senior staff	ältere Angestellte; Vorgesetzte *(pl.)*
to assist	helfen, unterstützen
duty	Pflicht, Aufgabe
to track	verfolgen, suchen
to monitor	überwachen
deadline	Frist
to research	heraussuchen, finden
travel connections	Verkehrsverbindungen
to arrange	planen, organisieren
to coordinate	aufeinander abstimmen, koordinieren
business trip	Geschäftsreise
to collect data	Daten zusammenstellen
analysis, *pl.* analyses	Analyse
executive	leitende(r) Angestellte(r), Führungskraft
to handle	bearbeiten
project data	Projektdaten
follow-up	Nachbereitung
meeting	Sitzung, Konferenz
meeting room	Sitzungs-, Konferenzraum
event	Veranstaltung
reception	Empfang
to support	unterstützen
customer-related	Kunden-, kundenbezogen
appointment	Termin
research	Nachforschung, Recherche
to direct	führen, (Weg etc.) weisen
insurance	Versicherung
work placement	Praktikum

2.5 The workplace

similarity	Ähnlichkeit
work environment	Arbeitsumfeld
layout	Anordnung, Gestaltung
health and safety issues	Arbeitsschutzfragen
fire escape	Feuerleiter
emergency exit	Fluchtweg, Notausgang
employee needs	Bedürfnisse der Mitarbeiter(innen)
wall unit	Wandschrank, -regal
filing cabinet	Aktenschrank
location	Standort
ventilation	Belüftung
seating arrangement	Sitzordnung

2.6 Office layouts: Pros and cons

content	Inhalt
home office	Büro zu Hause, häuslicher Arbeitsplatz
marking	Durchsicht/Bewertung von Arbeiten
sales staff	Verkaufspersonal
to equip	ausrüsten, ausstatten
once in a while	ab und zu
coffice *(Kombination aus coffee und office)*	Arbeitsplatz im Café
Wi-Fi	WLAN
relaxing environment	entspannende Umgebung
noise level	Lärmpegel, Geräuschkulisse
cabinet office	Büroflucht, -etage
secretariat	Sekretariat
to monitor	überwachen
disturbance	Störung
cubicle office	Zellenbüro
separate	(ab)getrennt
sound-absorbing partition wall	schalldämmende Trennwand
atmosphere of privacy	Privatsphäre
work area	Arbeitsfläche, -bereich
to overhear	zufällig (mit)hören, mitbekommen
exhausted	erschöpft
open-plan office	Großraumbüro
to cover	einnehmen
to group	anordnen
in a variety of ways	auf verschiedene Art und Weise
facilities	Möglichkeiten, Einrichtungen
recreation	Erholung, Entspannung
breakroom	Pausenraum
rest area	Ruhezone
office supplies and equipment	Bürogeräte und Büromaterial
visitor reception area	Besucherempfang(-szone)

Unit 3 Finding my way in the company

3.1 Learning about companies

to come across	zufällig treffen auf
field of activity	Tätigkeitsfeld
to be based in	Sitz haben in
findings	Ergebnisse, Resultate
similarity	Ähnlichkeit

3.2 Presenting a company

over a period of time	über eine Zeitspanne hinweg
range	Sortiment, Auswahl
service	Dienstleistung
to operate	tätig sein
furthermore	darüber hinaus
local community	Standortgemeinde
from outside	von außerhalb (der Firma)
trade partner	Geschäftspartner/in
general public	allgemeine Öffentlichkeit
approach	Herangehensweise
required	erforderlich
to make an effort	Anstrengung unternehmen
management team	Unternehmensleitung, Führungsmannschaft
head office	Hauptverwaltung
customer relations	Kundenbeziehungen
senior customer relations officer	Leiter/in der Abteilung Kundenbeziehungen
overview	Überblick
as we go along	bei Bedarf
to hesitate	zögern
to be precise	um genau zu sein
logistics services	Logistikdienstleistungen, Transportdienste
local farming community	landwirtschaftliche Betriebe hier vor Ort
sound	stabil, solide, ordentlich
customer base	Kundenstamm
firmly established	*hier*: gut aufgebaut
to branch out into	*hier*: Neuland betreten (mit)
farming supplies	landwirtschaftliche Güter
fertiliser	Düngemittel
seed(s)	Saatgut
pesticide	Pflanzenschutzmittel
farming equipment	Agrarmaschinen
network	Netz(werk)
sales outlet	Verkaufsstelle
neighbouring county	angrenzende Grafschaft
jointly responsible	gemeinsam verantwortlich
administration	Verwaltung
to retire	in Rente gehen
headquarters	Hauptverwaltung
central goods depot	zentrales Warenlager
sales	Absatz

to consolidate	das Erreichte festigen
to expand	sich ausbreiten, expandieren
to aim to	wollen, beabsichtigen
to build on that trust	auf dieser Vertrauensbasis aufbauen
specific needs	besondere Bedürfnisse
agricultural community	*hier*: Landwirtschaft
for the time being	zunächst einmal
to customise	auf die Kundenbedürfnisse zuschneiden
key account manager	Hauptkundenbetreuer/in
survey	Überblick
annual sales	Jahresumsatz
at home and abroad	im In-(land) und Ausland
affiliated company	angeschlossene Gesellschaft
current	jetzig
branch	Zweigstelle, Filiale
production plant	Werk, Produktionsstätte
subsidiary	Tochtergesellschaft
family-owned business	Familienunternehmen
to merge	(sich) zusammenschließen
to supply	liefern
to trade in	handeln mit
steady	stetig, kontinuierlich
turnover	Umsatz

3.3 Company organisation

company organisation	Unternehmensorganisation
organisational	Organisations-
hierarchical	hierarchisch
job title	Stellenbezeichnung
sales representative	Außendienstmitarbeiter/in
bookkeeper	Buchhalter/in
driver	Fahrer/in
managing director	Geschäftsführer/in
warehouse manager	Lagerleiter/in
wages clerk	Lohnbuchhalter/in
foreman	Meister/in, Vorarbeiter/in
product development officer	Produktentwickler/in
production manager	Produktionsleiter/in
accountant	Rechnungsführer/in
recruitment officer	Sachbearbeiter/in für Personaleinstellungen
sales manager	Verkaufsleiter/in
accounting manager	Leiter/in des Rechnungswesens
human resources manager	Leiter/in des Personalwesens
distribution manager	Vertriebsleiter/in
production controller	Produktionskontrolleur/in
marketing manager	Leiter/in der Marketing-Abteilung
junior accountant	Nachwuchskraft in der Buchhaltung
salary administration officer	Gehaltsbuchhalter/in
logistics officer	Leiter/in der Logistik
fitter	Schlosser, Monteur
dispatch manager	Versandleiter/in
facility manager	Objektleiter/in, Gebäudemanager/in
head buyer	Chef-Einkäufer/in
production supervisor	Produktionsleiter/in
project manager	Projektleiter/in
purchasing officer	Sachbearbeiter/in (im) Einkauf
quality controller	Qualitätskontrolleur/in
receptionist	Mitarbeiter/in am Empfang
sales agent	Verkäufer/in
software engineer	Software-Entwickler/in
warehouse worker	Lagerarbeiter/in
in the course of	im Verlaufe von

3.4 Telephoning

3.4.1 Some basics

ansaphone	Anrufbeantworter
area code	Vorwahlnummer
to dial	wählen
directory	(Telefon-)Verzeichnis
engaged	besetzt
extension	Durchwahlnummer, Nebenstelle
headset	Kopfhörer mit Mikrofon
landline	Festnetz
message	Nachricht
ringing tone	Klingelton
switchboard	Telefonzentrale
to key in	eingeben, eintasten
subscriber's number	Nummer des Teilnehmers
emergency	Notfall
caller	Anrufer/in
notepad	Notizblock

3.4.2 Telephone alphabet

equally	ebenso, ebenfalls

3.4.3 Good to know

asterisk	Sternchen
vertical bar/slash	senkrechter Strich
to underscore *[AE]*	unterstreichen

3.4.4 Telephone numbers

digit	Ziffer, Stelle
first name	Vorname
surname	Familienname

3.4.5 Telephone phrases

recorded message	automatische Ansage
out-of-office hours	außerhalb der Bürostunden/-zeiten
signal	Empfang
office number	dienstliche Nummer
home number	private Rufnummer
hotline, helpline	Notrufnummer, Beratungsstelle
to save	speichern
to delete	löschen, tilgen
tone	Tonsignal
to apologise	sich entschuldigen
to put so. through	jdn. durchstellen
to pass on a message	Nachricht weiterleiten
to not quite get sth.	etw. nicht ganz/genau verstehen
to leave a message	Nachricht hinterlassen
to take a message	Nachricht aufnehmen
to hold the line	in der Leitung/dran bleiben
to leave a number	Telefonnummer hinterlassen, jdm. die Nummer geben
urgent	dringend
participant	Teilnehmer/in
the day after tomorrow	übermorgen

Unit 4 Getting organised

4.1 From school to work

sheltered	geschützt
to reflect	widerspiegeln
world of business	Wirtschaftswelt
watershed	Wendepunkt, Zäsur
to take stock	Bilanz ziehen, Bestandsaufnahme machen

4.2 A beginner's experience

surroundings	Umgebung
habit	Gewohnheit
moving part	bewegliches Teil
division	*hier*: Abteilung, Sektion
to carry one's weight	voll mitziehen
to suffer	leiden
to interact	zusammenwirken, sich wechselseitig beeinflussen
accounting	Rechnungswesen, Buchhaltung
personnel	Personalwesen
legal	*hier*: Rechtsabteilung
to stutter	stottern
entry level	Eingangsstufe
to what extent	in welchem Umfang
a major part	ein bedeutender Teil
efficient	effizient, effektiv
to drag on	sich hinziehen
it is all about	es geht vor allem um …
to negotiate	verhandeln
delivery date	Liefertermin
salary	Gehalt
to meet a deadline	Frist/Liefertermin einhalten
to sulk	schmollen, üble Laune haben
to communicate effectively	wirkungsvoll kommunizieren
networking	Bildung von Netzwerken
to be repetitive	sich ständig wiederholen
to reckon	schätzen, damit rechnen
balance	Gleichgewicht, Ausgewogenheit
to just get on with sth.	einfach weitermachen/erledigen
to stall	zum Stillstand kommen
to pay off	sich auszahlen
sceptical	skeptisch

4.3 Organising my day

break	Pause
to paste	*hier*: einfügen
mailing list	Versandliste
to occur	vorkommen
to warm up to	sich erwärmen für
to be a bore	langweilig sein

4.4 How about filing?

(to do) filing	Ablage (machen)
parcel delivery	Paketauslieferung
to store	speichern
intranet	Intranet, firmeninternes Netz
to speed up	beschleunigen
no end	erheblich, mächtig
in a split second	im Bruchteil einer Sekunde
customer account number	Kundennummer
to draw up an agreement	Vereinbarung aufsetzen
circular	Rundschreiben
to draw up the minutes	Protokoll schreiben
to provide information	Informationen bereitstellen/geben
to come into its own	seine Berechtigung erhalten
for reference purposes	als Nachweis
by law	aufgrund gesetzlicher Vorschriften
to keep records	Unterlagen aufbewahren
tradesman	Handwerker
filing system	Ablagesystem
numerical system	Zahlensystem
hanging files	Hängeregistratur
folder	Aktenmappe
to stack up	aufstapeln
filing shelf	Regalschrank
to retrieve	hervorholen, auffinden

coding	Kodierung, Kennzeichnung
fastener	Halterung, Klammer
divider	Teiler
to be at hand	unmittelbar verfügbar sein
roller container	Rollcontainer
file storage	Aktenlagerung
to address an issue	Problem angehen

4.5 Organising my desk

creative	kreativ, schöpferisch
to clear away	beiseite räumen, wegräumen
to be there to stay	dauerhaft bleiben
to expand	erweitern
kingdom	Königreich
close at hand	in Reichweite
to figure out	herausfinden
receiver	(Telefon-)Hörer
workstation	Arbeitsplatz (*Tisch u. Stuhl*)
writing utensils	Schreibutensilien
stapler	Heftapparat, „Klammeraffe"
drawer	Schublade
currently	gegenwärtig, gerade jetzt, zur Zeit
file holder	Aktenablage, -mappe
in-tray	(Post-)Eingangskorb
out-tray	(Post-)Ausgangskorb
hanky *(coll.)*	Taschentuch
lunchbox	Brotdose
coffee mug	Kaffeetasse
tempting	verführerisch
pile	Haufen, Stapel
clutter	Durcheinander, Unordnung
to be under pressure	unter Druck/„Strom" stehen
screw	Schraube

4.6 Written communication

written communication	Schriftverkehr
purposefully designed	speziell entwickelt
stationery	(Firmen-)Briefpapier
to some extent	bis zu einem gewissen Grad
commercial register	Handelsregister
bank account number	Kontonummer
left-justified	linksbündig
justified text	Blocksatz

4.6.1 Sample letter

sample letter	Musterbrief
reference initials	Bezugszeichen
subject line	Betreffzeile
request for	Bitte um
salutation	Anrede
wide range	umfassendes Angebot
brochure	Broschüre
indication	Hinweis; Angabe
to contain	enthalten
to make arrangements	Vorkehrungen treffen, alles Nötige veranlassen
tour guide	Touristenführer/in
to suggest	vorschlagen, anregen
to get in touch	Kontakt aufnehmen
needs	Anforderungen
to look forward to sth.	sich auf etw. freuen
complimentary close	höfliche Schlussformel
enclosure	Anlage

4.6.2 British and American usage

convention	Standard
to apply	gelten
commonly	allgemein, häufig
to refer to	sich beziehen auf
punctuation	Interpunktion, Zeichensetzung
fairly common	sehr gebräuchlich, allgemein üblich
postal code *[BE]*; ZIP (zone improvement plan) code *[AE]*	Postleitzahl
to abbreviate	abkürzen
to precede	vorangehen (+ Dat)

4.6.3 E-mails

mobile messaging	Nachrichten-, Datenaustausch
at her/his convenience	nach Belieben, wann es ihm/ihr passt
requirements of form	formale Anforderungen
outside communication	Kommunikation mit Außenstehenden
inter-office	bürointern
carbon copy	Durchschlag
recipient	Empfänger/in
relevant	wichtig
to prioritise	nach Wichtigkeit ordnen
concise	präzise
seniors	Vorgesetzte, ältere Mitarbeiter/innen/ Kollegen/Kolleginnen
overlong	übermäßig lang
to clutter up	zumüllen
priority	Vorrangigkeit, Vorrang
irrelevant	nebensächlich
attachment	Anhang
to keep informed	auf dem Laufenden halten
apology	Entschuldigung
to cancel	stornieren, absagen
unfortunately	leider
initial	anfänglich, ursprünglich
urgent appointment	dringender Termin
on so.'s behalf	für jdm., in jds. Auftrag
organiser	Veranstalter
understanding	Verständnis
revolving door	Drehtür
power nap	Kurzschlaf
workmate	Kollege, Kollegin
to have a chat	ein Pläuschchen halten
to gossip	tratschen

Unit 5 Getting supplies

5.1 Where do companies shop?

office supplies	Büromaterial
buying channel	Einkaufs-, Bezugsquelle
potential	möglich, in Frage kommend
supplier	Lieferant
wholesaler	Großhändler
retailer	Einzelhändler
to relocate	umziehen
premises	Geschäfts-, Büroräume
downtown	*hier*: (im) (Stadt-)Zentrum, (in der) Innenstadt
to check out	etw. heraussuchen, sich schlau machen
office equipment	Büroausstattung
move	*hier*: Umzug
to be on the agenda	*hier*: anstehen
all sorts of	alle möglichen ...
on top	außerdem, dazu, zusätzlich
technical equipment	technische Ausstattung, Geräte
light fitting	Beleuchtungskörper
to give the green light	grünes Licht geben, zustimmen
offer	Angebot
good value for money	etw. Ordentliches für das Geld
to draft	entwerfen
catalog *[AE]*, catalogue *[BE]*	Katalog
to proceed	vorgehen, verfahren
to get going	sich dran/an die Arbeit machen

5.2 Making enquiries

5.2.1 Enquiry for office furniture

in addition to	zusätzlich, außer (+ Dat.)
Yellow Pages	Gelbe Seiten *(Branchenbuch mit Anschriften von Firmen)*
to come up with	vorschlagen, sich ausdenken
except for	außer (+Dat.)
high-end	hochwertig
attracted	*hier*: beeindruckt
variety	Vielfalt
design	Modell, Gestaltung
to display	zeigen, ausstellen
high-class	hochwertig
to enquire with so.	bei jdm. nachfragen
to recommend	empfehlen
medium-sized	mittelgroß, -ständisch
provider of IT support services	IT-Dienstleister
to distribute	vertreiben, verkaufen
illustrated	bebildert
to appreciate sth.	sich freuen(, wenn ...)
indication	Hinweis, Angabe
product line	Produktlinie, Sortiment
literature	Prospektmaterial
indicated below	unten angegeben
market offer	Angebot im Markt
customary reference	(branchen-)übliche Referenz
to place an order with so.	jdm. einen Auftrag erteilen
to thank so. for their kind attention (to the enquiry)	jdm. für die Bearbeitung (der Anfrage) danken
at your earliest convenience	sobald wie möglich, umgehend
competitive	umkämpft, wettbewerbsintensiv
to manufacture	herstellen, produzieren, (an)fertigen
terms and conditions	allgemeine Geschäftsbedingungen
sample	Muster, Probe
for testing purposes	für Prüfzwecke
current price-list	derzeit gültige Preisliste
discount	Rabatt, Nachlass
on behalf of	für, im Auftrag von
request	Anfrage, Bitte
draft	(Roh--)Entwurf

5.2.2 Write an e-mail enquiry

shortbread	Butterkeks
tartlet	Törtchen
agricultural fair	Landwirtschaftsmesse
market potential	Marktpotenzial
promising	vielversprechend
market research	Marktforschung
market share	Marktanteil
marketing campaign	Vermarktungskampagne
wholesale company	Großhandelsunternehmen
quantity discount	Mengenrabatt
hanging filing system	Hängeregistratur
product range	Verkaufsprogramm, Sortiment
to include (in)	aufnehmen in
discount for bulk orders	Mengenrabatt
grateful	dankbar

5.2.3 Make a telephone enquiry

purchasing department	Einkaufsabteilung
chain store	Filialkette
selected	ausgewählt
to get sth. done	etw. veranlassen
straightaway	sofort

5.3 Making an offer

prospective	möglich, in Frage kommend	to result in	zur Folge haben; *hier*: erbringen

5.3.1 Letter 1

comprehensive	umfassend	payment in full within a fortnight	vollständige Bezahlung innerhalb von zwei Wochen/14 Tagen
under separate cover	mit getrennter Post	receipt of invoice	Rechnungserhalt
renowned	namhaft, renommiert	to be subject to	unterliegen
manufacturer	Hersteller	cash discount	Barzahlungsrabatt, Skonto
high demand for	große Nachfrage nach	confident	zuversichtlich
workmanship	Verarbeitung	range of items	Sortiment
our prices are quoted net	unsere Preise sind Nettopreise	plenty of scope	viele Möglichkeiten
delivery	(Aus-)Lieferung	to furnish	einrichten, möblieren
date of your order	Termin/Datum der Auftragserteilung	further queries	weitere Fragen
to exceed	übersteigen	at your convenience	bei Gelegenheit, wenn Sie mögen
to grant	gewähren	to praise	herausstellen, anpreisen
volume discount	Mengenrabatt		

5.3.2 Letter 2

enclosed	in der Anlage, beigefügt	to approve	zustimmen
best-selling	meistverkauft	to complete the fitting	Einbau/Montage vornehmen
selection	Auswahl	illustrated	*hier*: abgebildet
to assess	feststellen	separately	*hier*: einzeln, als Einzelstücke
bespoke solution	kundenspezifische/individuelle/ maßgeschneiderte Lösung	long-standing experience	langjährige Erfahrung
to propose	vorschlagen	budget	Etat(-mittel)
to submit	vorlegen, unterbreiten	delivery period	Lieferfrist
all-in solution	Gesamtpaket, umfassende Lösung	practicability	Durchführ-, Umsetzbarkeit
to take into account	berücksichtigen	finishing	Endbearbeitung
showroom	Ausstellungsraum	reputation	(guter) Ruf
to finalise	abschließend bearbeiten, endgültig festlegen	fitting costs	Montage-, Einbaukosten
		storage	Archivierung; Lagerung

5.3.3 Phoning a potential supplier

to arrange an appointment	Termin vereinbaren	to prefer to do	am Liebsten tun
		to check	(ab)klären

5.3.4 Write an e-mail from notes

microfilter	Mikrofilter	terms of payment	Zahlungsbedingungen

5.4 Learning phrases

to standardise	normen, standardisieren	numeral	Zahlwort
to refer to	Bezug nehmen auf, verweisen auf	confusion	Verwirrung
with reference to	Bezug nehmend auf, unter Bezugnahme auf	hyphenated	mit Bindestrich
hyphen	Bindestrich	compound	zusammengesetztes Wort

Unit 6 Handling orders

6.1 Let's get going!

firmly established business relations	*hier*: feste Kundenbeziehung	terms of business	Geschäftsbedingungen
order form	Bestellformular	laid down	angegeben, niedergelegt
initial order	Erstauftrag	to transmit	übermitteln, übersenden
to confirm	bestätigen	to serve as proof	als Nachweis dienen

6.2 Placing a new order

demand (for)	Nachfrage (nach)
attached	beigefügt
order volume	Auftragsumfang
to reconsider	nochmals prüfen, überdenken
convinced	überzeugt
to understand	sich bewusst sein
to take up to	bis zu … dauern
charge	Gebühr
packing	Verpackung
herewith	hiermit
payment within a fortnight of receipt of invoice	Zahlung innerhalb von 14 Tagen nach Rechnungserhalt
30 days net	30 Tage netto
reference is made to …	bezüglich, wir beziehen uns auf
business relationship	Geschäftsbeziehung
to be entitled to	berechtigt sein zu, Anspruch haben auf
price negotiations	Preisverhandlungen
fair discount	Messerabatt
employee discount	Personalrabatt
seasonal	saisonal, jahreszeitlich
introductory discount	Einführungsrabatt
quotation	Preisangebot, Kostenvoranschlag
to be aware	sich bewusst sein
to quote a price	Preis nennen
trade discount	Wiederverkaufs-, Handelsrabatt
as requested	wie gewünscht, wunschgemäß
credit/bank transfer	Banküberweisung
invoice	Rechnung
to acknowledge	bestätigen
receipt	Empfang, Erhalt
query	Rückfrage

6.3 Placing a telephone order

to operate	*hier*: betreiben
curtain cloth	Vorhang-, Gardinenstoff
utterance	Äußerung
agent	*hier*: Sachbearbeiter/in
to conduct a telephone conversation	Gespräch/Telefonat führen
furnishings	*hier*: Möbel-, Einrichtungshaus
to require	benötigen
curtain fabrics	Gardinen-, Vorhangstoffe
to note down	aufschreiben, notieren

6.4 Order for office supplies

purchase order form	Bestellformular
hole	Loch
paper punch	Lochapparat, Locher
correction tape	Korrekturband
envelope	(Brief-)Umschlag
file holder	Aktenmappe, -ordner
padded mailer	gefütterte Versandtasche
self-adhesive	selbstklebend
tape dispenser	Klebebandspender
appointments book	Terminkalender
to notify	In Kenntnis setzen, informieren
to complete	*hier*: ausführen
by	*hier*: bis zu
specified	angegeben
shipping note *[AE]*	Lieferschein
purchasing agent	Sachbearbeiter/in (im) Einkauf
business discount	Firmenrabatt
two-digit	zweistellig

6.5 Chasing up a fax order

to chase up (sth.)	(einer Sache) nachjagen, etw. verfolgen
grant	Stipendium, Zuschuss
general administration department	Verwaltungsabteilung
order list	Auftrags-, Bestellliste
a couple of	ein paar, einige
not … either	auch nicht
cartridge	(Tinten-/Drucker-)Patrone
stuff	Zeug
in stock	auf Lager, vorrätig
van	Lieferwagen
first thing	als allererstes
ASAP (as soon as possible)	schnellstmöglich, sofort

6.6 Paying for goods and services

bank card	Bank-, Kundenkarte
electronic cash	elektronisches Geld
down-payment	Anzahlung
remainder	Rest(-betrag)
to hand over	übergeben
to pay upfront	im Voraus bezahlen
to trust	darauf vertrauen, dass
to return	(Waren) zurückschicken, -geben
sub-standard	von minderer Qualität
faulty	fehlerhaft
built-in	eingebaut
safety element	Sicherheitselement
purchasing transaction	Einkauf, Kauftransaktion
this goes for	das gilt für
extent	Umfang
to rely on	sich verlassen auf
way of thinking	Denkweise, „Denke"
contract of purchase	Kaufvertrag

to set out	darlegen
obligation	Verpflichtung, Pflicht
amount of money due	fälliger Geldbetrag
actually	tatsächlich
convenience	Bequemlichkeit
theft	Diebstahl
cash with order (CWO)	Zahlung bei Auftragserteilung
(to) buyer's specifications	(gemäß den, nach) Angaben des Käufers
cash/payment in advance (CIA/PIA)	gegen Vorkasse
shipment	Versand, Transport
to play safe	*(fig.)* „auf Numero sicher gehen"
cash on delivery (COD)	gegen/per Nachnahme
shipping company	Transportunternehmen
electronic means	elektronisch
letter of credit (L/C)	Akkreditiv, Kreditbrief
to be assured	*hier*: gewährleisten
to match	übereinstimmen mit
bill of lading (B/L)	Konnossement
reliability	Zuverlässigkeit
payment by bank transfer	*hier*: Zahlung per Überweisung
to claim back	zurückfordern
open account	laufendes Konto, Kontokorrentkonto
at regular intervals	in regelmäßigen Abständen
administration costs	Verwaltungskosten
to deduct	abziehen

6.7 Changing the terms – Reply

to weigh up	abwägen
to bear in mind	daran denken, nicht vergessen dürfen
pricing structure	Preisstruktur
to note	feststellen
to give careful thought to	sorgfältig prüfen
suggestion	Vorschlag, Anregung
to accommodate so.	jdm. entgegenkommen
goodwill	Wohlwollen, Kulanz
to promise	versprechen
in so.'s favour	zu jds. Gunsten
to extend	verlängern
time allowed for payment	Zahlungsfrist
due	fällig
to have (our) best attention	sorgfältig bearbeitet werden
to execute	*hier*: ausführen
option	Möglichkeit, Alternative
prompt(ly)	sofortig, sofort
expert	Spezialist/in, Experte/in; fachmännisch
to lend a hand	helfen
requirement	Erfordernis
to allow	*hier*: gewähren
on top of that	darüber hinaus, ferner
to upgrade	aufwerten, höherstufen
a variety of	verschiedene
at the latest	spätestens

Unit 7 From manufacturer to customer

7.2 Transport problems

Incorporated *[AE]*	*etwa:* GmbH od. AG
to ship	versenden, verschiffen, zum Transport aufgeben; transportieren
ready for shipment	versandfertig
haulier	Spediteur, Spedition; Transportunternehmer, -unternehmen
to let so. down	jdn. „hängen"/im Stich lassen
unfortunate	unglücklich, schlecht
to break down	liegen bleiben
tight	dicht, eng
delivery schedule	Liefer-, Belieferungsplan
to reschedule	umorganisieren, umplanen
transport capacity	Transportkapazität
available	verfügbar, zur Verfügung
at short notice	kurzfristig
costly	teuer, kostspielig
annoying	ärgerlich
to make a firm promise	fest versprechen, feste Zusage machen
to hold responsible	verantwortlich machen
if that fails	wenn das nicht klappt/funktioniert
to persuade	überzeugen
delay in delivery	Lieferverzug
delivery plan	Lieferplan
freight capacity	Fracht-, Transportkapazität
ready for dispatch	versandbereit, -fertig
to provide so. with	jdn. beliefern/versorgen mit
surgery	Arztpraxis
medical supplies	Medizinbedarf, Sanitätsartikel
treatment	Behandlung
goods-in department	Wareneingang(-sabteilung)
delivery	*hier*: An-, Belieferung
delay	Verzögerung, Verzug
shipment	Versand, Belieferung; Sendung
route	*hier*: Streckenführung, -plan
delivery time	Lieferzeit
to offer one's apologies	sich entschuldigen
rather unfortunate	*hier*: nicht gut
to insist on	bestehen auf
to cope	klar-, zurechtkommen
case of emergency	Notfall(-situation)
to appreciate	zu schätzen wissen
effort	Anstrengung

7.3 Dispatching goods

7.3.1 Yet more paperwork?!?

dispatch(ing)	Versand
to require	erfordern, verlangen
attention	Aufmerksamkeit
delivery note	Lieferschein
packaging	Verpackung
to dispatch	versenden
damaged	schadhaft, beschädigt
to ensure	sicherstellen
packing list	Pack-, Versandliste
satisfied	zufrieden
appearance	Aussehen, Erscheinungsbild
to leave a good impression	einen guten Eindruck machen
dispatch date	Versandtermin
consignment	Sendung, Partie
advice of dispatch	Versandanzeige
record	*hier*: Nachweis
signature	Unterschrift
document	*hier*: Unterlage
order number	Auftragsnummer
delivery address	Lieferanschrift

7.3.2 Shipping terms

carriage forward (C/F)	unfrei
carriage paid (C/P)	Fracht bezahlt, frachtfrei, franco
deadweight (dwt)	Eigen-, Totgewicht; Bruttotragfähigkeit
duty forward	unverzollt
duty paid	Zoll bezahlt, verzollt
exclusive of freight	ausschließlich/zuzüglich Fracht
free at the receiving/arrival station	frei Empfangsbahnhof/-station
freight	Fracht(-kosten/-gebühren)
freight collect	unfrei, Fracht bezahlt Empfänger
freight paid	Fracht bezahlt
freight prepaid	frachtfrei, Fracht im Voraus bezahlt
gross weight (gr. wt.)	Bruttogewicht
inclusive (of freight)	einschließlich (Fracht)
franco domicile	frei Haus
net weight (nt. wt.)	Netto-, Füllgewicht
customs duties	Zollgebühren
all-inclusive	alles eingerechnet
carrier	Spediteur, Transportunternehmen
carrying weight	Tragegewicht
transport charges	Transportgebühren, -kosten
carriage	Transport, Beförderung
means of transport	Transportmittel
mode of transport	Verkehrsträger, Transportart

7.4 Advice of dispatch

contract of sale	Kaufvertrag
freight charges	Frachtkosten
haulage company	(Straßen-)Transportunternehmen
in good order	in gutem Zustand
to advise	informieren, in Kenntnis setzen
to pick up	*hier*: abholen
works	Fabrik, Werk
to trust	hoffen, davon ausgehen

7.5 Receiving goods

receipt of shipment	Sendungsannahme
to document	dokumentieren, erfassen
to keep track	nachverfolgen
goods received	Wareneingang, eingegangene Ware
accounting department	Abteilung Rechnungswesen, Buchhaltung
documentation	*hier:* Unterlagen, Belege
discrepancy	Abweichung, Unstimmigkeit
to solve	lösen
claim	Forderung, Anspruch
receipt of goods	Warenannahme
movement of goods	Warenbewegung
goods-in area	Warenannahme(-bereich)
warehouse	Waren-, Materiallager
purchase order number	Bestellnummer
quantity	Menge
specification	Angabe, Spezifikation
visible	sichtbar
damage	Beschädigung, Schaden
delivery slip	Lieferschein
spot check	Stichprobenkontrolle
defective	fehler-, mangelhaft
relevant	*hier*: zuständig
accounts department	Buchhaltung(-sabteilung)
physical inspection	genaue/eingehende Untersuchung
to record	erfassen
shipper	Spediteur
to reject	ablehnen, zurückweisen
incorrect	falsch
replacement	Ersatz(-lieferung)
to update	auf den neuesten Stand bringen, aktualisieren
goods received record	Nachweis der Warenannahme
to weigh	(ab)wiegen
sequence	(Ab-)Folge
to unload	ent-, ausladen
to put into storage	einlagern, auf Lager nehmen
close inspection	genaue Prüfung

7.6 Incoterms® 2020

terms and conditions of trading	Handelsbedingungen
to specify	im Einzelnen festlegen
party to the sales contract	Partei des Verkaufsvertrages
import and export clearance	Abfertigung zur Ein- und Ausfuhr
journey	*hier*: Transportweg
to pass from … to …	übergehen von … auf …
mode of transport	Transportart
inland waterway transport	Binnenschifffahrt
carrier	Frachtführer, Beförderer
alongside	längsseits
freight	Frachtgebühren
carriage	Fracht-, Transport(kosten)
delivered at	angeliefert in
unloaded	entladen
duty paid	verzollt
at buyer's disposal	nach Wahl des Käufers
vessel	Schiff
named	angegeben
packaging	Verpackung
loading charges	Verladekosten
port	Hafen
export duty	Ausfuhrabgaben
customs clearance	Ausfuhrabfertigung
origin terminal charges	Abfertigungsgebühren am Abgangsort
loading on carriage	Verladung auf Transportmittel
carriage charges	Transportkosten
negotiable	verhandelbar
destination terminal charges	Gebühren am Zielort
delivery to destination	Lieferung an den Bestimmungsort
customs clearance	Verzollung

Revision

parcel	Päckchen, Paket
delivery van	Lieferwagen
to cause	verursachen
to prove	be-, nachweisen
in good order and condition	in gutem/einwandfreiem Zustand
adequate	angemessen, gut
speedy	schnell
to report missing	als fehlend melden
job	Aufgabe, (Arbeits-)Auftrag
previous	vorherig
to satisfy	zufriedenstellen
demanding	anspruchsvoll, schwierig

7.7 Invoicing

invoicing	Rechnungsstellung
reference number	Bezugsnummer, Kennziffer
invoice item	Rechnungsposten
net price overall	Nettopreis insgesamt
number of units per item	Stückzahl pro Bestellnummer
percentage rate	Prozentsatz
value added tax (VAT)	Mehrwertsteuer (MwSt)
price per item	Preis pro Position/Stück
product description	Produktbezeichnung
sub-total	Zwischensumme
total amount payable	zu zahlender Gesamtbetrag
to identify	genau bestimmen
winegrower	Winzer, Weinbauer
property	Eigentum
to pay in full	vollständig bezahlen
to be of service again	*hier*: wieder beliefern
in the near future	bald
due date	Fälligkeitstermin
currency	Währung
interest	Zinsen
pan head	Flachkopf-
screw	Schraube
hexagon	Sechskant-
exchange rate	Wechselkurs

7.8 Making payment

to recognise	erkennen
cheque	Scheck
credit card	Kreditkarte
debit card	Debit-, Kundenkarte
direct debit(ing)	Lastschrift(-verfahren)
online transfer	elektronische Überweisung
standing order	Dauerauftrag
payee	Zahlungsempfänger/in
to get so. to do sth.	jdn. bitten/veranlassen etw. zu tun
to withdraw	(Geld) abheben
to pass on to	weiterreichen/-leiten an
to transfer	überweisen
to obtain	erhalten, bekommen
sort code *[BE]*	Bankleitzahl
PIN (personal identification number)	PIN (Geheimzahl)
cash receipt	Kassenquittung, -bon
purchase	(Ein-)Kauf
to set up	einrichten
button	Knopf, Taste
to instruct	beauftragen
account data	Kontendaten
IBAN (international bank account number)	IBAN-Nummer
BIC (bank identifier code)	BIC (Bankleitzahl)
reference	Hinweis, Verweis
to authorise	bevollmächtigen, autorisieren

TAN (transaction number)	TAN (Transaktionsnummer)
multi-part	mehrteilig
transfer form	Überweisungsformular
finally	schließlich, zuletzt
to enter	eingeben
to process	ver-, bearbeiten
online banking	Online-Bankverkehr
receipt	Quittung
period of validity	Gültigkeitsdauer
statement	*hier*: Aufstellung, Liste
annual	(all)jährlich
insurance premium	Versicherungsprämie
ink cartridge	Tintenpatrone
roll	Brötchen
stay	Aufenthalt

7.9 Looking ahead

altogether	gänzlich, vollständig
to get rid of	loswerden, abschaffen
shopkeeper	Ladenbesitzer/in, Geschäftsinhaber/in
day's takings	Tageseinnahmen, -losung
purse	Geldbörse
wallet	Brieftasche, Portemonnaie

Unit 8 How to deal with complaints

8.1 Let's get going!

to complain	sich beschweren
complaint	Beschwerde, Mängelrüge

8.2 A sympathetic way of handling a complaint

in actual fact	tatsächlich
business transaction	Geschäftsvorgang
to go about it	etw. machen
opportunity	Gelegenheit, Möglichkeit
out of the ordinary	außergewöhnlich
confused by	verwirrt wegen
used to do	oft getan haben
top	Oberseite
loaf	Brot(-laib)
retail company	Einzelhandelsunternehmen
customer support manager	Kundendienstmitarbeiter/in
blotch	Fleck(en)
stripe	Streifen
stripey	gestreift
gift card	Geschenkgutschein
sweeties	Süßigkeiten
to publicise	viel berichten
to give in to	nachgeben
recipe	Rezept
voucher	Gutschein

8.3 Can a customer complaint be a gift?

on the contrary	im Gegenteil
gift	Geschenk
valuable	wertvoll
to spend money on sth.	Geld ausgeben für etw.
to care about	*hier*: sich Gedanken machen wegen, (jdm.) wichtig sein
relationship with	Beziehung zu
to fix a problem	Problem lösen
to take one's business elsewhere	woanders hingehen/einkaufen
to handle	*hier*: umgehen mit
profitable	gewinnbringend, profitabel
business relationship	Geschäftsbeziehung
to treat	behandeln
to work	funktionieren
to focus on	sich konzentrieren auf
to be within so.'s control	beeinflussen können
to be out of so.'s control	nicht beeinflussen können
to follow sth. up	(einer Sache) nachgehen
to give feedback	sich zurückmelden, Rückmeldung geben
to emphasise	hervorheben, betonen
rather than	(an)statt
frustrated	unzufrieden, frustriert
recommendation	Empfehlung
solution	Lösung
investigation	Untersuchung, Nachforschung
to interrupt	unterbrechen
to draw so.'s attention to	(jdn.) aufmerksam machen auf

8.4 Learning to be polite

inconvenience	Unannehmlichkeit
to come back to so.	sich (bei jdm.) wieder melden
much to our regret	sehr zu unserem Bedauern, wir bedauern sehr
sub-standard	minderwertig
suitable	geeignet
substitute(e)	Ersatz(-ware)
china set	Porzellanservice
to meet	*hier*: entsprechen, erfüllen

8.5 A very angry customer

plastic wrapping	Plastikhülle
transport pallet	Transportpalette
case	Karton, Kiste
to check against	abgleichen mit
invoice amount	Rechnungsbetrag
to make a note of sth.	sich etw. notieren
to take sth. up with so.	etw. mit jdm. besprechen
to cross-check	genauestens prüfen
dispatch department	Versandabteilung
to suffer a loss	Verlust erleiden
short delivery	Minderlieferung
our fault	unser (eigenes) Verschulden
current wine list	neue/aktuelle Weinliste

8.6 Role play

to indicate	andeuten
shipping agent	Spediteur, Versandbeauftragter
delivery company	Lieferfirma, Zustelldienst
arrival	Ankunft
to report	anzeigen
on-carrier	Weiterbeförderer
outcome	Ergebnis
throughout	während

8.7 Satisfying customers is a must

standing	Ruf, Ansehen
incident	Vorfall, Vorkommnis
to maintain	aufrechterhalten
after-sales service	Kundendienst
to implement	umsetzen, realisieren
output	(Produktions-)Ausstoß
target	(Produktions-)Ziel
outgoing goods	Warenausgang, abgehende Ware
quality assurance	Qualitätssicherung
objective	Ziel(-setzung)
money-back guarantee	Geldrückgabegarantie
random	zufällig, Zufalls-
quality check	Qualitätskontrolle
to involve	beteiligen, miteinbeziehen
quality improvement measure	Maßnahme zur Qualitätsverbesserung
staff suggestions	Mitarbeitervorschläge
to monitor	überwachen, kontrollieren
refund	Rückerstattung
helpline service	Notruf-, Hotline-Dienst
rejects	Ausschuss(-stücke)
to render (a service)	(Dienstleistung) erbringen
to reward	belohnen
as a matter of routine	routine-, regelmäßig
to spot-check	Stichproben machen
outgoing consignment	abgehende Sendung
training	Schulung
conflict management	Konfliktbewältigung
key priority	oberste Priorität
complaints procedure	Beschwerdeverfahren
hot dog seller	Würstchenverkäufer/in
diner	*hier*: Gast
gas supply company	Gaslieferant

Unit 9 Customer acquisition

9.0

customer acquisition	(Neu-)Kundengewinnung

9.1 Let's get going!

print advertising	Werbung in Druckmedien
to persuade	überreden
advertising	Werbung
part and parcel	fester Bestandteil
to advertise (for)	bewerben, Werbung machen für
to attract	locken, anziehen
billboard	Plakatwand
hoarding	Werbefläche
leaflet	Faltblatt
banner advertising	Bannerwerbung
perimeter advertising	Bandenwerbung
freebie	Gratiszeitung
poster	Plakat
ad(vert), advertisement	Inserat, Anzeige
neon sign	Leuchtreklame
product launch	Produkteinführung
to place (an ad(vert))	(Anzeige) platzieren

9.2 Purposes and means of advertising

purpose	Zweck
means	Mittel
sales advertising	Verkaufswerbung
to involve	beinhalten
to approach	ansprechen, zugehen auf
existing customer	bestehender Kunde
advertiser	Werbetreibende/r
personal selling	persönlicher Verkauf
word of mouth	Mundpropaganda
fair	Messe, Verkaufsausstellung
media contact	Medienkontakt
outdoor display	Außenanzeige
to be out to do	darauf aus sein, zu tun
persuasion	Überredung
creation	Schaffung
commercial	Werbespot
image brochure	Imagebroschüre
display stand	(Verkaufs-)Ständer
freesheet	Gratiszeitung
give-away	Kunden-, Werbegeschenk
mail circular	Postwurfsendung
supplement	Beilage
product demonstration	Produktvorführung
product tasting	(Waren-)Verkostung
stand-up display	(Werbe-)Aufsteller
window display	Schaufensterauslage
sales promotion activity	Verkaufsförderungsmaßnahme
print(ed) medium (*pl.* media)	Druckmedium
raw material	Rohstoff
finished goods	Fertigwaren
supply chain	Liefer-, Wertschöpfungskette
state-of-the-art	allerneuest, hochmodern
quality test lab	Labor für Qualitätsprüfung
tool	*hier*: Werkzeug(-maschine)
to go toe-to-toe	in direktem Wettbewerb stehen
fraction	Bruchteil
middle man	Großhandel

9.3 Preparing an advertising campaign

advertising campaign	Werbekampagne
bakery	Bäckerei
confectionery	Konditorei
oatcake	Haferplätzchen
to get a foothold	Fuß fassen
product manager	Produktleiter/in
to be engaged in	dabei sein, beschäftigt sein mit
MD (managing director)	Geschäftsführer/in
buyer	Einkäufer/in
food retailing company	Lebensmitteleinzelhandelsunternehmen
food retailer	Lebensmitteleinzelhändler
ordinary shopper	*hier*: einfache/r Kunde/in
one size fits all	eins passt für alle
to be driving at sth.	auf etw. hinauswollen
to come in (on sth.)	*hier*: mal einhaken
trade fair	Fachmesse
to look into sth.	einer Sache nachgehen
venue	Veranstaltungsort
to report back to so.	jdm. berichten
to come back to sth.	(wieder) zurückkommen auf
expense	Kosten, Ausgaben
in terms of	*hier*: für
fair stand hire	Standmiete
to go over the top	*hier*: übertreiben
low-cost	niedrigpreisig
profit margin	Gewinnspanne
convincing	überzeugend
retail chain	Filialist, Einzelhandelskette
upfront	im Voraus, zuerst einmal
to be a bit of a gamble	etw. riskant sein
to throw out	verwerfen
face-to-face	direkt, persönlich
effective	wirkungsvoll
mailshot	(Post-)Wurfsendung
to come into the picture	ins Bild kommen
to take into consideration	berücksichtigen
to tackle	angehen, bewältigen

9.4 Minutes of a meeting

minutes	Protokoll
intern	Praktikant/in
extract	Auszug
chair	Vorsitz
attendee	Anwesende/r
minute taker	Protokollant/in
review and adoption	*hier*: Verabschiedung
agenda	Tagesordnung
reading and approval	*hier*: Genehmigung
any other business	Verschiedenes
item	Tagesordnungspunkt
appropriate	angemessen, richtig
to bring up (an idea)	(Gedanken) zur Sprache bringen
involved	*hier*: damit verbunden
grocery chain	Lebensmittelkette
for the time being	vorläufig, bis auf weiteres
to schedule	planen
action to be taken	zu treffende Maßnahmen

9.5 Minutes writing: The dos and don'ts

procedure	Verfahren
to circularise	verteilen, versenden
to give an account	*hier*: informieren
action point	Aktionspunkt
history/process log	Verlaufsprotokoll
motion	Antrag

to adopt a motion	Antrag annehmen	beforehand	vorher
to vote on	abstimmen über	clarification	Erläuterung
summary minutes, results log	Ergebnisprotokoll	wording	Wortlaut
to cover	abdecken, behandeln	voting result	Abstimmungsergebnis
approval	Zustimmung	option discussed	diskutierte Alternative
chairperson	Vorsitzende/r	modification	Veränderung
agenda item/point	Tagesordnungspunkt	to table a motion	Antrag stellen/einbringen
in favour	dafür	to second	unterstützen
against	dagegen	to carry a motion	Antrag annehmen
abstention	Enthaltung	to fail	*hier*: abgelehnt werden
to highlight	hervorheben	shorter and snappier	kürzer und knapper

9.6 Coming to a decision

marketing drive	Marketingoffensive	responsible	*hier*: zuständig
according to	jdm. zufolge	information pack	Info(rmations)paket
stand rent	Standmiete	to object	einwenden
fair booth construction	Bau des Messestands	consumer	Verbraucher
accommodation	Unterkunft	to launch	starten

9.7 Developing and maintaining a customer base

permanent	dauerhaft	sales representative	Vertriebsmitarbeiter/in
feedback	Rückmeldung	equivalent	Entsprechung
(technical) support	(technische) Unterstützung	booklet	Büchlein
customer relationship management	Kundenbeziehungsmanagement	flyer, handbill	Flugblatt, Handzettel
		handbook	Handbuch
circularisation	Verteilung von Werbematerial	instruction manual	Bedienungs-, Betriebsanleitung
cold calls	Telefonwerbung	(product) get-up	(Produkt-)Aufmachung
customer care	Kundenbetreuung	recipe book	Kochbuch
customer loyalty	Kundentreue	labelling	Etikettierung, Kennzeichnung
customer needs	Kundenbedürfnisse	high street	Hauptgeschäftsstraße
pricing strategy	Preispolitik	passer-by	Passant/in
sales promotion	Verkaufsförderung	wrapping	Verpackung

9.8 A circular to buyers

to opt for	sich entscheiden für	refreshment	kleine Stärkung, Häppchen
approval	Zustimmung	excellent	ausgezeichnet
to select	auswählen	snack	Imbiss
launch	Markteinführung	to enjoy	genießen
potential	Potenzial	delicious	köstlich
major player	wichtiger Akteur	addition	Ergänzung
grocery market	Lebensmittelmarkt	at leisure	in aller Ruhe
to carry	führen, listen	exquisite	erlesen, fein
outlet	Laden	anticipating	in Erwartung
taste	Geschmack	representative	repräsentativ
preference	Vorliebe	to whet so.'s appetite	jdm. Appetit machen

9.9 A buyer reacts

attractive(ly)	ansprechend	to advertise for a product	Produkt bewerben
listing	Listung	pricing	Preisgestaltung

Unit 10 Dealing with visitors

10.1 Let's get going!

arrangement	Vorbereitung

10.2 Gearing up to a visit from partners

staff meeting	Mitarbeitertreffen
head	Leiter/in
quality control department	Abt. Qualitätskontrolle
officer	Sach-, Mitarbeiter/in
sister company	Schwestergesellschaft
first-hand	aus erster Hand
insight (into)	Einblick (in)
PR (public relations)	(Abt.) Öffentlichkeitsarbeit
quality regulations	Qualitätsvorschriften
stuff	Kram, Zeug
health and safety regulations	Arbeitsschutzbestimmungen
to sort out	klären, erledigen
transfer	Transfer, Fahrt
staff canteen	Personalkantine
hospitality	Bewirtung
to attend	dabei/anwesend sein
to clarify	herausfinden
trust you	typisch
to assume	annehmen
to go down well	sich gut machen
progress	Fortschritt
group	Konzern
parent *[BE]*/mother *[AE]* company	Muttergesellschaft, Konzernmutter
subsidiary *[BE]*, daughter company *[AE]*	Tochter(-gesellschaft)
sister company	Schwestergesellschaft, Konzernschwester
to see to sth.	sich um etw. kümmern
welcome pack	Begrüßungspaket, -mappe

10.3 The next step

availability	Verfügbarkeit
to negotiate	aushandeln
I hadn't realised	das war mir nicht klar
charge	*hier*: Preis
to charge	berechnen
there is … off	der Preis reduziert sich um …
to be due to do	etw. tun sollen
company booking	Buchung für ein Unternehmen
business rate	Preis für ein Unternehmen
standing arrangement	feste Vereinbarung
internet access	Internetzugang
free of charge	kostenlos
priceworthiness	Preiswürdigkeit
fare	Tarif, Fahrpreis
ingredient	*hier*: Bestandteil

10.4 Getting things organised

arrangement	Anordnung
timetable	Fahrplan; Zeit-, Ablaufplan
Tourist Information Office	Fremdenverkehrsbüro, Touristeninformation
name tag	Namensschild(chen)
to collect	abholen
taxi ride	Taxifahrt

10.5 Passing on information

counterpart	Kollege/in
to be on the safe side	auf „Numero sicher“ gehen
factory tour	Fabrikbesichtigung
minster	Münster, Dom

10.7.1 Greeting people

to offend	beleidigen

10.7.2 Small-talk – Introduction

icebreaker	Eisbrecher
relaxation	Entspannung
definitely	ganz bestimmt
pastime	Freizeitbeschäftigung
to feel confident	sich zutrauen
to go a long way	ein großer Schritt sein
to establish	*hier*: anbahnen
customs	Bräuche, Brauchtum
to celebrate	feiern

10.7.3 Hospitality and politeness

hospitality	*hier*: Gastfreundschaft

10.8 Business cards

advertising tool	Werbemittel
cardholder	Karteninhaber/in
first and foremost	zuallererst aber
let alone	geschweige denn
to keep in touch	in Kontakt bleiben
job title	Stellenbezeichnung
university degree	Hochschulabschluss
modesty	Bescheidenheit
to make contact	Kontakt aufnehmen
extension	Erweiterung
reverse	Rückseite
due respect	gebührender Respekt
etiquette	Verhaltensregel
to observe	*hier*: einhalten
to bow	sich verbeugen

Unit 11 What it takes: Events and projects

11.2 Getting ready for the event

stage	Stadium
to take care of	sich kümmern um
field sales staff	Außendienstmitarbeiter *(pl.)*
training centre	Ausbildungszentrum
staff canteen	Personalkantine
division director	Bereichsleiter/in
departmental staff	Mitarbeiter/innen der Abteilung
time slot	Zeitfenster
return	*hier*: Rücksendung
attendance form	*hier*: Anmeldeformular
reimbursement	Erstattung
travel expenses	Reisekosten
room requirements	Raumbedarf
timeline	Zeitleiste
to pencil in	eintragen
interim report	Zwischenbericht

11.3 Problems with room bookings

conference facilities	*hier*: Konferenzräumlichkeiten
family reception	*hier*: Familienfeier
fully booked	ausgebucht
to wrap up *(coll.)*	*hier*: abschließen
dinner party	festliches Abendessen
that would do the trick	das ist die Lösung
function	*hier*: Veranstaltung
training session	*hier*: Seminarsitzung
thereabouts	so ungefähr, (oder) um den Dreh
be in the clear	*hier*: OK sein, in Ordnung gehen
provisional	vorläufig
entry	Eintrag
note	Notiz
confirmation	Bestätigung
seating	mit einer Platzkapazität von
event organiser	*hier*: Veranstalter
to stagger	staffeln
service staff	Bedienung(-spersonal)
slot	Zeit(-fenster)
original(ly)	ursprünglich
coach	Ausbilder/in, Trainer/in
to conduct	leiten, durchführen
to be to (do)	(tun) sollen

11.4 Getting geared up for the training

training seminar	Schulung(-sveranstaltung)
utensils	Gerätschaften
to make available	zur Verfügung stellen
ballpoint pen	Kugelschreiber
erasable	löschbar
crockery	Porzellan
cutlery	Besteck
cooler	Kühler
evaluation sheet	Bewertungsbogen
laser pointer	Laserleuchtstift
extension cable	Verlängerungskabel
facilitator's toolbox	Moderatorenkoffer
name tag	Namensschildchen
pinboard	Pinwand
waste bin	Abfallbehälter
wiper	Wischer

11.5 Events as a marketing tool

scope	Spielraum
interaction	soziale Interaktion
business-related	geschäftlich
bonding	Vertiefung von Kontakten
networking	Vernetzung, Knüpfung von Kontakten
professional development	berufliche Entwicklung
seminar hotel	Tagungshotel
residential seminar	mehrtägiges Seminar
overnight stay	Übernachtung
webinar	Web-Seminar
awareness	Bewusstsein
to sponsor	fördern, unterstützen
roadshow	*etwa:* mobile Verkaufsveranstaltung
prize-giving	Preisverleihung
festivities	Fest
session	Sitzung
to neglect	vernachlässigen
primary	oberste(r, s)
customer handling	Umgang mit Kunden
telephone manners	Verhalten am Telefon
as the need arises	nach Bedarf
to familiarise	vertraut machen
factory tour	Fabrikbesichtigung, -rundgang
focused	zentriert
stand	(Ausstellungs-)Stand
corporate name	Firmenname
colour coding	*hier*: Firmenfarben
in-house	(firmen)intern
as of (+ Zeitangabe)	von … an
coaching session	Training, Schulung

11.6 Project work

to argue	behaupten
to initiate	einleiten, beginnen
implementation	Umsetzung
conceptualisation	Konzepterstellung
conclusion	Abschluss
documentation	Erstellung von Unterlagen
communicating	Informations-, Gedankenaustausch
milestone report	Meilenstein-, Zwischenbericht
engineering department	Entwicklungsabteilung
conveyor belt	Transportband
to get into a muddle	durcheinander geraten
ambitious	ehrgeizig
buffer time	Pufferzeit
cost estimate	Kostenschätzung, -voranschlag
final report	Abschlussbericht
interim report	Zwischenbericht
network/critical path analysis	Netzplantechnik
progress report	Fortschrittsbericht
project acceptance/ approval	Projektabnahme
project stage	Projektstadium, -stufe, -phase
schedule/progress control	Terminkontrolle
steering committee	Lenkungs-, Steuerungsausschuss
time schedule	Zeit-, Ablaufplan
transaction number	Vorgangsnummer
work package	Arbeitspaket

Unit 12 Presenting

12.1 Let's get going!

to blow away	vom Hocker hauen/reißen, begeistern

12.2 Preparing a presentation

to avoid	vermeiden
desperate	verzweifelt
to rehearse	einüben
to not have a clue	keine Ahnung haben
hairy	heikel
target audience	Zielpublikum
to learn by heart	auswendig lernen
to be agonising	eine Qual sein
seemingly	scheinbar
flawless	makellos
mess	Chaos
unintelligible	unverständlich
appropriate	angemessen, passend
ample	reichlich, genügend
to outline	umreißen, skizzieren
hype	Rummel, Wirbel
durable	strapazier-, widerstandsfähig
productive	leistungsfähig, ertragreich
phenomenal	phänomenal
efficient	wirkungsvoll, wirksam
awesome	großartig, toll
outstanding	hervorragend, ausgezeichnet
stunning	verblüffend, umwerfend
remarkable	bemerkenswert, erstaunlich
premium	hochwertig
top-notch	erstklassig
pleasure	Vergnügen
superb	hervorragend, erstklassig
breakthrough	Durchbruch; *hier:* bahnbrechend
advanced	fortschrittlich, fortgeschritten
engineering	*hier*: Ingenieurskunst, -leistung

12.3 Project: Presenting your company

legal form	Rechtsform
CEO (chief executive officer)	Vorstandsvorsitzende/r
merger	Fusion, Zusammenschluss
takeover	Übernahme
acquisition	Aufkauf
template	Vorlage
corporate design	einheitliches Firmendesign
slide	Folie
contrasting	sich abhebend, kontrastierend
font	Schrift(art)
engaging	*hier*: einnehmend, fesselnd
poor	dürftig, schlecht
comprehensible	nachvollziehbar, verständlich
visualisation	Visualisierung, Veranschaulichung
meaningful	aussagekräftig
appealing	ansprechend
prompt card	Stichwortkarte
articulation	Aussprache
emphasis	Betonung
suitable	passend
facial expression	Mimik
confident	selbstbewusst, souverän
exaggerated	übertrieben
stiff	steif
gestures	Gestik
posture	Körperhaltung
to fidget around	herumzappeln
punctuating	*hier etwa*: unterstreichend, mit Hervorhebung wichtiger Punkte

12.4 Describing graphs & diagrams

real estate	Immobilie(n)
property development	Grundstückserschließung, Immobilienentwicklung
commercial property	Gewerbeimmobilie
competitor	Wettbewerber, Konkurrent

12.4.1 Pie chart

percentage	*hier*: prozentualer Anteil
share	Anteil
revenue	Erlöse, Umsatz(-volumen)
quarter	Quartal
approximate	ungefähr, circa
to account for	ausmachen, entfallen auf, betragen
slice	Anteil, (Kuchen-)Stück
to constitute	ausmachen, darstellen
significant	wesentlich, bedeutend
negligible	vernachlässigbar, unbedeutend
proportion	Anteil

12.4.2 Bar chart

staffing level	Personal(be)stand
quarterly result	Quartalsergebnis
business unit	Geschäftsbereich, -einheit
profitability	Rentabilität, Gewinnsituation
to render	wiedergeben, übertragen
all-time high	Allzeithoch
to amount to	betragen, sich belaufen auf
by … per cent	um … Prozent
to continue	anhalten, weiter bestehen
to reach	erreichen
thus	somit
compared with/to	verglichen mit/zu
year before/earlier	Vorjahr

12.4.3 Line chart

turnover	Umsatz
marketing spending	Marketingausgaben
to slump	*hier:* abstürzen
gradual	stetig, kontinuierlich
slight	geringfügig, leicht
axis	Achse
to recover	sich erholen
housing market	Wohnungsmarkt
boom	Hochkonjunktur
competition	Konkurrenz; Wettbewerber
to lay off	freisetzen, entlassen
value	Wert
striking	auffällig
relevant	bedeutsam, wichtig
all-time	Allzeit-
high	Hoch, Höchststand
low	Tief, Tiefststand
to lose momentum	an Fahrt verlieren
to emerge	auftreten, sich herausbilden
cost-cutting programme	Sparprogramm
department head	Abteilungsleiter/in

12.4.4 Preparing and presenting data

to compile	zusammenstellen, sammeln
expenditure	Ausgaben, Aufwendungen
temporary	zeitlich befristet, Zeit-; vorübergehend
composition	Zusammensetzung
spreadsheet software	Tabellenkalkulationsprogramm

Unit 13 Going to a trade fair

13.1 Let's get going!

trade fair	(Handels-)Messe, Ausstellung

13.2 Getting information

engineering company	Maschinenbauunternehmen
measuring and testing equipment	Mess- und Prüfgeräte
to make a push	energisch daran gehen
representative	(Außendienst-)Vertreter/in
management team	Führungsmannschaft
specialist trade fair	Fachmesse
industrial sector	Branche
engineering industry	Maschinenbau
relevant	einschlägig
facilities	*hier*: Angebot für Aussteller
costs involved	*hier*: anfallende Kosten
exhibition centre	Messezentrum
to host	veranstalten, ausrichten
major	groß
manufacturing industry	verarbeitende Industrie
to be aimed at	sich richten an
business public	*hier*: Fachpublikum
DIY (do it yourself) enthusiast	interessierte/r Heimwerker/in
in view of	*hier*: wenn man … bedenkt, im Hinblick auf
participation	Teilnahme
exhibitor	Aussteller
exhibition space	Ausstellungsgelände, -fläche
to showcase	zeigen, ausstellen
engineering testing	technische Erprobung
business services	Dienstleistungen für Unternehmen
dealings	Geschäfte, Geschäftsmöglichkeiten
related field	*hier*: verwandter/angrenzender Sektor
repairs and maintenance	Wartung & Instandhaltung
education & training	Bildung & Ausbildung
aero engineering	Luftfahrt(-technik)
networking	Vernetzung, Netzwerkaktivitäten
design	Gestaltung
assembly	Montage, Zusammenbau
components	*hier*: Komponentenbau
MRO engineering	Instandhaltungs-, Reparatur- & Betriebstechnik
aeronautics engineering	Flugzeugbau
related field	*hier*: verwandtes Gebiet
component supplier	Zulieferer für Bauteile
strong views	klare/eindeutige Meinung
to participate in	teilnehmen an

13.3 Fair business in Germany

to stage	veranstalten, ausrichten
fair venue	Messestandort
fair visitor	Messebesucher/in
p. a. (per annum)	jährlich
trade fair business	Messegeschäft
to enjoy	*hier*: haben
far beyond	weit über … hinaus
in the very centre	mitten in
on the doorstep	vor der Haustür
trade and industry	Handwerk und Gewerbe
generally speaking	allgemein gesehen
specialisation	Spezialisierung
internationalisation	Internationalisierung
attending fairs	Messebesuch(e)
service provider	Dienstleister
commerce	Handel
distributor	Vertriebsgesellschaft
wholesale trade	Großhandel
retail trade	Einzelhandel
to keep up to date	sich auf dem Laufenden halten
to run a business	Unternehmen leiten
public at large	breite Öffentlichkeit
ideally suited	gut geeignet
respective	jeweilig
in terms of	hinsichtlich
fair booth	Messestand
in its own right	für sich (genommen)
fairgoer	Messebesucher/in
oral(ly)	mündlich
to sample	probieren
competing product	Konkurrenzprodukt
marketing tool	Marketinginstrument
fair stand designer	Messestandgestalter
vehicle production	Fahrzeugbau
printing	Druckereigewerbe
food	Nahrungsmittel(-industrie)
hotel and catering	Hotel- & Gaststättengewerbe
aviation	Luftfahrt(-industrie)
leather goods	Lederwaren(-industrie)
jewellery	Schmuckwaren(-industrie)
outdoor sports	Outdoor-Sport(-industrie)
caravanning	Wohnwagenbau-Industrie, Caravanning
equestrianism	Reitsport

13.4 Preparing for the fair

strategy meeting	Strategietreffen
to set about	sich dranmachen

13.4.1 Things to do

access	Zugang	travel arrangements	Reisevorbereitungen
exhibition grounds	Messegelände	to market	*hier*: bekannt machen; vermarkten
contractor	Auftragnehmer	fair participation	Messeteilnahme
stand space	Standfläche	trade magazine	Fachzeitschrift
flowchart	Flussdiagramm	sales literature	Verkaufsprospekte
fair organiser	Messegesellschaft	to recruit	anwerben, einstellen
to make transport arrangements	*hier*: Transport organisieren	complimentary ticket	Freikarte

13.4.2 Action plan

action plan	Aktionsplan	to rehearse	proben
business objective	Geschäftsziel	rota	Dienstplan
to get a quote	Angebot einholen	approximate(ly)	ungefähr
floor space	*hier*: Standfläche	timeframe	Zeitfenster, -raum
electrics	Elektrik	follow-up work	Nachbereitung
to double-check	nochmals prüfen	to follow up	nachverfolgen
staff briefing	Anweisungen ans Personal		

13.5 Contacting customers

trade magazine	Fachzeitschrift	to explore	erkunden, ausloten
to pencil in	eintragen	cooperation	Zusammenarbeit
diary	Kalender	aisle	Gang
fair organiser	Messeveranstalter	to redeem	einlösen, eintauschen
aeronautics design	Konstruktion im Flugzeugbau	cordial(ly)	(sehr) herzlich
to set aside	*hier*: zur Verfügung stellen	slip	Zettel, Abschnitt
highlight	Höhepunkt	product innovation	Produktneuheit

13.6 Changing a reservation

language skills	Sprachkompetenz	cancellation	Stornierung
evening class	Abendkurs		

13.7 How to get there

advice	Rat(schläge)	to go for so.	auf jdn. zutreffen, für jdn. gelten
beforehand	vorab	sat nav (satellite navigation)	Navigationsgerät
to know one's way about	sich auskennen		

13.7.1 Learn to read a site map

site map	Lage-, Übersichtsplan	colour coding	Farbmarkierung
to give directions	Weg erklären	to find one's way around	sich zurechtfinden

The map

disability	Behinderung	shuttle bus	Pendelbus
outdoor exhibition area	Außengelände	(motorway) junction	(Autobahn-)Anschlussstelle

13.7.2 Learn to give directions

speed restriction	Geschwindigkeitsbeschränkung	dual carriageway	vierspurige Straße
filter	*hier*: (Abbiege-)Spur		

Unit 14 Working in human resources (HR)

14.1 Let's get started!

human resources	Personalwesen
HR department	Personalabteilung
to complete	*hier*: beenden, abschließen
factor of production	Produktionsfaktor
soil	Boden
labour	Arbeit

14.2 Interview with an HR manager

HR manager	Personalleiter/in, -chef/in
food processing company	Lebensmittel verarbeitendes Unternehmen
red and black currants	rote u. schwarze Johannisbeeren
fruit preserves	Fruchtkonserven
hotel and catering trade	Hotel- & Gaststättengewerbe
recruitment	Personalbeschaffung
to assess	bemessen, bewerten
harassment	Belästigung
to dismiss	entlassen
dispute	Streit(igkeit), Auseinandersetzung
to tolerate	dulden
bullying	Mobbing
superior	Vorgesetzte/r
on the factory floor	*hier*: in der Produktion
admin	*(coll.)* Verwaltung
appraisal interview	Mitarbeitergespräch
performance	Leistung
appreciation	Wertschätzung
contract of employment	Arbeitsvertrag
to lay down	niederlegen
job title	Stellenbezeichnung
holiday entitlement	Urlaubsanspruch
promotion	Beförderung
empowerment	Ermächtigung, Vergrößerung der Entscheidungsspielräume
transfer	Versetzung
tool(s)	Werkzeug, Instrumente
recruitment from within	interne Personalbeschaffung
exceptional	außergewöhnlich
pay rise	Gehaltserhöhung
to cut jobs	Stellen streichen
to make redundant	(Personal) entlassen
emotional strain	seelische Belastung
to re-invent	neu erfinden
to advertise	*hier*: ausschreiben
vacancy	freie Stelle
job agency	Personalvermittler
unacceptable	nicht hinnehmbar
offensive behaviour	beleidigendes Verhalten
it goes without saying	selbstverständlich, es versteht sich von selbst
initial training	Erstausbildung
on the shop floor	in der Fertigung/Produktion
to upgrade	aktualisieren, ausbauen
in-house	(firmen)intern
to outsource	fremdvergeben, auslagern
to settle	beilegen
to get out of hand	außer Kontrolle geraten
mediator	Vermittler/in
recruiting	Personalbeschaffung
to contribute	Beitrag leisten
continuing education	Weiterbildung
firing *(coll.)*	Entlassung
lay-off	Freisetzung
job posting	Stellenausschreibung
performance bonus	Leistungsprämie
achievement measurement	Leistungsmessung
performance review	Leistungsbeurteilung
to reward	belohnen
to recruit	(Personal) einstellen, beschaffen
wages and salaries	Löhne und Gehälter

14.3 Activities in the HR department

administrative activities	Verwaltungs-, Bürotätigkeiten
dismissal	Kündigung
redundancy	Entlassung
performance interview	Mitarbeitergespräch
data input	Dateneingabe
return	Rückgabe
assessment interview report	Bericht über das Mitarbeitergespräch
questionnaire	Fragebogen
records	*hier*: (Personal-)Akte
notice	Mitteilung, Ankündigung
redundancy plan	Sozialplan
vacancy notice	Stellenausschreibung
letter of dismissal	Kündigungsschreiben
promotion notice	Beförderungsmitteilung
payroll clerk	Lohnbuchhalter/in
appraisal document	Beurteilungsbogen

Revision

printer toner	Druckertoner
stationer's	Schreibwarengeschäft

14.4 An interesting job advertisement

extensive	umfangreich
property development company	Immobilienentwicklungsgesellschaft
work experience	Praktikum
property company	Immobiliengesellschaft
enterprise	Unternehmen
to implement	umsetzen
to regenerate	*hier*: sanieren
property management	Immobilienverwaltung
creative	gestalterisch, kreativ
state-of-the-art	hochmodern
to generate	erzeugen, schaffen
occupier	Nutzer/in, Bewohner/in
fair	angemessen
return	Ertrag
urban	städtisch
keen	*hier*: hochmotiviert
to perform	ausführen, erledigen
data entry	Dateneingabe
to top up	auffüllen
stationery	Büromaterial, Schreibwaren
fluent	fließend
proficient	kompetent
interpersonal skills	soziale Kompetenz
proactive	Initiative ergreifend
demeanour	Auftreten
eager	begierig, bemüht
CV (curriculum vitae)	Lebenslauf
probationary period	Probezeit
cover letter	An-, Begleitschreiben

14.5 Applying for a job

in terms of	was … anbelangt
appearance	Erscheinungsbild; *hier*: Form und Gestaltung
recruiter	Personalbeschaffer/in
on average	durchschnittlich
concise	knapp
time waster	Zeitverschwender

14.5.1 How to present yourself in a CV

résumé	Lebenslauf
extra-curricular	außerschulisch
part-time	Teilzeit(-)
coherence	Zusammenhang
school leaver	Schulabgänger/in
organisational	Organisations-
effective	wirksam, effektiv
ICT (information & computer technology)	Computer- und Informationstechnologie
shelf-filling	Auffüllen der Regale
stockroom	Lager
nursing home	Pflegeheim
publishing (house)	*hier*: Verlag
work-shadowing	Hospitation
keyboarding skills	Texterfassungskompetenz
intermediate	*hier*: Zwischenstufe
reference	Empfehlungsschreiben
completion	Abschluss, Beendigung

14.5.2 The cover letter

profile	Kurzbiographie
personal data sheet (PDS)	Personalbogen, Lebenslauf
relevant	einschlägig, wichtig
suitability	Eignung
availability	Verfügbarkeit
personal profile	persönliches Profil
posting	Anzeige, Inserat
hands-on	praxisbezogen
approach	Ansatz
to acquire	sich aneignen, erwerben
colour coding	farbliche Kennzeichnung
insight (into)	Einblick in
sound grounding	solides Fundament
negotiable	verhandelbar
period of notice	Kündigungsfrist

Country	Inhabitants	Adjective	Language(s)	Currency/Code & Symbol
Australia	Australian	Australian	English	Austral. dollar (AUD – A$)
Austria	Austrian	Austrian	German	euro (EUR – €)
Belgium	Belgian	Belgian	French, Flemish, German	euro (EUR – €)
Brazil	Brazilian	Brazilian	Portuguese	real (BRL – R$)
Canada	Canadian	Canadian	English, French	Canad. dollar (CAD – Can$)
Czech Republic	Czech	Czech	Czech	Czech koruna (CZK – Kč)
China	Chinese	Chinese	Chinese (Mandarin), Cantonese	yuan renminbi (CNY – ¥)
Denmark	Dane	Danish	Danish	Danish krone (DKK – Dkr)
Egypt	Egyptian	Egyptian	Arabic	Egyptian pound (EGP – £)
Finland	Finnish	Finnish	Finnish	euro (EUR – €)
France	French	French	French	euro (EUR – €)
Great Britain (England, Scotland, Wales); UK = Great Britain + Northern Ireland	British, Briton, (English, Scot, Welsh)	British (English, Scottish, Welsh)	English	pound (sterling) (GBP – £)
Greece	Greek	Greek	Greek	euro (EUR – €)
India	Indian	Indian	Hindi, English, Urdu	rupee (INR – ₹ [Re/Rs])
Indonesia	Indonesian	Indonesian	Indonesian	Indonesian rupiah (IDR – rp)
Iran	Iranian	Iranian	Persian	Iranian rial (IRR – ریال)
Ireland	Irish	Irish	English	euro (EUR – €)
Italy	Italian	Italian	Italian	euro (EUR – €)
Japan	Japanese	Japanese	Japanese	yen (JPY – ¥)
Luxembourg	Luxembourg citizen	Luxembourg	French, German	euro (EUR – €)
Mexico	Mexican	Mexican	Spanish	Mex. peso (MXN – Mex$)
(the) Netherlands	Dutch	Dutch	Dutch	euro (EUR– €)
New Zealand	New Zealander	New Zealand	English	NZ dollar (NZD – NZ$)
Norway	Norwegian	Norwegian	Norwegian	Norw. krone (NOK – kr)
Poland	Pole	Polish	Polish	zloty (PLN – zł)
Portugal	Portuguese	Portuguese	Portuguese	euro (EUR – €)
Russia	Russian	Russian	Russian	rouble (RUB – руб)
South Africa	South African	South African	English, Afrikaans	rand (ZAR – R)
Spain	Spaniard, Spanish	Spanish	Spanish	euro (EUR – €)
Sweden	Swede	Swedish	Swedish	Swedish krona (SEK – kr)
Switzerland	Swiss	Swiss	German, French, Italian	Swiss franc (CHF – Sfr)
Turkey	Turkish	Turkish	Turkish	Turkish lira (TRL – ₺)
U.S.A.	(US) American	American	English, Spanish	dollar (USD – $)